OUR OWN

OUR OWN

Adopting and Parenting the Older Child

Trish Maskew

Morton Grove, Illinois

Jacket design by Randall Van Vynckt

Snowcap Press
9500 Oriole Ave.
Morton Grove, IL 60053-1012
www.snowcappress.com; info@snowcappress.com

Publisher's Cataloging-in-Publication Data
Maskew, Trish.
Our own: adopting and parenting the older child / Trish Maskew.
p. cm.
Includes bibliographical references (p. 270-275) and index.
ISBN 0-9669701-5-2 (pbk.)
1. Older child adoption—United States. 2. Adopted children—psychology. I. Title
HV875.55 .M34 1999
362.73'4–dc21   2003111480

Printed in the United States of America

Third printing (first softcover edition), September 2003

To my children, Meghan, Patrick, and Connor,
who fill my days with love and laughter

And to my "heart" children, Vince, Amanda, and Jen,
for allowing me to share in your lives
and for all that you've taught me

❖ Acknowledgments ❖

I would like to extend special thanks to my editor, Virginia Van Vynckt, for all her advice, patience, and encouragement in making this mutual dream a reality. I would also like to thank my copy editor, Marv Weinstein, for working his magic on my manuscript. I couldn't have done it without either of you.

Thanks to AnnaMarie Merrill, Kristie McKinney, Donna Class, Joanne Weaver, and Jon Pennington for their invaluable input in reviewing the final manuscript.

I am especially grateful to the fifty families and adult adoptees who shared their stories and thoughts with me. Their experiences, insights and advice make this truly a parent-to-parent book. A special thank you to Carole H., Sarah P., and Susan H. for going above and beyond the call of duty.

I would also like to thank Judith Ashton, Teri Bell, Linda Grillo, Dr. Jerri Jenista, Dee Paddock, Dr. Joyce Maguire Pavao, Sandra Russell, Joanne Weaver, and Adoptive Families Together for their professional insights.

I would not have been able to survive the process of writing this book without the support, encouragement, and mutual kvetching of my family and friends. A special thanks to novelist Cathryn Alpert for her encouragement and for sharing the agony of writer's block with me.

I owe my biggest debt of gratitude to my husband, Mike, and to my kids, Meghan, Patrick, and Connor, who did more than their fair share of the cooking and cleaning while I worked on the book and who graciously endured my long hours at the computer.

One of my greatest pleasures is hearing from adoptive parents who have found this book helpful, and who share their experiences and insights. Many thanks to all of you.

—*Trish Maskew*

❖ Contents ❖

❖ Introduction ❖

At least once a week someone will approach me and my obviously adopted children and ask, "Do you have children of your own, too?" Or, if my birthdaughter is with me, "And *she* is your own, right?" My standard response is, "They are *all* my own." Some people get it, others don't.

In talking to many families, I've found that people often ask adoptive parents the most personal questions about their children. At the least these unwanted conversations can be annoying; at worst they are hurtful to both me and my children, who are old enough to understand the implication.

As committed parents who love our children, we find it maddening that others don't see our family as real. *Our adopted children are our own, completely and truly.* Once I made a commitment to parenting my adopted children—and especially after the initial adjustment period when they were no longer "strangers" to us—they did truly become *my own.*

My husband and I have parented a birthchild, done foster care, and adopted two older children. To us, all of those kids, regardless of how old they were when they joined our family or how much time they spent in our home, are our own. They have a piece of our hearts and our lives. Adopting older children has brought a new dimension to our family, and our kids have taught us and given us more than we could ever hope to give them.

When we first considered older child adoption, there were very few resources to answer our questions. Even now, some ten years later, adoptive parents have few choices, and many of the books and articles out there emphasize the clinical over the practical. Over the years, I came to the conclusion that what adoptive parents needed, what *we* needed, was a book about older child adoption from those who had lived it every day. From parents to parents.

I hope you will find *Our Own* helpful as you make the journey from prospective adoptive parent to new parent to experienced parent. For this book, I interviewed about forty families with adopted children and also asked several adults who had been adopted about their experiences. Although I consulted experienced adoption professionals and have read many clinical works, this is not intended as professional advice. It is rather the sum of my experiences as a parent, coupled with the experiences of many families, some with as many as twenty children. *Our Own* contains the stories of real people. Whatever conclusions it draws as to what children do and why they do it are the conclusions of those who have lived older child adoption day in and day out for years. The identities of all the families and individuals in this book (except for people quoted in a professional context), as well as a few details, have been changed to protect the families' privacy.

It is my hope that as you read *Our Own* you will be enriched by the experiences of others, educated about the feelings and events that shape adopted children and their families, and encouraged to make an older child part of your family. As adoptive families, it often falls to us to educate others, even adoption professionals, about what adoption really entails. It is my hope that as we share our experiences, both good and bad, we will inspire more people to view adoption as a legitimate, normal way to form families. Most of all, it is my hope that this book will play a small part in teaching the world that our adopted children really are *our own.*

❖ 1 ❖

The Decision to Adopt

Have you ever stood in front of a mirror and asked yourself, "Am I crazy?"

If you're considering adopting an older child, you will. It's a perfectly honest and normal reaction to a decision that will change your family's life forever.

I vividly remember the night I asked myself this question. Our second son, five years old, had been home about a month. His previous adoptive placement hadn't worked out and he was scared and sad. I slept lightly, afraid that I would not hear his soft crying if he woke up in the dark. Our ten-year-old son was having trouble, too. His brother's arrival sparked memories of his own move eighteen months before. He was afraid we wouldn't want him anymore now that we had a "smaller, cuter son," and he was angry at the disruption of his calm, happy life. To top it all off, our nine-year-old daughter had decided that she'd had enough of her needy brothers and she wanted attention.

When I finally got them all down for the night, I wrapped myself up in a blanket, collapsed on the bed and cried my eyes out. I kept asking myself, "Why did I do this? Am I crazy?" I just knew I had really messed up this time! Thankfully, I fell into a deep sleep and woke up refreshed and ready to start another day. That night was the turning point for us, but for a few hours there I had serious questions about my sanity.

"Are you crazy?" is also the reaction, spoken or unspoken, that you'll get from many of your friends and relatives, particularly if you're adopting a child with special medical or emotional needs. Complete strangers will walk up to you and say, "I could never do what you did!" This may mean that they admire you for your decision. But it also just as likely means, "You're really crazy! I would never do that!" Adopting an older child—pre-school age and older for the purposes of this book—is just something a lot of people cannot understand, and never will. Meanwhile, you'll read and hear media stories of adoptions gone "bad" and families in chaos. You may begin to wonder if older child adoptions are always a disaster.

The good news is that you are not crazy for considering older child adoption. Most families with older adopted children do quite well. Surveys have shown that about 70 to 75 percent of families who adopt a child over the age of four consider the adoption successful. The adoptions that don't work out well often involve children who have serious behavioral problems due to trauma in their early lives.

Most families feel adoption is one of the best things they ever did. The Joneses adopted three children, ages eleven, twelve, and thirteen, from Vietnam. They say, "These children are the joy of our life! They are our reward and they have brought us so much more than we expected. We would do it again in a minute." Many adoptive families are approached by people telling them how lucky their children are to have been adopted. But adoptive parents almost uniformly respond, "We are the lucky ones!"

That doesn't mean that the families do not face problems, often for years. These children have suffered abandonment, rejection, and often abuse, and may struggle with grief, anger, fear, homesickness, and loss of self-esteem. Most, however, will grow up to lead fulfilling lives.

Even those families who have endured difficulties often think positively about adoption because it puts the rest of life into perspective. These kids are great examples of the ability of the human spirit to overcome adversity. They bring their families back down to the basics: love for family, the desire to do good for others, and the benefits of enduring difficulties together. It is difficult to get upset because you can't get a reservation at your favorite restaurant when all you can think about is how grateful you are that your son made it home from the other side of the world. It is hard to be concerned with how fashionable your clothes are while rejoicing that your daughter with learning disabilities has finally read her first book.

In *Our Own,* I hope to bring the reality of older-child adoption into focus. By dispelling myths, both good and bad, this book will help you make better decisions about whether older child adoption is for you. Learning about common adjustment issues can help banish some of your fear and uncertainty. Families who are informed, educated, and prepared make better homes for kids whose lives have already been shattered by insecurity, rejection, and hopelessness.

"Am I crazy" is probably just one of the many questions on your mind as you pursue the adoption of an older child. Others include:

- ❖ Why do families adopt?
- ❖ Why do I want to adopt an older child?
- ❖ Who are the children available for adoption, and why?
- ❖ Do I have what it takes to successfully adopt and parent an older child?
- ❖ What kind of support and resources can I rely on?

Carefully considering these questions and their answers can help you decide if adopting an older child is really for you.

Why Do Families Adopt?

Generally, parents who adopt infants admit that adoption was not their first choice. Many come to adoption after learning that they could not have biological children, and often after spending years and thousands of dollars on infertility treatments. Many who adopt children who are no longer babies, on the other hand, report having always had the desire to adopt older kids, including those with special medical or emotional needs. Some even view it as a calling of sorts, something they feel compelled to do.

Brent, a single dad who adopted two boys, six and eight, from India, was in high school when a doctor in his church adopted a Vietnamese refugee. That first sparked his interest in older child adoption.

Tara, mother of two boys adopted at ages eight and five, says that as a teenager, she would see news segments about waiting kids and know that she would someday adopt an older child.

For some parents, the decision is influenced by their ages and, often, whether they already have kids.

"We'd done the 'baby thing,'" says Gail, "and while it was fun, we figured we were getting too old to deal with bottles and car seats and dirty diapers. Plus, we wanted a kid closer in age to our daughter so she'd have somebody to play with."

Single parents are becoming more and more acceptable to many—but not all—adoption agencies. The reasons singles choose older child adoption are varied, although it is clear that some think they have no other choice.

Nancy, a single woman in her thirties, started thinking of the things she hadn't achieved and finally concluded, "I really don't care if I get married—if I do, fine, if not, fine. But if I get to sixty-five, what am I going to look back on and regret, and I realized I'd regret not having children." Her state agency told Nancy that, because she was single, she could adopt only older children. She felt fortunate to get a seven-year-old girl. A few weeks after her daughter was placed with her for adoption, the same agency placed a healthy biracial infant with her because they couldn't find a home for him elsewhere.

Occasionally, parents will see something in the news and suddenly decide to pursue adoption, never having considered it before. "I saw a picture in the paper one morning with just a few lines of text about Jim. He was nine years old and deaf, and was living in an orphanage in Asia," says Shirley, a single mom in her late fifties. "I felt like I could handle it so I thought I would call and ask for information, although I was sure I would not qualify. I was wrong!" Almost a year later, Jim joined his new family and is now learning sign language and making good progress in school.

Liam and Colleen, a couple in their mid-twenties, had unsuccessfully pursued infant adoption before finding a photolisting of available children on the Internet. Colleen explains, "There were so many children in this age group [six- to nine-year-olds] and so few infants. Why would we want to adopt an infant? They'll always be adopted, they'll always find homes."

Allison and her husband, Shawn, had talked about adoption on and off for almost five years before answering an ad in the paper for prospective parents for infants from China. After finding out they were ineligible "for about thirty different reasons," they received a call from a social worker asking them to review a video of two children, ages six and four, in a Russian orphanage. "After we saw it, that was it!" Allison says. "We knew these were our children."

Why Do I Want to Adopt?

Your answers to this question will be as individual as you are. But it pays to carefully examine your motives in adopting.

Are you pursuing an older child adoption purely as a way to help a "needy" or "hurt" child? While altruism is worthy, adoption professionals warn against choosing a child solely for such reasons. The fantasy "rescued waif" will soon become the reality of a flesh-and-blood child complete with personality, behavioral habits, and emotional issues.

Myth: Children will be eternally grateful to you for rescuing them from their terrible life.

Fact: No child can be perfect enough to fulfill your expectation of "grateful orphan."

It is hard for some to believe that children who have endured abuse, famine, abandonment, or institutionalization will ever be ungrateful. But the life the child is living is, at least, familiar. Even children who live in abusive or neglectful homes consider them "home," and few would ever choose to leave. To the child, adoption is not rescue, it is change—and change is scary. Many children who live in orphanages come to view them as home, too. We can't expect that children will be grateful just because we have met some of their needs. How many of us would be so grateful to neighbors who brought us food when we were ill that we would graciously turn our lives over to their control? Altruism by itself is not a good reason to adopt.

Whether they give birth or adopt, people always have selfish reasons for choosing to become parents. Pure selfishness, however, like pure altruism, can create problems. If you adopt only for yourself, to have the child you never had, then you may be expecting your child to live up to the fantasy of a perfect child. You cannot mold your child, biological or adopted, to fit an ideal or to fill all the "gaps" in your life. Nor can you adopt to impress others. No one else has to live with the child twenty-four hours a day, seven days a week. If your expectations are not realistic, the adoption will be in trouble before it has ever begun.

You should strive for a balance of selfish and altruistic goals in adoption. This allows you the rewards of meeting personal goals, helping a child, and at the same time allowing her to exercise her personal feelings and independence in an environment of acceptance and realism. Most families sum up this balance with a single statement: "We wanted to *parent* a child." Parenting consists of meeting a child's physical, emotional, and spiritual needs. Parents gain satisfaction in their job by imparting their cherished values and ideas, and by watching their child achieve his or her full potential, whatever that potential might be.

Gail, adoptive mother of two, expresses it this way: "Parenting gives you a fresh outlook on the world. It's hard to be jaded when a kid excitedly says, 'Mom, look at that rainbow!' Parenting also challenges you like nothing else on earth. I figure if you're a successful Mom or Dad, you—and your kids—can be anything."

Who Are the Children Available?

There are some 500,000 children in America's foster care system at any given time, with approximately 100,000 available for adoption. Two-thirds of these children are over the age of five. Another 29 percent are between ages one and five. There are countless more throughout the world waiting for families.

The United States is one of a handful of countries that remove children from their biological parents for reasons of abuse and neglect. Many countries do not, simply because the state does not have the means to support them. Children seldom enter America's foster care system as true orphans. Most have suffered years of neglect and/or abuse. Often, the children who eventually become available for adoption have moved in and out of foster care numerous times. Many are continually returned to abusive or neglectful homes after parents take minimal steps to convince the court that they have changed. Children are seldom returned to the same foster family when they reenter care, further disrupting their lives.

Trina's son Ryan was removed from his home by the police

and placed in a foster home, where he stayed for two weeks. He was returned to his birthmom, and lived with her for five more months. Trina isn't sure he lived with his birthmother exclusively during that time, as she reportedly left him with people she considered very close friends. He was again put into foster care, where he stayed until he was placed with Trina's family nine months later. In those intervening nine months he was moved seven times, Trina says. When she counted up all the times he was moved from one home to another, including back and forth to his birthmom and her friends, she realized her son had experienced at least eleven moves in just twenty-six months.

Some children have physical disabilities that require special care. Often these children have spent much of their life in foster care. Almost all children available for adoption will certainly have the normal adoption issues of feeling abandoned and rejected. A large percentage will have serious abuse issues as well, and require long-term counseling. Children who were seriously abused or neglected as infants, or who have moved many times, may find it difficult, even impossible, to attach to their new families. Some children were exposed prenatally to drugs and alcohol, causing lifelong emotional and physical difficulties. Others are basically healthy emotionally, but wait simply because of their race or age, or because they have siblings who must be placed with them.

Jason, who is African-American, entered the state foster care system at the age of three. He spent almost six years in different foster homes, including two pre-adoptive placements that did not work out, before he finally found his forever family. He has settled in nicely with his parents and three siblings, and his adoption has been finalized.

Internationally, some children are removed from their homes for abuse and neglect, but many enter orphanages either because their parents have died or because poverty makes it impossible for their families to support them. Some have medical conditions that can't be easily treated in their countries or that would pose impossible financial or emotional hardships for them and their families. Available children may suffer from malnutrition or other physical effects of poverty. Many will have experienced the death of their parents. Some suffer from fetal alcohol syndrome or the long-term effects of institutionalization, such as developmental delays or attachment difficulties. Many older children wait simply because they are boys, and most internationally adopting families request girls.

Myth: All these children need is love and a good home and they'll be fine.

Fact: Most available children, both in the United States and abroad, will have adoption issues that "love and a good home" alone cannot fix. Regardless of how good their new homes are, they will have to work through fears and anger related to abandonment and rejection. These fears and anger often surface during the teen years as adopted children attempt to form an identity and struggle to decide which qualities of both families to retain.

Myth: Most of these kids will never recover from their abusive experiences. They will never attach to their new families and will grow up to be criminals.

Fact: While some children are indeed so damaged by long-term abuse or neglect that they will never overcome their legacy of pain and violence, most of these kids will attach to their new families and become productive adults.

You do, however, need to educate yourself thoroughly about the effects of long-term abuse and/or neglect, multiple foster care placements, or life in an institution before you even begin the process to adopt. Read as many books as possible, and talk to as many people as you can who have adopted older children.

Parents and professionals debate endlessly over whether children adopted domestically or internationally tend to fare better. Internationally, children are less likely to have come into care for abuse and less likely to have been moved countless times—making it more likely they'll be able to attach to their new families and overcome previous trauma. Some countries do rival the U.S. system in the number of children who will have long-term behavioral or emotional problems.

On the other hand, if you adopt internationally you must deal with language difficulties, cultural differences, sketchy or nonexistent family history, and possibly undiagnosed medical problems. The largest difference, however, is cost. Foreign adoptions cost on average $15,000 to $25,000, a sum many families simply cannot afford.

Nancy, a single mom of four adopted children, has adopted older children from both the States and Asia. She says she doesn't understand why people will pay $20,000 or more to adopt a child from Europe when they can adopt children here who have the same or fewer problems. However, she adds, "I started a foster parent association and have been active in a local adoption group. I don't know anyone who has adopted domestically who hasn't had major problems, and I know a lot of families." After research, Nancy decided to adopt her second older child from Asia, as she found that many experienced parents believe children from Asia have fewer problems.

Some adoption professionals agree with that assessment, some do not. Kids can have problems regardless of which country they are from. They all have different family histories, different orphanage experiences, and different temperaments.

Countless families have adopted domestically with good results. Alan and Theresa, parents of twelve children, adopted four siblings several years ago. Although the children had been abused, they are attached to their adoptive family and functioning well in their new home. Even many families who have children with severe special needs advocate for domestic adoption. Trina and her husband Doug, adoptive parents to three older children, deal with autism and cerebral palsy on a daily basis. However, Trina reports that all of her children are fully attached and doing well. "Domestic adoption is cheaper, it is safer and we have just as many kids who need homes here as they do in Europe or South America," she says.

All debate aside, it is, of course, up to you to decide whether international or domestic adoption is right for you.

Do I Have What It Takes?

You owe it to yourself and your future kids to determine whether you have the resources and qualities needed to make adoption a success. Adoptive parents are not special. Some find that parenting comes naturally, while others have to really work at it. Many

❖ How Would You React? ❖

1. Your son is throwing another tantrum, as he has done daily for the last year. He is twelve.

2. You watch in amazement as your new daughter eats her sixth banana today.

3. Your son is ten and knows better, but is disobeying. Your friends tell you not to discipline him. After all, "he's had a horrible life."

4. This week your nine-year-old son has destroyed two appliances and three sets of clothes, and broken every house rule. When you correct him, he bursts into tears.

5. Your eight-year-old son, home three weeks, is noisily devouring his dinner, eating with his hands. Your parents look on with horror.

6. In a state of numbing exhaustion, you pour vegetable oil instead of vinegar into your mop water and proceed to wash the kitchen floor.

7. You've exhausted all avenues of outpatient therapy and your daughter is still a risk to herself and the family.

8. Your son tells your spouse that you locked him in his room today, and you are amazed to see your spouse looking at you suspiciously.

9. Your daughter, six, has just suffered two hours of night terrors, as she has each and every night for the last six weeks.

10. Each night for the last six months, you've stood at the washing machine, bleary-eyed, putting urine-soaked sheets in to soak.

11. You'd like to go out for the evening, but now that the neighbors have heard the story of how your daughter locked your friend in the bath for two hours, you doubt you'll find a baby-sitter.

12. Each night after you kiss your daughter goodnight, you lock her in her room so she cannot molest her siblings while you sleep.

13. Your family and friends have stood by you for a year, but some of your new son's behavior is not improving. As the final straw, your daughter says she's sorry you ever brought him into the family.

14. The special ed team at your son's school has just informed you that he is not simply learning English slowly. He has permanent learning disabilities, most likely from prenatal alcohol exposure.

15. Your son, ten, refuses to sleep alone in his room and screams until you let him sleep with you.

16. You come home from work to find a police officer waiting for you with your daughter, eleven. She was caught shoplifting.

17. Your daughter, ten, leans back in her restaurant chair and sucks her thumb.

18. Your son refuses to eat, although he is very malnourished.

19. Your newly arrived son, age eight, is groping for your breast and wants you to nurse him.

20. Your daughter, who's been in the family for six years now, doesn't want you to be her parents anymore.

people underestimate their own ability to handle difficult circumstances. Families often find that weathering difficulties and successfully emerging on the other side enriches their lives. Still, no family, regardless of how many children they have raised, can be sure how they will handle a given situation.

On the opposite page is a list of questions that can help you evaluate whether you're ready for older child adoption. These scenarios are drawn from adoptive families' real-life experiences. As you rate your reaction to each situation, pay particular attention to your initial response, as it is often the most honest.

Which of the following thoughts would you most likely have if faced with this situation?

a) This is perfectly normal given the situation.

b) Okay, this is a little tough. I need to do some reading or talk to my support group about this.

c) I need to call the social worker and/or therapist *now*!"

d) This is hopeless and I can't handle any more. The child will have to leave."

Add up your total score, using the following: a=1; b=2; c=3; d=4. I based the following evaluations on the opinions and experiences of many adoptive families. But keep in mind that there are no "right" answers to any of these questions. Only you can decide whether older child adoption is for you. Two people can react to identical situations in entirely different ways that are appropriate for their particular families.

Total score under 40: You display a high level of confidence in your parenting abilities. Experienced families with strong support systems can often weather difficult times amazingly well. Parents who have gained knowledge and experience about the difficulties older children sometimes face are generally well equipped to handle the behaviors that these kids bring with them.

On the other hand, you may need to question whether you are being realistic about how difficult some of the above situations can be—even for experienced families. Situations 7, 12, and 14 are extremely difficult and require the help of therapists or other professionals.

40 to 60 points: You have lots of company if you scored in this range. Successful adoptive parents realize that virtually all newly adopted children experience some of these behaviors, especially those involving eating, sleeping, and regression. On the other hand, realizing that difficulties involving prenatal exposure to drugs and alcohol, attachment difficulties, and abuse are always possible can make even experienced parents anxious. This mix of optimism and awareness is typical of the successful adoptive families I've talked with.

60 to 80 points: If you scored in this range, it's possible that this is your first look at the types of behaviors older kids can exhibit. Or perhaps you have never parented before and have little confidence in your abilities. A high score does not necessarily mean that older child adoption is not for you. However, you may want to discuss some of these behaviors with your social worker or support group and do some additional reading on adoption issues. Preparation is a key element in adoption success.

While a few of the above situations are extreme, most of them fall into the "normal" range of experiences for children adopted at an older age. Most of these behaviors diminish greatly after the child feels secure in his new home. Prolonged abuse and neglect can aggravate normal adjustment behaviors, and family counseling is usually necessary in that case. While these experiences are difficult, most families find a way to work through them.

Although you need to be prepared for the worst, undue worry about the possibility of extreme behavior can be harmful as well.

Successfully handling situations such as those described requires commitment, flexibility, empathy, and intuition, as well as a strong support system.

Commitment

Are you willing to commit yourself to being this child's parent forever? Parenthood is *not* a disposable commodity. Children available for adoption may be poor, malnourished, or orphaned or have serious behavioral difficulties, but they are human. They deserve and need the same love and security that you do.

Most parents who have infants the "regular" way expect a couple of years of sleepless nights and family turmoil. They expect that their child will go through annoying phases, get sick now and then, and not always reach milestones on "schedule." Imagine, if you will, a couple entering their pediatrician's office. They are worn out, pale and shaken. Their son by birth, four months old, has colic. He cries nightly, sometimes for hours, and their lack of sleep is taking its toll. They are at the end of their rope. They say to their doctor, "We can't take it anymore. This is not the type of child we expected and we don't think we can keep him. You'll have to find another home for him."

Or imagine a frustrated mom speaking with a school psychologist. Her birthdaughter has failed fourth grade, again. Her learning disabilities are profound and progress is slow. In addition, her work habits are sloppy, making academics a failing proposition. Her mother has tried all the methods, spent thousands of dollars on tutors, and tried every disciplinary technique she knows. She tells the psychologist to call the state and have her daughter removed from her home.

Do these situations strike you as preposterous? Of course. Few parents would willingly relinquish their birthchildren because developmental, medical, or behavioral problems made them difficult to raise. However, some families have disrupted adoptive placements (returned the child to state or agency custody) for these reasons.

Chloe and her husband Stan adopted a young boy whose previous adoptive family had relinquished custody. "According to the agency, the family was upset because he had night terrors every night, sometimes for a couple of hours," says Chloe. "After a few weeks, they couldn't take it anymore."

Agencies occasionally get shocking reminders that not all adopting parents take their commitment to their children seriously. One agency received a phone call from a prospective client who asked, "What is your return policy?"

Another agency worker reports hearing about a couple who became pregnant after they had adopted a Russian baby. They wanted to know what to do about "the other one."

While shocking, these examples drive home the point that commitment is vital, and that many in our society consider adoption "second best." Each move a child experiences reduces the chances that he'll find a permanent home. Simply put, you should be willing to commit to your adopted children as deeply and unequivocally as you would your birthchildren. All children can have medical problems, learning disabilities, and behavioral problems. Parenthood does not come with guarantees. The one thing the successful adoptive parents I've talked to have in common is that they view themselves as parents, unconditionally.

But what if the child has serious emotional issues? Perhaps a child has true attachment difficulties and is a danger to herself and the family. Or perhaps she has fetal alcohol syndrome and is barely functioning in school. Should families disrupt adoptions for these reasons? While it is understandable that families cannot continue to live in a dangerous situation, there are options short of disruption, which is permanent. Children with attachment difficulties often require residential treatment, meaning the child lives in a home away from her family. Parents do sometimes simply disrupt the placement when the child is removed from their home. However, many families choose to continue their family bonds although their child does not live with them. They visit or call the child, and still call her their daughter. Such a commitment proves to the child that she is still loved and accepted, even if she cannot live at home.

It is unfair to say that adoptive placements should *never* disrupt; in some cases, disruption may be in the child's best interests. Adoptive parents should, however, be determined to stick with the placement until no other option is available. The trusted adults in their lives have hurt these children, often repeatedly. Many of them will not survive yet another rejection.

Flexibility

Agencies look for parents who are flexible and have realistic expectations. To be a successful parent, you have to be willing to accommodate different personalities and to concentrate on the most serious behavior problems first, leaving the minor things for later. If your child has been abused or has serious developmental delays, she may never meet your initial expectations. You have to alter your expectations, not the child.

Many times parents have a picture of what their child will be like, and spend much time planning how they will relate to their fantasy child. However, seldom does the reality mesh with the fantasy. Parents who adopt children internationally often have only a picture or video to base their expectations on. Colleen, whose daughter arrived from Russia at age seven, recalls, "From what they wrote about her, we were expecting a shy, little demure girl—that she would be meek. She's so different. She is a big ham and performer."

Veronica, who adopted nine-year-old Jason from the U.S. system, recalls imagining him as "smart, well-behaved, adoring, loving, accepting." She says he met almost all her expectations except that the "loving part is still well in the works. He definitely keeps his emotional walls up."

Other expectations center on age. You may be quite tolerant of a three-year-old sucking her thumb, but mortified at a ten-year-old doing so. However, it's normal for children to regress to earlier stages of development when they join a new family. Often, the move brings back memories of prior losses and children regress to the age they were then. Or, in an effort to establish appropriate parent-child bonds, the child may regress to an age where he can feel "babied."

Children generally arrive in their families with numerous behaviors that need to be adjusted. Many families address the most serious behaviors first and leave minor ones until the child has settled in. This may mean that small but annoying issues, like table manners, are not addressed for quite some time. In the exhausting first weeks of placement, it is unreasonable for a parent or child to attempt to change every behavior. Deanna and her husband adopted an eight-year-old boy. Deanna says they've had to pick their battles with their new son, and this perceived "unfairness" has been particularly hard on their daughter. "She does not believe that I pick my battles with her, too." Other children in the home can become upset if they see the new child "getting away" with something they would not be allowed to do. It's a good idea for parents to prepare their other children for this situation.

Parents sometimes have to change their long-term expectations, too. A parent who feels education is a top priority may have trouble accepting a child who turns out to have learning disabilities. This scenario often plays out in biological families as well. It can be difficult for a parent who is expecting his son to attend university to accept that the child may finish high school only with great effort. Children who arrive at an older age may already have ideas about their career choices, too, and may not listen to your suggestions.

Empathy

Empathy is the ability to identify mentally with a person so that you can understand his feelings. Empathy is a must for adoptive parents. Children who have lost their birthfamilies, for whatever reason, will feel abandoned and rejected. You must be able to see things through your child's eyes.

You can use the memories of your most profound losses to help you relate to your children. If you have experienced infertility, you know how hard it was, and still is, at times, to accept that you can't have biological children. All your hopes and dreams for the child you imagined having together are gone, and that hurts, badly. You may grow to accept your infertility and you will love your adopted children truly as your "own," but the loss is still there. In a similar way, no matter how much they grow to love their adoptive parents, adopted children will always feel the loss of their birthparents. If you have lost someone close to you, through death, divorce, or estrangement, even as an adult, you will be better able to empathize with your child as well. Losing a parent is a traumatic experience, even for adults with mature coping skills. How much more so is it for a child?

Adopted children also feel that they're powerless, that others are controlling their lives, for better or worse. As an adoptive parent, you should be able to relate to that as well. Throughout the adoption process, most families feel powerless; their lives and schedules are at the mercy of agencies and government officials. You may start out by having a good relationship with your social worker. However, once the home study is complete and you're forced to wait and to navigate an often-frustrating system, this may change. Even though your personal worker may not be responsible for the delays and setbacks, you may well take your frustration out on her. In much the same way, children will dump their emotional baggage on the people who are the closest and most trusted—their parents.

If you can draw on your own issues of separation and loss, you'll be better equipped to handle your child's emotional needs. There will be days when your child will wish she was not adopted, regardless of how much she loves you. There will always be missing pieces in her life, and you will not be able to supply them. It is difficult to watch your child struggle with her sadness and anger, but true empathy, offered at the proper time, will help.

Intuition

Intuition, the ability to discern what is happening in a situation without being told, is also an essential quality for parents. Intuition gives you the ability to see when emotional issues are masquerading as behavioral problems. Parents who have children by birth or who adopted them as infants can often tell when a kid is having a lousy day, is tired, or is not feeling well. It can be considerably harder to make those calls if you've known your eight-year-old for only six months! However, if he's normally well-behaved, and then acts totally obnoxious several days in a row, it's a pretty safe bet that something is going on emotionally. Instead of focusing on how his behavior affects you, stand back and see if there is a pattern that will explain his actions.

"One week Simon was horrid. He broke one house rule after another, and I was furious. It was so unlike him," says Tara about her son. "After a couple of days of grumbling about how awful this usually good kid was being, I decided to ask him why he was doing so many bad things. He broke down crying and told me that he was a bad kid—always had been and always would be. All of a sudden his actions made sense. He was acting out his feelings of low self-worth. After a long talk, he was back to his old bubbly self again."

What Kind of Support Will I Have?

During the initial stages of adoption especially, you will need plenty of support. It is difficult to deal with behavioral problems when your friends and family keep insisting that you "send him back." If you're married, it's absolutely essential that both of you want to pursue this adoption. Children are master manipulators, especially if they have experienced abusive pasts, and your child will test your relationship. She will check to see if either parent has easier standards and may attempt to break you apart if she is uncomfortable with one of you. You should seriously consider how strong your marriage is before you adopt.

It is especially important for single parents to make sure they have strong support systems in place. Having friends and family available to discuss things, encourage you to keep going, and provide respite (short-term substitute) care if needed is essential.

Seek out those who share your desire and who can give balanced information on the joys and challenges of older child adoption. To get information:

❖ Read everything you can find of both general adoption literature and that specific to older child adoption.

You'll find a detailed list of suggested reading materials in Appendix C, but these titles are a good place to start:

Raising Adopted Children, by Lois Melina (Harper and Row, 1989)

Adopting the Older Child, by Claudia Jewett (Harvard Common Press, 1978)

Adopting the Hurt Child, by Dr. Gregory Keck and Regina Kupecky (Pinon Press, 1995)

Toddler Adoption: the Weaver's Craft, by Mary Hopkins Best (Perspectives Press, 1997)

Real Parents, Real Children by Holly van Gulden and Lisa M. Bartels-Robb (Crossroad Publishing, 1997)

Personal Accounts:

Gift Children, by J. Douglas Bates (Ticknor and Fields, 1993)

They Came to Stay, by Marjorie Margolies and Ruth Gruber (Coward, McCann & Geoghegan, 1976)

❖ Attend informational meetings.

Both public and private agencies hold meetings for those interested in adoption. Once you begin your home study, public agencies, as well as certain private agencies, conduct seminars designed to prepare families for older child adoption. These classes are not only valuable sources of information, but also are a good way to meet other adoptive families.

❖ Search the Internet.

There are numerous e-mail lists that provide information and support to present and future adoptive families. Groups may discuss adoption in general, specific issues such as special needs, or a specific country. Be careful, though—information on these lists, especially about particular agencies or procedures, is not always accurate and unbiased. Always try to get information from more than one source, and verify it independently if possible.

There also are several online magazines that deal exclusively with adoption. General adoption-related Web sites are prolific. You can research agencies, find explanations of how subsidies work, search photolistings of available children, and learn about legal, moral, and emotional issues relevant to adoption.

Trust Yourself

While it is important to discuss all the issues and spend time preparing for adoption, you must trust your own instincts. No one knows your desires and needs like you do. No one else can tell you that you do or do not have what it takes to be a successful parent. It's great to seek support from family and friends, and even better to get advice and comfort from adoptive parent support groups. But ultimately you'll have to advocate for yourself and your child. At times, you may be guided by nothing more than instinct, and you will simply have to trust yourself!

❖ 2 ❖
Getting Started

Once you decide to adopt, it's natural to want to get everything done quickly and get your child home. Unfortunately, the actual adoption process tends to be slow and difficult. In theory it would seem easy—children need parents, parents want children—just match them up! However, the decision to adopt is merely the first step. So, where do you begin?

Many will tell you that the first step is the home study, a close look at your life conducted by your state or a private agency to see if you would make suitable parents.

However, there are several things that you (and your spouse, if you're married) should think about before you set up your home study, simply because different agencies and different types of adoptions require different home studies. Some things you need to consider first are:

- ❖ How many children do I want to adopt?
- ❖ What age child(ren) do I want?
- ❖ Do I want to adopt across racial or ethnic lines?
- ❖ What kinds of disabilities am I comfortable with?
- ❖ Do I want to adopt domestically or internationally?
- ❖ Can I afford all the potential costs of this adoption?

How Many Children Do I Want to Adopt?

Do you want to adopt a single child or a sibling group? Many families feel more comfortable adding children to their family one at a time. Professionals agree that it is the most natural way to build a family. Each child has the chance to be in the family spotlight, and parents have more time to spend helping the child adjust to his new family. Adding a sibling group can aggravate adjustment issues, and make the new parents feel even more exhausted. If one sibling has severe behavioral problems, it may strain the placement for all the kids.

However, adopting siblings has its benefits, too. Many children feel more comfortable moving into a new home when they have support from loving siblings. The kids can help each other remember the events of their lives. They also maintain a biological bond that many adoptees feel is missing in their lives. Many parents who have adopted siblings feel that the benefits outweigh the additional stresses.

❖ The Home Study ❖

In order to adopt, you must have a completed home study. The home study process usually includes one or two visits to your agency, tons of paperwork, and a visit or two by the social worker to your home to make sure it's safe and suitable for children.

This two-way process doesn't just scrutinize you as potential parents. It also helps you prepare for the adoption. This is the time to bring up any concerns or questions you have about parenting, older child adoption, or this adoption in particular. Your worker can help you explore such issues, or point you to other parents or professionals who can help.

The worker will ask you why you want to adopt and what you think you have to offer a child. You will be asked about your marriage, your ideas on parenting and discipline, and your infertility if applicable. You will also be asked to provide references, health statements from your doctor, a police clearance letter and possibly fingerprints, and a financial statement. If you work, the agency will want to know about your plans to take family leave. Many agencies require that you take some time off work even if you are adopting school-age children.

During your home visits, the worker will want to know where your child will sleep and what you have done to prepare a space for him. She may check for basic safety precautions: that poisons are properly stored, that any firearms are locked up, and that you have working smoke detectors. Some agencies require that you have fire extinguishers.

Home studies for older children or for transracial adoption usually involve additional questions about the challenges you will face as a family. You may be required to do additional reading or to take parenting classes.

You may be tempted to adopt more than one child at a time, especially if you're adopting internationally, because it usually costs less than doing two separate adoptions, and you don't have to endure the long process of adopting again. If a sibling group is not available, you may try to adopt two unrelated children. Most parents and professionals advise being very careful about adopting non-related kids at the same time, and many agencies strongly discourage the practice or even disallow it.

In many cases, the kids feel intense competition for their parents' time. They have to adjust to new siblings at the same time they are adjusting to new parents, and unlike the parents' birthchildren, the other child doesn't have a bond with the parents either. This friction can lead to long-standing animosity between the kids and a long, difficult adjustment for the whole family. The effects of adopting unrelated kids may be lessened if you adopt children who have lived together most of their lives, or who shared a strong sibling-like bond in the orphanage.

You also need to consider how you might feel about adopting only one or two kids out of a sibling group. While many parents and professionals say it's almost always better to keep brothers and sisters together, agencies will sometimes split up siblings if they cannot find a family to adopt all of them. Some countries resist placing two children at a time, even if they're birthsiblings. In domestic adoption, it's not uncommon for siblings to have been raised in different foster families. One might be adopted by his foster family, while the other is not. Unless the siblings have been in close contact, they may face some of the issues unrelated children do when adopted together.

What Age Child Do I Want?

When you picture your child in your mind, what age is he? This is one indication of the age you are most comfortable with. Some families have a maximum age that they don't want to exceed. Perhaps a child who is just starting school is best for you. Some families think they could add a child up to age ten, while others are comfortable adding teens to their family.

There are several things to think about when deciding on an age. The first is your age. Some countries and agencies have age requirements for parents. Vietnamese law, for example, requires that adoptive parents be twenty years older than the child they are adopting. Many domestic agencies have maximum age restrictions. In some instances, age requirements are lifted for children over school age. If your age could be considered a liability—that is, if you are under thirty or over fifty—find out which agencies and/or countries consider you eligible.

Consider the ages of the children already in your family. Do you want your new child to be the oldest or the youngest or somewhere in the middle? For many years, agencies insisted that families not disturb the birth order of their children. Many still feel that it is best for the newest child to be the youngest in the family. These rules are not set in stone, however, and agencies do make exceptions. How do you decide what is best? If your oldest daughter has a strong personality and is a natural leader, it may be difficult for her to relinquish her role as the oldest child. On the other hand, a child who is shy or easygoing may not mind having an older sibling.

"When we talked to our kids about adoption, one of the prerequisites, especially for our second-born, Brittany, was 'nobody older than me,'" say Denise and Bruce, parents of sixteen children, twelve of them adopted. "There was a sib group but one of the three was older than Brittany. The agency offered to split them up, but we didn't want to do that. But changing the birth order on Brittany was a huge problem—probably the biggest our family has ever faced. You could just feel the tension. She told us it was okay, but later she told us that she only did because she didn't want to feel guilty about splitting them up. She carried that bitterness for several years. Dawn seemed a lot younger than her, but to Brittany it didn't really matter—there was just something about the fact that she was older. They wouldn't sit by each other, wouldn't speak to each other, wouldn't walk to the bus together."

On the other hand, Tara and Eric adopted a boy who was nine months older than their birthdaughter, and report no problems. "Julie wanted a new sibling so badly that she didn't really care that he was older by a few months, and they don't seem to compete much either," says Eric. "Of course, they're different sexes, which we know helps. Julie would have had a much harder time with another girl, we think."

Some families find that getting children younger than their other kids, the most accepted practice because it is the most natural, is also troublesome. After all, some kids are invested in being the "baby" of the family. Allison says that when her new kids came home, her daughter Caitlyn had a really hard time. She was used to being the baby of the family and was quite upset that she was being "replaced."

Twinning, the pairing of two non-related children of the same age, is becoming more common. However, most social workers caution families against twinning children of the same sex, as the competition can be fierce. You should take the time to think about how difficult it would be if one daughter entered puberty much earlier than the other, or what difficulties could arise if both your sons liked the same girl, or if one son was a much better student than the other. Many agencies will not let families twin same-sex children at all. However, in some cases, such decisions are left solely to each family.

Do I Want to Adopt Across Racial or Ethnic Lines?

Many families adopt transracially with great success, but not all people think transracial adoption is good for the child. In 1972, the National Association of Black Social Workers issued a statement condemning transracial adoption. They felt that placing black children with white parents was cultural genocide and that there were plenty of black families willing to adopt the children, but that agencies did not pursue them enough. For many years, there were policies making transracial placement difficult. That changed with the passage of the Multi-Ethnic Placement Act in 1994, which prohibits discrimination against an adoptive family solely on the basis of race. However, it is customary for agencies to seek parents of the same race first. This can be extremely frustrating for some adoptive parents.

Brenda, a single woman in her forties, is trying to adopt two school-age children. She located two Asian boys in a western state and inquired about them. She says, "I was told, 'You need to wait at least six months to call back about these kids because we will be looking for other families first, in this order: A two-parent Asian family locally, or at least in state. Then a two-parent Asian family on the West Coast or, barring that, in the rest of the United States. Then we'd accept a two-parent family where both parents are fluent in [the children's] original language, first in the city, then the state, or rest of the country. Then we'd seek a two-parent family which has a child of this racial background who is fluent ... then a two-parent family with an Asian child who is not necessarily fluent in this language. After we have exhausted all those possibilities, we will seek a single man who meets the above requirements. Lastly, we would look for a single woman with these specifications. So, you shouldn't even bother to apply for at least six to nine months, and even then it is probably not likely.' " Not all agencies go to these lengths to find same-race families first. Later, this caseworker was removed from the boys' case and they were immediately placed in a non-Asian two-parent family.

In deciding to adopt across racial or ethnic lines it is important to consider how your extended family and community will react. Many parents find that their parents or siblings don't support transracial adoption. Too, each of us must confront our own feelings about race. People often have unacknowledged prejudices. A good rule of thumb is, "Can I picture myself married to a person of this race or ethnic group?" If not, perhaps you should not adopt a child of that race either.

Cassandra, who has adopted two children from Asia, reports that her parents are mortified that she and her husband would adopt children who are so "dark." She says, "Although my parents make an effort to disguise their racism, I know that deep down my parents will never understand why Rupert and I adopted children of a different race, and they will never love them as much as their white grandchildren."

Only you can decide whether you need full family support for your adoption. Keep in mind, though, that children are often very aware of the subtle nonverbal reactions of people and may sense underlying prejudice. Some families report, however, that family members were non-supportive before the adoption, but changed their minds once they met the child.

Allison reports that before the adoption her parents were very opposed to her and Shawn adopting from overseas. But once Emily and Tyler arrived, their grandparents became their biggest cheerleaders and supporters.

Where you live also matters in transracial adoption. Do you live in a multicultural area, or is your town predominantly one race? Cities with racial diversity are often more accepting of multiracial families and offer more opportunities for cultural exploration.

Gail, mother of two Asian children, says, "Before we brought home Laura, my husband and I had planned to move to a small town. But then we realized this would not be a good idea with a Chinese-born child in our family. I wasn't worried about overt racism or hostility as much as I was about isolation. There couldn't have been more than a handful of Asian-Americans in that entire county, and I knew she would forever be 'the Chinese kid.' Who needs that?"

Multiracial families draw attention. This can be especially difficult if you have other children. If you adopt transracially, you should be willing and able to explore your child's culture and to develop ties with her racial or ethnic community. For an in-depth discussion of these topics, see Chapter 8.

What Disabilities Am I Comfortable With?

During your home study, you will likely be handed a form asking you to indicate which disabilities—physical, emotional, and behavioral—you are willing to accept. Some parents feel pressured into accepting disabilities they are not comfortable with so as not to appear too "picky." Most social workers, however, understand that families have different expectations and limits. You will not be doing yourself, your agency, or your child any favors by accepting a disability that you don't feel qualified to deal with.

Many items, especially on international adoption forms, may be unfamiliar. For example, forms may list illnesses such as atresia, hyperbilirubinemia, or hemophilia. Few of us know immediately what those terms mean. Research each item so that you feel capable of making a decision. A good medical encyclopedia usually can give you a general idea about an illness and its prognosis. Disabilities that have emotional and behavioral components are more difficult to evaluate. You should become familiar with conditions older adopted children are at greater than average risk for, such as attachment difficulties, fetal alcohol syndrome, sensory integration disorder, and attention deficit disorder.

Often the child acceptance forms will have a place to check yes, no, or maybe. "Maybe" is a safe bet. You can research a condition more fully after a child has been referred to you.

One way to become familiar with the reality of living with certain types of disabilities is to join a support group of adoptive parents who can share their experiences. Families who have adopted children with similar diagnoses can be great sources of information. There are national information centers for patients with hepatitis, cerebral palsy, cystic fibrosis, and other illnesses that can send you information and connect you with local families whose children have similar diseases. Public libraries are often good sources of information as well.

During her search for children, Trina was offered a child who had spina bifida. "I found that for me, the issue of 'disability' was one that I needed to explore more," she says. "With a lot of help, I learned [enough] about spina bifida to know that, contrary to what I thought, it was indeed a disability that would be appropriate for our family. We ended up not adopting her because it was a baby, which we weren't looking for, and because we have a lot of stairs. But the aspect of raising a child with spina bifida was no longer uncomfortable to me."

Domestic or International?

Often, the single most important factor in the international vs. domestic decision is cost. Beyond that, families who adopt domestically generally feel that there are more than enough children here who need permanent homes. They also cite the availability of information regarding their child's medical, social, and educational past as a definite plus, and enjoy having the opportunity to meet their child before the adoption. Families who adopt internationally often mention the fact that it is easier to find available children without apparent major emotional or physical disabilities.

Some families turn to international adoption after years of trying to adopt domestically but being turned away because the child they were hoping to adopt could not be moved past county or state lines or the parents were considered too old, or because there were several families vying for the same child. There are usually more families available for children who are younger or are emotionally healthy, and some families find that they are only referred children with serious problems. One social worker told Brenda, a single woman in her mid-forties, that she would only be considered for teenage girls who had been sexually abused. Other reasons given for choosing international adoption are: less fear of birthparent interference, shorter waiting times, the desire to help needy children around the world, and the opportunity for travel.

Can I Afford All the Potential Costs?

The most obvious costs are the agency and legal fees needed to actually adopt the child. But that is just the tip of the iceberg. In virtually all cases, domestic adoption costs less than international adoption. State agencies do free home studies for parents desiring to adopt special needs children. Most states define special needs as children older than toddlers, or of minority heritage, or children with physical, emotional, or behavioral problems. Some families have home studies done by private agencies, however, because it is often faster and because it is easier to have the home study sent to many different states, making it easier to locate a child. Home study costs range from $500 to $3,000, with most agencies charging between $1,500 and $2,000.

Subsidies to care for adopted children are common in domestic adoption. Generally, any special needs child will receive a subsidy of some kind if adopted through the state or county agency. Subsidies are available for medical expenses, therapy, and everyday child-rearing expenses. In some cases, states also reimburse parents for their or the child's visits prior to adoption. Parents who qualify for a medical or support subsidy also usually qualify for a one-time payment for nonrecurring expenses, such as legal fees and agency fees, if any. Some states offer clothing reimbursements at the time of adoption. Subsidies vary widely from state to state and child to child. It's up to you to become familiar with the subsidy rules for your state.

In most cases, subsidies have to be negotiated *before* adoption. They can be difficult to renegotiate later, so ask for a clause agreeing to possible changes if your state allows it. Some states also may require you to relinquish custody of your child should it become necessary to place him in residential treatment. Addressing these questions ahead of time can prevent considerable trouble later. For a discussion of subsidies, see Appendix A.

In contrast, few services are available to counter the cost of international adoption. You'll most likely have to work with at least two different agencies. Many international adoption agencies provide home studies for local families, but if you live outside their service area you will need a local agency to do your study. Adoption fees and restrictions vary widely from country to country and from agency to agency. Check with several agencies before selecting a program.

Agencies sometimes discount fees for the adoption of older children, so when calling, ask if their program fees apply to infants or older children. Even agencies that do not advertise discounted fees will sometimes lower fees for a family that is interested in a child who is difficult to place. Travel costs for international adoptions can be quite high. Your agency should be able to give you approximate costs for travel to pick up your child and may work with a travel agency that offers discounts. A few countries allow children to be escorted to the United States, and your agency will be able to inform you about escort fees as well. When discussing travel with your agency, be sure figures include lodging, meals, and in-country travel (which may or may not be included in the agency fees). These costs can be substantial.

Allison and Shawn adopted two children from Russia. They were initially quoted $12,000 plus travel expenses, "but somehow it just kept growing and growing," and eventually the adoption cost them almost $28,000, Allison says.

There are several fees besides those mentioned above. The Bureau of Citizenship and Immigration Services (BCIS) requires a hefty fee for the filing of an I-600A form, the petition for adoption of a foreign-born child. You will also be required to file a dossier (a collection of documents). In some cases you will need multiple birth certificates, marriage certificates, and other documents whose costs vary from state to state. State certification can run as high as $20 per document, and you may need to have the documents translated, certified by the U.S. State Department, and approved by the foreign country's embassy.

As for initial medical and dental insurance, the Health Insurance Portability and Accountability Act of 1996 bans group health insurance carriers from using pre-existing condition limitations to exclude newly adopted children from coverage. Pre-existing conditions *must* be covered. Parents must give written notice to the carriers within thirty days of the adoption to ensure coverage. It is possible that insurance will not cover initial blood tests or tests for parasites which are recommended on your child's arrival. Some families find that the costs of "catch-up" immunizations are substantial and often not covered by insurance. Because the law covers only *group* insurance, check to see if your individual or self-employment health insurance will cover your child. Many agencies require that you provide written proof that your child will be covered. Even if they don't, a written statement from your insurance company may prevent filing problems later on.

One large expense that often catches families by surprise is dental work. Dental care is often lacking in orphanages and in some countries is virtually nonexistent. If your child came from a neglectful birthfamily, it's unlikely they took him to the dentist very often, if at all. Children may need multiple cleanings as well as extensive repair work. Shirley, who adopted two older boys from Asia, says her son Brian's teeth looked beautiful, but were a mess on the inside. He had to have $2,500 of dental care on his arrival, and her insurance covered only half of it.

Sometimes a family is able to find a professional willing to donate services. A local dentist offered to do the work on Colin and Bridget, Liam and Colleen's children, without charge. "If he hadn't we would have really been in a bind," they say.

Children adopted at an older age often need psychological

counseling. Can you afford long-term counseling if needed? Counseling can be $100 a session or more. There is no way to determine ahead of time what types of medical or psychological care will be necessary. Be prepared for all the possibilities.

Many agencies require at least one parent to take a leave of absence from work after the child's arrival. While some agencies dictate a certain length of time, others require parents to take as much time as is needed for the child to settle in. With the passage of the 1993 Family Medical Leave Act, all employees who work for companies with more than fifty employees are eligible to take up to twelve weeks of *unpaid* leave for the adoption of a child. To be eligible, you must have worked at the same company for at least 1,250 hours during the last calendar year. Check with your employer for details of your company's plan.

Consider, too, the costs of clothing and bedroom furniture. Children who come from deprived backgrounds often grow incredibly fast. One family reports that their son grew twelve inches and gained fifty pounds in the first two years! Most towns have shops that stock good-quality used clothing, and many families frequent yard sales as they struggle to keep up with their child's growth. Toys or sporting equipment such as bikes or skates can add to your initial cost as well. By counting all the costs ahead of time, you can save yourself considerable stress during the adoption process.

"How do families afford to do it?" you may ask. Here are some sources that families have used to help finance adoption:

- ❖ Grants from the National Adoption Foundation. It helps a small number of families each year. (See Appendix C.)
- ❖ Assistance from employers. Many companies now offer adoption benefits.
- ❖ The adoption tax credit. While this won't finance an adoption, it can help ease finances after the adoption is final. The amount of the federal tax credit, based on adjusted gross income, can be as high as $10,000. You may also be able to exclude from income any amounts paid by your employer for adoption expenses. Check with the Internal Revenue Service and/or your adoption agency for details.
- ❖ Military subsidies (for active-duty personnel).

❖ Home equity loans. These offer a lower interest rate and more flexible rules than most other loans. The interest may be tax-deductible. It may also be possible to refinance your initial mortgage at a lower interest rate. Home equity loans do put your home at risk if you default.

❖ Adoption loans. MBNA America offers an adoption line of credit of up to $25,000 at an interest rate of prime plus 4.9 percent. (See Appendix C.)

❖ Consumer loans. Many banks offer consumer loans that can be used for adoption. Credit unions may offer "signature" loans that require no collateral.

❖ Low-interest-rate credit cards. Beware of cards with teaser rates that rise suddenly six months later. And note that cash advances usually don't qualify for the low interest rates or the grace periods that purchases do.

❖ Personal loans from family and friends.

❖ Donations from churches or civic groups.

❖ Fund-raisers such as bake sales, car washes, or yard sales.

❖ Rearranging priorities, such as trading expensive newer cars for older ones, or removing "extras" from budgets to allow room for savings and/or loan payments.

❖ Bartering, such as offering computer skills in return for medical or dental services.

Finding Your Child in the United States

If you have decided to adopt domestically, you need to contact your local department of social services or find a local agency to do your home study.

If you want to adopt locally only, it's probably best to have your home study done by your local office of social services. However, if you're open to adopting a child from any state, you may have more success if a private agency does your study.

"It's always in your best interest to have a private home study done, even if it costs you a couple of thousand dollars," says Trina, an adoptive mother who has worked with the state system for twelve years. "A private home study will allow you to pursue any child in any state, because you will be able to send out copies of your home study yourself without involving a social worker. This saves time, aggravation, and puts you in charge of your search."

Not all social services departments are difficult to work with, obviously. Try contacting your local department first. If they are very helpful and quick to respond to your questions, you may feel comfortable working with them. If, however, your calls go unanswered or unreturned for long periods of time, your agency fails to tell you about informational meetings, or your inquiries are met with a pessimistic "there are probably no children who meet your criteria," then you may need to look elsewhere.

When looking for a private agency, ask each agency you contact how much experience it has in placing older kids, what its requirements are for adoptive parents, what post-placement services it offers, and what percentage of its older-child placements disrupt. Most state agencies require prospective parents to attend classes that look at common behavioral and adjustment issues adopted kids face. These classes are invaluable and a great source of support. Not all private agencies offer classes and post-placement support, so you may need to seek outside assistance. You should also ask the agency for a list of families who have adopted older children through them. Keep in mind, however, that agencies rarely give unbiased information and you will likely not hear from families who have been displeased. Asking other adoptive parents which agency they used may prove to be more useful in finding a good agency.

Parents often feel intimidated by social workers. They feel that the worker has the power to decide whether they get a child. Few social workers are really that tough to deal with. Many families clean furiously before a scheduled home visit only to be disappointed when the worker barely glances at the house, never mind under the beds and in the closets. The sense of intimidation can cause more serious difficulties if parents feel unable to speak out when things are not progressing as they had hoped. It sometimes takes repeated phone calls to get answers, and many families become frustrated.

Trina offers this advice: "This is the social worker's job, one that extends from eight to five, and includes sick days, vacation days, and sometimes just plain old 'out of the office' days. This is your *life*. It is the essence of who you are, who you plan to be, and how you intend to follow your bliss for the rest of your days. It is fundamental to your happiness, your peace of mind, and your well-being. So, you have every right to protect yourself and if that means to call, to continue to call, to call every day, then do so without the usual social guilt that would leave you feeling pushy or ill-mannered. These do not apply to this situation. If you need to make repeated phone calls, it's because the people at the other end are making it necessary to call repeatedly. Just do it politely."

After your home study is complete, you are ready to find a child. Some families wait for their worker to find a child for them, growing frustrated as the wait lengthens. Many parents who successfully adopt domestically, however, take a very active role in finding their child. Here are some tips on how to find a child in the United States.

❖ Do not limit yourself to your state and its social services department. Find out which states currently favor placing their children out of state. Ask which private agencies place kids in state custody; more and more private agencies are working with public departments to place older children.

❖ Use the Internet. Find the adoption-related Web sites and the e-mail lists and talk to people. Join parent support groups, meet people, go on chats, ask questions and make yourself and your search known. The more networking you do the faster you can find a child. Sometimes all it takes is finding one person who knows someone else, who knows of a child who needs a home.

❖ Check photolistings. There are two kinds of photolistings, paper and Internet. Net sites are generally updated less frequently than paper listings. Provide your agency with addresses to order photolistings that you find on the Internet. You may have to call and order them yourself. Some states will send photolistings to parents as well as agencies. Some states have centralized exchanges, and you cannot apply for a child unless you are in the database.

❖ Consider your local foster-to-adopt program. Many states are implementing these programs, in which children are placed in foster families likely to adopt them. This benefits both the child and the family.

❖ Make yourself known to every social worker you can. One family made up a packet of information that included pictures, brief essays on their family concerning holidays, education, discipline, and religion, and their home study. They kept names and numbers of everyone who received it and followed up at least once a month.

❖ Join your local foster parent support group. Sometimes children remain in limbo, not becoming legally free for adoption until a qualified family shows interest in them. States prefer not to terminate parental rights until a family is found so that the child is not left an "orphan." Once an interested family is located, parental rights are terminated quickly. Your local foster parent association may know of kids like these.

Domestic adoption requires persistence, patience, and lots of time and effort. Most parents will tell you that it is worth it.

Adopting Internationally

If you adopt internationally, you will most likely be working with two, even three, different agencies. As in domestic adoption, your choice of local agency will be the most important regarding such things as home studies, local support groups, and your relationship with your social worker. Many local agencies have a particular international agency that they work with. Ask about this before you sign on with them, as it could limit your choices of countries and children.

Many parents today search the Internet photolistings of available international children before they choose an agency. Agencies spend a considerable amount of time and money listing children on photolistings and it is important that you use only the listing agency to adopt those children. Thoroughly check out the agency. Finding a child you feel a connection with will do you no good if you can't bring your child home!

How do you find a good international agency?

❖ The *first* thing you should do is order the *Report on Intercountry Adoption* from International Concerns for Children (see Appendix C). It includes descriptions of adoption agencies with their requirements and fees, as well as articles on foreign adoptions and photos of some waiting children, and is updated regularly. If an agency is not listed in this report, ask some serious questions. Be sure to ask which *overseas* agency or facilitator the agency uses too, and ask other parents about their experiences with them.

❖ Is your agency licensed? It may sound like an agency and look like an agency, but if it is not licensed by the state(s) in which it does adoptions, ask some hard questions. Facilitators are unlicensed individuals or organizations that match children and parents and oversee the paperwork process. Many are reputable, but many are not. They are not subject to the kind of official review that licensed agencies undergo, and rarely offer in-depth support services to families when an adoption runs into trouble.

❖ What are the fees and will the agency tell you how they break down? If not, consider using a different agency.

❖ How long has the agency been in business? ICC won't include agencies less than two years old in its report. You probably don't want to be a guinea pig for a new agency. However, if your agency is working with a well-known, well-established, reputable agency or facilitator overseas, you're probably okay.

❖ Order information packets from at least half a dozen agencies. Does the packet leave you with fewer or more questions? If you have an uneasy feeling, or if the information feels less than complete, ask questions, or move on.

❖ Get on the Internet adoption e-mail lists and ask for agency recommendations. Ask lots of questions. If there is a rash of people posting agency recommendations unasked all of a sudden, be suspicious. An agency may be using such stories to attract customers. Anyone can set up a Web site for a little money—be a smart consumer. Your time would be better spent signing onto an e-mail list of parents who are adopting or have adopted from the country you're interested in. Ask fellow list members which agencies they recommend and why.

❖ Beware of any agency (or facilitator) that claims it can do adoptions faster, cheaper, and better than anyone else. If a relatively new agency claims it can do things better than one in business twenty years, you should be cautious. There have been agencies that claimed they could skip some "nonessential" steps to save time and money. They rarely stay in business long. On the other hand, be cautious about an agency or facilitator that seems to be charging much more than the norm.

Choosing a country is easier for most parents. You may already have an idea of which country you'd like to adopt from. If not, browsing international photolistings can give you an idea of which children appeal to you the most. The night my husband and I looked at the photolistings for the first time, there were many children we liked, but it was the Vietnamese children who sold us on international adoption. For some reason, they appealed to us in a way the others didn't. Remember, this is *your* adoption. Even if you can't justify your choice to others, or quite make sense of it yourself, your gut instincts count.

Ask experienced parents and professionals about adoption from the country you are interested in. What kind of process is involved? How do the fees compare to those of other countries? What are the orphanage conditions (they can vary widely from country to country and even from institution to institution)? How long do you usually have to wait for a referral and to travel? Do you meet the requirements for that country? Is travel required and for what length of time? For what reasons are children generally relinquished? Is contact between the birthfamily and adoptive family possible? International adoption is one of the largest, most expensive decisions you will ever make. Do it carefully and methodically and you will limit the potential for problems.

The Referral

One day, after the reams and reams of paperwork and the seemingly endless bureaucratic red tape, the day arrives when your social worker calls to tell you you've been matched with a child. This day is one of the most exciting *and* one of the most panic-provoking of the entire adoption process. Such panic is normal.

After all, this is a life-changing decision.

The referral should include photos of your child and all the information available to the agency. If you are adopting domestically, the referral should include medical, psychological, educational, and family histories. If any of this information is missing, ask for it. It is, unfortunately, not unusual for social workers to leave out pertinent information that could negatively affect your decision. If there seem to be large gaps in the information, dig a little deeper. If possible, talk to foster parents, teachers, counselors, and previous social workers. Agencies often have frequent turnovers in staff, and the current worker may not know the complete history of your child.

With international adoption, it is likely that you will receive only basic information. Our older son's referral stated that he was healthy and in the third grade. It had some information about his family history. It did not, however, contain information about his height or weight, his grades in school, or his emotional health. Your agency should send you everything it has available. If you have more questions, your agency may be able to contact the overseas workers to find out more. However, be prepared to receive little information. If possible, ask for a video of your child and watch how he interacts with adults and peers. Look for signs of medical conditions, although the most obvious ones are rarely overlooked. You should also check the relinquishment documents carefully to make sure that the appropriate releases have been signed and that your child meets the United States' legal definition of "orphan." (See Appendix B.)

Take whatever medical information you are given to your doctor for an evaluation. If your doctor is unfamiliar with the medical problems of international adoptees, you can have a clinic experienced in international adoption review them for you, either in person or by mail or phone. (See Appendix C.)

Sometimes, a family that has asked for one child may receive a referral of a child with siblings. If this is the first mention of adopting siblings, take the time to really consider it. Don't feel pressured to accept more than one child if it doesn't feel right to you. Review your family's circumstances, finances, and expectations before deciding. Sibling adoptions usually turn out very well, but the initial adjustment can be especially difficult.

In some cases, families have accepted the referral of a single child only to find out later that the child had available siblings, or siblings who were placed elsewhere. This seems to be a more common occurrence in orphanages overseas than it is in the States. If at all possible, it is preferable for siblings to be placed together. Leaving behind brothers and sisters is another loss for children. Many kids mourn the loss of their siblings even more than they do the loss of birthparents. This seems to especially be the case in abusive or neglectful families where brothers and sisters stuck together and protected each other. Some families have returned to their child's birthcountry or home state to adopt the remaining siblings. Others have arranged for birthsiblings adopted by different families to remain in contact with each other.

One family received a shock when they traveled to pick up their seven-year-old daughter. They met the girl, talked with her and showed her pictures of her new home. She was shy and somber. A short time later, an orphanage worker came in and asked a question, and a heated argument broke out among the orphanage staff. The family kept asking the interpreter what was happening and finally she said, "They say she has a brother." The worker brought in an eleven-year-old boy and their daughter's face lit up with joy. The parents say they knew then that they could not leave the country without him. They miraculously managed to finish his paperwork and bring him to the United States too. He had a difficult adjustment, but the children are both now doing well.

Although this scenario is unusual, it pays to ask about siblings when you receive the referral, and scrutinize the paperwork for clues that the child might have brothers or sisters. For example, in some cultures, kids are often given numbers as names, to show their place in the family. If your child is "number three," you can bet he has, or at least had, older siblings. Another clue is if the birthparents have been married many years and this is supposedly their only child. Many families do not learn of their child's siblings (who may or may not be available for adoption) until their child has been home for many months.

You may be referred a child who has had one or more previous adopted placements that disrupted (meaning the parents returned the child to state or agency custody). The mere fact that the placements disrupted does not necessarily mean the child's behavioral or emotional problems are severe. It may simply mean she and the previous family did not "mesh" well or were not really ready for the adoption, or that the family wasn't able to weather typical adjustment behavior. However, to the extent that you can, find out why the previous placement(s) disrupted. A series of disrupted placements can signal trouble—ask as many questions as you can of the agency and previous caregivers or professionals who have dealt with the child. Listen carefully to the answers; if they strike you as too vague, keep pressing.

As you read the descriptions of the child in the referral paperwork, keep in mind that it is a social worker's job to place children. Workers understandably want to present children in the most favorable light. For this reason, you must ask questions, especially if you believe the information you have received is too superficial. Many times, photolisting write-ups and referrals contain only basic information.

Nancy, whose daughter has serious attachment problems, says, "The write-up they did on my daughter was hysterical. It was this beautiful picture with a bow in her hair. She looked so charming. It said she was a straight A student and in Girl Scouts, and they didn't get into any of it and I thought [later], 'How scary!'" Haley's write-up didn't mention that she ate out of garbage cans or that she had tried to kill a baby while in a foster home. (Haley is now in residential treatment.)

Deciding whether to accept a referral can be difficult. You should not feel pressured to accept a child you do not really want. You should talk with your agency about any concerns you have before accepting the referral. Most agencies will understand if you feel unable to parent a child with disabilities. Sometimes, parents are tempted to accept a child with significant disabilities that they feel unable to cope with. Try to remember that this adoption is fulfilling your needs, too.

Trina puts it this way: "You are entitled to protect what you want here. Yes, he may need help, and he may find that in your home, but he may not. He has social workers, therapists, supervisors, teachers, and foster families to help him. It is their responsibility. You are looking to build a family. If you think this little one is the Child of Your Heart, then by all means go for it, but adopt him because he will fulfill any longing you have for a child, not because you fear for the quality of his life."

Once you do find the child of your heart, you're well on your way to becoming a parent. You're also on the brink of one of the most difficult times in the adoption process—the wait.

❖ 'Decoding' a Photolisting ❖

I asked several experienced families how they would interpret a few phrases commonly used in photolistings. Some of their answers were humorous, some were scary, but all pointed out that you cannot rely on a photolisting to tell the whole story.

"This very active child..."

It may mean, "This kid bounces off the walls. Think ADHD."

"Will need help to work out issues of his past..."

It may mean, "This child has serious emotional difficulties from past experiences."

"Loves to be the center of attention..."

It may mean, "This child will have difficulty sharing you with siblings." Or, "This child is so wounded he may not be able to let you out of his sight."

"Should be the only or youngest child in the home..."

It may mean, "She may hurt younger children." Or, "This child has attachment difficulties."

"Needs a strong, consistent, two-parent family."

It may mean, "It will take two of you to hold him down!"

"Has come far since entering placement."

It may mean, "Not far enough!"

Families also shared comments that they consider positive.

"This child is a leader."

"Gets along well with peers and adults alike."

"Bright and inquisitive..."

"Enjoys playing with his friends and frequently wins..."

"Is anxious to have a family of his own..."

❖ 3 ❖
Surviving the Wait

It was the day we took the final plunge and signed the referral papers that my son became real to me. The decision had been made and I was officially waiting. We felt we had really accomplished something—so much thought and work had gone into getting that far—but I had no idea that the next four months would test my commitment over and over again. We adoptive parents are different from birthparents in a profound way because each and every day of the adoption process grants us another opportunity to change our minds. You will likely find yourself questioning your decision many times during "the wait."

Although the wait may be longer for international adopters, it can be lengthy for domestic families as well. You may be required to visit your daughter many times before she moves in with you. The adoption may be delayed while your son finishes out a school year in his foster home. If you are adopting internationally, your wait will usually be at least three or four months. It may be a year or longer.

"It's like your whole life stops," says Cassandra, who survived the wait twice in adopting her daughters from Asia. "You can't get anything done, it's all you think about. It's the worst feeling of suspended animation I have ever been stuck in."

The wait *is* difficult, more so than anyone imagines before beginning the process. However, it can also be a time of intense preparation and activity. One of the first things parents do after the referral is announce the imminent arrival of their child to family and friends. Some families have long discussions with family and friends before they actually decide to adopt. If you have strong, supportive friends and relatives who can discuss the pros and cons of adoption in a balanced way, you may find such discussions helpful and informative. However, most families I talked with waited until after they received the referral to tell their loved ones. The most common reason given is fear that something will go wrong or that they will change their minds, and the adoption will fall through. Another significant reason parents wait is the fear that family and friends will not approve and may try to influence their decision. Sadly, this is often true.

Allison says, "My mother just plainly said, 'We could never love a child who is not ours!' It upset me so much and it really put a damper on things. My parents are very concerned with what others think and they didn't think Russian grandchildren would go over too well in their circle of friends. Once they found out their friends thought it was a good thing they started saying things like, 'Ooh, we have the most beautiful grandchildren in the whole world and they're extremely bright too!' The whole thing was a really bad experience."

My own parents were very troubled about our plans to adopt. They imagined all the worst things that could happen. As difficult as that was to deal with, I knew they were motivated by concern for our welfare. They feared we would make a decision that would adversely affect our lives forever. Parents are parents for life—it doesn't stop when your child is eighteen or twenty. If you run into family opposition, try to keep in mind that in most cases, it's provoked by love and fear for your future. Just knowing that, though, is not enough. You must also know how to cope with it. I asked several families how they dealt with negative reactions from family or friends. They suggest:

❖ Be sure of what *you* want before you tell them and be ready to explain *why* you have made this decision.

❖ Bring up some of your own concerns about adoption, how you addressed them, and your conclusions.

❖ Acknowledge the risks involved in adopting an older child and what you plan to do in case of severe emotional or behavioral problems.

❖ If your child has known disabilities, explain the problem and your child's limitations openly and honestly.

❖ Answer any questions they have if they present those questions in a calm, rational way.

❖ Explain how you think the adoption will affect your other kids, and what you're doing to prepare and protect them.

❖ Remind them that this is *your* decision, that you made it carefully, and that you would appreciate their support.

❖ Offer to give them names and numbers of other grandparents or extended families for support or to sign them up for a grandparents group if your agency offers one.

❖ Recommend books and articles about adoption.

❖ Remember that even if you do all these things, your family and friends may still not support your decision, so seek out other adopting parents for support.

❖ Keep your hopes up. Most families do come around after the children are home.

Losing a Referral

Sadly, some parents become attached to a child through a picture or report, only to lose the referral later. The reasons for lost referrals vary. In the case of international adoptions, referrals can be lost when the birthfamily reclaims a child from the orphanage. Occasionally, agencies will refer the same child to two families, trying to ensure placement.

"I saw a photo of an adorable 3 1/2-year-old boy I just knew was 'the one.' We sent our dossier in, and heard a week or so later that his birthfamily had decided to raise him after all," says Gail. "I was thunderstruck. This kid had been in the orphanage more than two years, and nearly adopted twice before. I remember going to a business conference that week and at one point just hiding in a bathroom stall and crying and crying."

Chloe and her husband, Stan, accepted a legal-risk placement of a teenage girl. All the workers expected that she would be with them permanently as her mother had made no effort to meet the court's requirements for her return home. After the girl had been with them for three months, the birthmother was granted custody in a court hearing after her abusive husband had committed suicide. Chloe and Stan were devastated that the girl they considered truly "theirs" was taken from their custody.

In domestic adoptions, legal-risk placement, like the one Chloe and Stan participated in, is fairly common. You should be ready for the possibility, however remote it seems, that a birthparent may reclaim the child if you accept a placement for a child who has not been legally freed for adoption yet. In some cases, the courts or social services assume that termination of parental rights will happen quickly, but circumstances can change.

How do parents cope with the loss of a referral? Gail suggests performing some type of "funeral" for the child. She says, "I did a little ritual where I quietly shredded all the referral paperwork and said goodbye to him and wished him and his family luck. You really do have to say goodbye to this kid who's occupied your heart for weeks or months."

Preparing for Your Child

Although it is difficult to know exactly what you will face when your child gets home, it's important to try to prepare yourself for the huge change that your family is about to experience. If you haven't already started, now is the time to begin reading everything you can find about older child adoption. Start with the most upbeat, balanced accounts and work your way up to books dealing with more serious issues, such as *Adopting the Hurt Child* by Keck and Kupecky (Pinon Press, 1995). Familiarize yourself with the major issues of adoption—and do so fully.

The old adage, "a little bit of knowledge is a dangerous thing," holds true here. Many parents have small bits of information about reactive attachment disorder (RAD), for instance. In the last few years, news stories about children with RAD have abounded, and agencies have made a greater effort to educate parents. However, most people know little more than the signs of RAD (see Chapter 11). That kind of surface education can actually be a disservice to parents. Virtually *all* newly adopted older children show some symptoms of attachment difficulties. That's why some professionals suggest that parents wait at least a year before having a child diagnosed. There are other illnesses and learning disabilities that can look like RAD to the untrained eye. You should be educated enough so that you don't immediately jump to the wrong conclusion. Learn about the different possibilities—for your sake as well as your child's.

Some families say they hesitated to explore the serious issues and, in fact, some agencies seem leery of educating parents fully. Why? They worry about putting unrealistic fears into parents' minds. Not all social workers feel this way. Teri Bell, social worker with Americans for International Aid and Adoption, says, "If reading about it or talking about it scares parents so much they decide not to adopt, imagine what a real kid would do to them!"

I asked a group of parents if their agencies had prepared them for the realities of older child adoption. Parents who adopted domestically and had been required to take pre-adoptive classes felt prepared for the most part. However, most of the people who adopted domestically through private agencies or who adopted internationally said they were not adequately prepared. In response to the question, "What did your agency do to prepare you?" Allison and Shawn replied, "Nothing. Nada. No classes, no recommended reading list, nothing. We had to do it ourselves. We got on the Internet and read and asked questions. We learned a tremendous amount that way."

They are not alone. Most parents were left to navigate the education process on their own. Several families mentioned the helpfulness of online adoption support groups. They read any information they could find, and they sought out experienced adoptive parents. One thing that parents mentioned over and over again was that it would have been very helpful if the agency had paired them with a "buddy" family or had provided a panel of experienced parents to question.

Most agencies acknowledge that parental preparation is important. However, many local agencies, the ones who do home studies and have the most contact with parents, simply have not worked with enough adoptive parents of older children to make support groups feasible. Many international adopters use facilitators, people or organizations who do not have adoption agency licenses and who may have no background in adoption, social work, or psychology.

As the number of families adopting older children grows, it has become more and more obvious that agencies have an obligation to prepare families for the realities of older child adoption. Dee Paddock, adoption therapist and adoptive mother of three, tells agencies: "When I was pregnant, taking Lamaze classes, the worst thing anyone said could happen was that we might have to have a C-section. We did not ever talk about babies who die, or babies born with birth defects. It was considered too negative for prospective parents. But when my baby died and the Lamaze coach wanted to visit me, I refused. I was angry that she *didn't tell me,* she kept it all positive and nice, so when it happened I became the exception, the freak. If you don't prepare your clients and tell them the truth, when it happens to them, they too become the exception and you add to their pain. Parents need to hear that sometimes kids have problems and that grief isn't pretty."

Adoptive parents have to do their part, too. Professionals say some parents won't admit that their child may have problems. Agencies can require classes, reading, and discussion, but many feel that parents come into these activities with a "that won't happen to me" attitude. They are often the same parents who later say, "No one told me this could happen."

"I want parents to read about adoption, seek out experienced families, and ask questions," says one social worker. "And most importantly, I wish they would let go of their fantasies and *get real.* We can try to educate them, but if they don't want to hear what can happen and really think about it, they won't be prepared."

Sandra Russell of Heaven Sent Children wants parents to realize that they may have to wait for the rewards. "Adopting older children is not for wimps, and the parents need to have a strong ego system which is not based on the need to have love returned immediately," she says. "We try to get parents to read, talk to others, learn developmental issues and then really soul-search, but most learn the hard way."

Experienced parents and professionals urge new parents to really think about the possibilities before adopting. It is human nature to want to avoid the difficult stories, but don't make the mistake of assuming everyone else is just jaded and negative.

Preparing Siblings

If you already have children in your home, preparing them for the adoption is a must. Many children are excited about the idea of getting a sibling, while others are hesitant. While the decision to adopt should be yours, taking your children's feelings into account is vital. If they're old enough to comprehend both the rewards and the difficulties coming up, they should be able to voice an opinion. Successful older child adoption requires commitment on the part of the parents, the adopted child, *and* your other children. A child who is totally opposed to the idea of a new sibling could possibly disrupt a placement.

Having a realistic discussion with your children about the pros and cons of adopting can uncover their reservations or objections. Then, as a family, you can discuss ways to make your children more comfortable with the idea. Often, children can think of many good things about having another sibling, but are unrealistic about the adjustment period. It may be hard for them to comprehend a brother who breaks his toys in a fit of jealousy or a sister who refuses to speak to them for days.

One way to prepare the kids is to role-play possible scenarios. This is especially helpful if your child is under the age of seven. You pretend to be the new sibling and create a disturbance. Say, "I don't like you and you're not my brother and if you tell Mom I said this I'm going to beat you up tonight when she's asleep!" How does your child handle it? Then you can demonstrate to your son how to confront his brother, or when to tell you about his sister's behavior.

If your other children are adopted, their feelings about their adoption may surface or recur. Gail and William found that their adoption of a four-year-old son brought out feelings of abandonment and insecurity in their daughter, who had been adopted as a baby. "I'm just going to have to find a new home," sobbed Laura shortly after her new brother arrived. If your adopted child is voicing opposition to the upcoming placement, it could be that he is afraid that a new child will take his place and he will have to leave, or that you will love him less. This feeling is normal for any kid who gets a new sibling, but for the adopted child it may be more intense. Regardless of how irrational his fears seem to you, and maybe even to him, they are likely very real. Memories of a former home or move can raise feelings of abandonment and rejection in our children. They may *know* their place in the family is secure, but may *feel* very differently. Sometimes they have trouble putting those feelings into words and express their fear by their behavior.

Many parents and professionals recommend waiting at least a year between adoptions. That way the first child has a chance to adjust before another kid joins the family.

If your child is reacting badly to the idea of a new sibling, you may have to summon up much patience and encouragement to help him through it. Most children will regain their equilibrium after the adoption occurs and they see that their place in the family is secure. But be prepared for some rocky days before and immediately after placement. Being aware of the probability of adoption feelings resurfacing and being willing to discuss them, sometimes repeatedly, with your child will go a long way toward easing the adjustment.

Language and Culture

If you are adopting internationally, learn about your child's language and culture. Few adoptive parents become fluent in their child's native language, but learning some phrases can make the transition easier. Your child will be intensely scared and confused the first few weeks in your home. If you can ask basic questions, such as "Are you okay?" or "Are you hungry?" you may be able to ease some of her frustration. You may be surprised how much you and your child can communicate with gestures and a few key words. You'll also be amazed at how quickly she picks up English.

If possible, find someone locally who is willing to interpret for you in an emergency or if you need to discuss something that requires better language skills. If you don't know someone personally, try calling a local university or college. A child who is old enough to read may be able to use a bilingual dictionary.

If you are adopting across ethnic or racial lines, you'll want to learn about the culture of your child's country or ethnic group. Many families spend a lot of time preparing for language difficulties, only to find cultural differences to be a far bigger problem. Prepare yourself not only for your travel to his country, but also for your child's arrival here.

Deanna and Gary traveled with their two older children to adopt Aaron, age eight. Deanna says they read about Vietnamese culture from one end to the other, mostly as a way to prepare their kids for traveling to Vietnam, rather than a way to think about Aaron's cultural issues. They just didn't think it would be a long-term issue. "I think that was the biggest piece of information we could have had." Try to learn about your child's cultural adjustments from *his* viewpoint before his arrival. Culture is discussed more fully in Chapter 8.

Some travel guides, such as the *Lonely Planet* series, can give you a good overview of a country, its people, and its basic cultural customs and taboos. *Culture Shock,* another series of travel books designed for business travelers, provides guidance for such things as official greetings, gift giving, etiquette, and celebrations. The books also familiarize the reader with family structure and daily habits. (For details, see Appendix C.)

Preparing the Child

The agency or social worker representing your child will play the primary role in preparing him for adoption. If you're adopting domestically, the social worker may help the child prepare a life book, which contains photographs, drawings, stories, and other keepsakes, and which chronicles his life from birth to adoption. Life books are especially useful for children who have been moved many times. A child who has had many different homes and caregivers may confuse people and places.

If your child does not have a life book before he enters your family, you may want to help him make one. A life book can help answer the big questions kids have about who they are, why they lost their birthfamilies and what is happening to them. It can also show that the adults in their lives were responsible for the choices made, and clarify any misconceptions that kids have about when they moved. A life book can point out that the decision to separate the child from his birthfamily happened well before the adoptive parents came onto the scene. Your child may not show much interest in his life book at first, but later he may, especially in his early teens as he tries to understand how his history affects who he is.

Parents are often asked to send a photo album or book to their child before placement, both domestically and overseas. These photos are used to familiarize the child with your family and her new home. Photos can also help assure a child that the parents who come to pick her up are the right people. Check with your agency about what to put in the album, but generally it should contain photos of all family members, preferably engaged in everyday activities. Include pictures of the house, yard, pets, and rooms of the house—especially the child's room.

Deanna prepared an album for Aaron before his arrival. She says, "We sent lots of photos in a series over about six months' time while we waited to travel. We sent an initial set of pictures that were immediate and extended family, animals, and house. The next set was summer activities. Another included leaf rak-

❖ Making a Photo Album ❖

Families give the following suggestions for your child's album:

Make sure it's sturdy so it can be looked at repeatedly.

Gear the book to your child's age. The older the child, the more words of explanation you will need.

Consider including balloons, stickers, or other things for your child to share with his friends.

If you have other children, send a ribbon cut to the height of your tallest child. Mark the heights of the other kids on it. Your child will know how big his new siblings are in relation to him.

Send a map to show where she is now and where you live in relationship to it.

Leave a few blank pages so that the child can add letters or pictures as they are sent.

Write things that show you are including her in your family. One family wrote, "This is our house, which we will be painting this summer. What color do you think is best?"

Include not only photos of your family and your pets, but also pictures of your house, your place of worship, her school, your cars, stores you frequent—anywhere the child is likely to spend a lot of time on a regular basis.

Include pages showing "a day in our life" activities to help your child feel more secure about her new home.

ing and autumn woods walks. We sent a set of winter photos with sled and snowmen. Since we came home this has been Aaron's reference book for family life. We have been able to use those photos to explain we were going for a walk in the woods or to a festival."

Preparing a room for your son or daughter is one of the few fun aspects of waiting. Most families put a lot of thought and effort into the bedroom as a way of "claiming" their child. Children enjoy seeing that their families have a place for them and that you are preparing for their arrival. You may want to leave some things undone so that they can pick out things they like. Some families let their child choose the color of the paint, for example. However, it may be easier to leave things such as wall decorations for well after arrival. You may all be too tired and too stressed to worry about painting and decorating right after the child comes home. Experienced parents warn against overwhelming a newly arrived child with too many clothes or toys. Excitement-filled vacations like a trip to Disney World may also be too intense in the first few weeks.

Now What?

While families are usually eager to prepare a room and a book for their new child, these activities occur fairly early on during the waiting period. After that initial flurry of activity, the wait seems to stretch before you like a never-ending road. What can you do to pass the time? A group of families shares these suggestions for waiting parents:

- ❖ Join a support group for adoptive parents, either on the Internet or in your community.
- ❖ Read, read, read. Read books about adoption, parenting, culture, and travel.
- ❖ Gather medical supplies or other needed donations for orphanages and hospitals overseas.
- ❖ Remodel a section of your house.
- ❖ Take a trip.
- ❖ Go on with your life. Accept invitations and go to community events or work extra hours.
- ❖ Clean out your closets.

- ❖ Install safety gadgets in your house.
- ❖ Host an exchange student, if you feel that you can accommodate both children after your child comes home.
- ❖ Double your agency's estimated "wait time" so you'll be pleasantly surprised.
- ❖ Learn to cook food from your child's culture
- ❖ Put loose photos in albums. Your child will love looking at them when he gets home.
- ❖ Take a class in CPR or first aid.
- ❖ Call your agency with endless questions!

Traveling to Get Your Child

If you are adopting from overseas, or even out of state, you may have to travel to pick up your child. A few countries allow children to be escorted, but many agencies feel it is much easier on the child if the parent goes to get them. Travel, especially to a foreign country, can be exciting and fun. It can also be stressful. All of those feelings are heightened by adoption. The additional anxiety that you feel when you are meeting your child for the first time can make the stress of being far from home almost unbearable. Finding out as much as you can about your destination before you go can ease the discomfort. Many families find their trips enjoyable, especially after meeting their child.

Traveling to your child's country can be an essential part of understanding him and where he comes from. You will be able to meet the people, view the culture, and watch your child's reactions in familiar surroundings. It is easier for him to get used to you if he is not trying to adjust to completely new foods, smells, and activities at the same time. Your child's memories of his homeland will dim with time and your memories of the sights and sounds of his country can be invaluable to him.

If you have other children, you have to decide whether to take them when you travel. For many, if not most, families the decision is made by finances. International travel is expensive. If you do have a choice, carefully consider the pros and cons of letting them accompany you.

Many families feel that they want the time to focus solely on their new son or daughter. Other families feel that travel is vital for the whole family. Deanna and Gary took their two older children, ages ten and twelve, to Vietnam when they adopted Aaron. "This child had been somewhere for eight years and these guys [his brother and sister] needed to know where that is," Deanna said. "They were willing to make all the commitments they needed to make, like shots and agreeing to follow some basic health and safety regulations. I think the whole adjustment has gone better than it would have without them going."

There are many things to consider when deciding whether to take your children with you. What kind of travelers are they? Are they upset by changes? Do they like to try new foods or will they die without pizza and hamburgers? Will they be able to let their new brother or sister be the focus of everyone's attention for at least a few days? Are there health risks associated with the country you are traveling to? Are they willing to have the necessary immunizations and to take necessary safety precautions while in the country? As with most things, only you can decide what is best for your family.

If you'll be traveling overseas, you should consult—or have your family doctor look up—current recommendations from the Centers for Disease Control (CDC) concerning immunizations and food and water safety. Your doctor may be willing to prescribe antibiotics and anti-diarrheal and anti-nausea medications for you to take along. Take over-the-counter medicines that may not be available where you're going. Many children have respiratory or ear infections and parasites such as lice or scabies.

Buying clothes for a child you haven't seen can be tricky. Experienced parents suggest that you buy clothes such as T-shirts, sweat pants, or leggings, which don't have to be an exact size. You can always buy two or three outfits, as well as shoes or sandals, in the child's country and leave the rest of the shopping until you get home. You should, however, have enough clothing to get through the first few weeks, as you may not want to take on a major shopping expedition immediately after arrival.

Children who have been living in deprived conditions often grow incredibly fast in their new home. Some families have found themselves buying three or four complete wardrobes in the first year alone. For this reason, some shop yard sales and consignment stores for lower-priced clothing. Although some kids, especially those who have been in foster care for a long time, may object to used clothing, most will be okay with it if they have several new outfits, too.

You may wish to bring a couple of small gifts to give your child when you first meet. This can often break the ice and make everyone more comfortable. If your child is in an orphanage or group home, bring something small for the other children as well. Parents have mentioned that balloons, stickers, water guns, inflatable beach balls, sidewalk chalk, play jewelry, and bubbles

❖ Important Travel Items ❖

Some parents who have adopted internationally say these were some of the most useful things they took along:

Duct tape (for fixing suitcases, shoes, glasses, strollers, backpacks, toys, you name it)

Camera

A good attitude

A carry-on bag with essential items—luggage does get lost!

Medical kit

Swiss army knife

Moistened towelettes

Carsickness bags (many kids get carsick on the drive back from the orphanage)

An extra pair of glasses or a copy of your eyeglass prescription

Baggies

Ear plugs

Waterless antibacterial soap

A good backpack

Siblings

Copies of paperwork (including your receipt that proves you sent your visa cable in case your paperwork doesn't arrive)

Insect repellent

Journal

Cash in small denominations

Small tape player and tapes

were big hits. Several families have suggested bringing a Polaroid camera to the orphanage so that you can take pictures of the children and give them to them. It may be the first photograph of themselves they have ever seen. Parents also recommend that you take the time during the wait to travel to write a list of questions to ask your child's caregiver when you meet. You will probably be too flustered during the initial meeting to think of things to ask.

The most important thing to take with you, by far, is a good attitude. You will be tired and nervous. Paperwork problems do arise, and accommodations may not be what you are accustomed to. A sense of adventure and awe, and plenty of patience and optimism, will make your visit more enjoyable for you and your hosts. Keep in mind, too, that some people distrust our motives for adoption. In some countries, rumors have circulated that Americans adopt children to use them as servants or even organ donors. In other countries, Americans have a reputation for being pushy, brash, and arrogant. Your conduct and demeanor can either hinder or help other families and the future of international adoptions.

Pre-placement Visits

If you are adopting domestically within your state, you will likely have the opportunity to visit with your child before she moves in with you. For many parents this is an exciting time; for others, it's unrelenting agony. Most parents suggest that you limit the number of visits as much as you can. They say your child will simply feel like a visitor until she actually moves in with you.

You may set up unrealistic expectations of your family life if you fill your visits with outings and endless family fun. Nicole, who adopted three boys from the foster care system, says, "We spent many of our visits at McDonald's or local parks. We purposely did not take them to places where there were lots of distractions because we wanted to interact with them and help them get to know us." She and her husband took along a Polaroid camera on their visits so that the children could immediately have pictures of them as a family. She feels that it provided a good way for the boys to process meeting them.

Parents, too, can form unrealistic expectations when visits go extremely well. Kids often put their best foot forward during visitation, waiting until they are home and really comfortable before unleashing the true testing behavior. Many parents are amazed when the happy, sunny child they visited with moves in and turns into a misbehaving, surly one. You should be prepared for all the normal adjustment problems even if your visits go smoothly.

Some parents adopt children they have foster-parented for years. For some kids, the transition from foster care to adoption can be traumatic. Adoption carries a message of permanence that can throw the child off balance. In foster care, they can protect their feelings of abandonment and rejection by reminding themselves that their stay is temporary. In adoption, they have to commit to the family, and doing so may be just as scary for them as for children who move to a new home.

A foster parent or social worker will probably accompany your child when you meet. A supportive foster parent can make the transition easier. Chloe's youngest son was escorted to their home by his foster mother. She stayed for a weekend to ease the transition and redirected his requests by saying, "Why don't you ask your Mommy?" Chloe feels that her son benefited from being granted permission to change his loyalties and from seeing that the foster mother trusted his new parents.

Social workers often use life books to ease the transition from one home to another. Some parents try to ease the transition by discussing the move during the last visit and making plans for what they will do the day the child moves in. Knowing what to expect may help kids feel less anxious on moving day.

The Initial Meeting

Although it seems the day will never arrive, the first meeting with your child can come with little advance warning. At first, finally meeting your child may feel like the *end* of the road, especially if your journey to adoption has been long and frustrating. Some parents report feeling unprepared to actually meet the child simply because they had focused on the process and its many hurdles so much that she never seemed real. Others are relieved to be dealing with a real person instead of simply imagining or worrying about all the things that might go wrong.

Whether you adopt domestically or internationally, one feeling that is almost universal—and completely normal—is panic. Even parents who are generally unflappable or who have adopted before report a sudden rush of panic when they meet their child. I remember calling our social worker right before we traveled in a state of blind panic, wondering what on earth was wrong with me. She chuckled and said, "You're going halfway around the world to see a nine-year-old child you've never met, to bring him home to be your son. Why on earth would you be scared?" To which I replied, "Oh, well, since you put it *that* way!"

This tendency to push the panic button is one reason that many parents feel you shouldn't travel alone. Your traveling companion may be able to calm your fears. Allison talked about her panic and her husband's response. She said, "I didn't have any serious fears until the day I met them. Then I got so scared—not because there was anything wrong with them—it was just the enormity of it all! Shawn was so good. He just kept repeating over and over that it would be okay. I don't know what I would have done if he hadn't been there."

Most parents report that their surge of panic subsided within twenty-four hours of meeting their child. You will likely continue to be on edge and hyperaware of your child's every move, but the desire to bail out usually fades quickly. In its place comes a surreal sense of the rest of the world hurrying by while you and your child stand still. Most parents recall little of what happened around them after they met their child.

There is no way of predicting what meeting your child will feel like. Parents do, however, caution against expecting your child to rush to see you, even if other children do. They also say you should not expect eye contact, affection, happiness, or gratitude. If you are scared, imagine what your child must be feeling. One thing you can count on is that you will never forget that first meeting.

❖ 4 ❖

The Family in Shock

"I loved that kid before I ever walked across the courtyard to give him a hug; I didn't like him for probably three to six weeks after that," says Deanna about her son, adopted at age eight. "He came with an incredibly annoying Woody Woodpecker laugh." Deanna knew it must have been nervousness on his part, but it was still hard to deal with.

Many parents have similar reactions to their new children. This is just one of the many profound differences between older child adoption and infant adoption. When your child is old enough to have developed personality traits, there may be some you wish he didn't have. Deanna, however, reports that after the initial adjustment her son became more relaxed and dropped some of his most annoying habits.

Other parents find something else even harder to deal with— their lack of parental feelings for their new kids.

Allison speaks of meeting her two Russian children, ages four and six: "When I gave birth to all four of my birthkids, the world shifted, and I didn't feel that way about them [the older kids] at first. And I thought, 'Oh God, what's wrong with you? What's going to happen and should I just leave Russia now?' It took me three weeks to love them. But because it had been such a powerful thing with my birthchildren, it never dawned on me that this would happen."

Allison's husband, Shawn, however, thought it was a perfectly normal reaction. He likens it to the type of bonding that fathers feel with their birthchildren. He told Allison, "You were in love with two cells the minute you knew you were pregnant. I had to *learn* to love my child."

When I met my sons, I truly cared for them, I ached for their losses and pain, and I rejoiced in the happy moments, but it was several weeks before I felt true love for them. Liam, who with his wife, Colleen, adopted two children from Russia, says, "Was it love at first sight? No, I think it was acceptance at first sight— love took a while. It took a *long* time." Colleen adds, "We had an open heart, we had acceptance and we wanted to love [our son], but it was tough." Perhaps "infatuation at first sight" best describes parents' initial feelings. You'll probably be happy to have your child home, but at the same time not be truly comfortable with him. Your child will no doubt feel the same way.

The Honeymoon

Many adopted children will let you enjoy a honeymoon—a period of near-perfect behavior. Honeymoon periods can last as long as a year; some are barely perceptible.

Generally, the honeymoon is a time for your child to size you up and figure out where you are coming from and what it means for her. It may be fairer to say that the entire family goes through a honeymoon. There is a period of hyperawareness right after placement, where the whole family is tuned in to making the new child feel at home. You may lighten routines, relax limits, and put forth an extra effort to make her feel welcome. Your other children will likely be willing to share their belongings and go out of their way to make their new sibling feel special.

You are, in fact, living with a stranger. She may feel more like a houseguest at first. As much as we like entertaining company, it upsets the balance in our homes. No matter how much fun guests are, or how much you truly care for them, it's still a relief when they leave and your life settles back to normal. Similarly with older kids, there will be good aspects to the first weeks, but it is still a strain. Don't be surprised if you think, "Whew! I'll be glad when this kid's parents come to pick her up!"

Your child, too, will be feeling the strain. He may feel as though he's living in a fishbowl, with everyone watching his every move. Some kids love the attention, and will strive to do all the right things to make it last. Other kids are intensely aware of feeling they have to perform, and begin to crack under the strain. Either way, children feel the need to act perfectly in order to be accepted. In the beginning such acceptance comes more easily, as the whole family is willing to accept the newcomer at face value. But soon, you and your children will desire a return to routine and the strain of living artificially will become too much. You will begin expecting more from the new kid, and having less patience. Your children will tire of giving in and want your attention. And your new child will still not know where he fits in. The family honeymoon is over and the adjustment begins.

Your Adjustment

If you are one of those unfortunate few who don't have a honeymoon period, your child will drop you into reality very quickly. Whether your family goes through a honeymoon period or not, the sooner you begin to relax and act normally, the sooner your child will settle in. It is impossible for a child to know how to act and what to think if there aren't any rules to follow. As parents, we often think of how hard the adjustment is going to be on our child, or on our other children. But we seldom think about how difficult it will really be for *us*. The mixed feelings can catch us unaware. Try to give yourself the same amount of patience and understanding that you give to others. Attachment to your child will progress slowly.

"At first it was all wonderful and 'honeymoonish' and we were so thrilled to have him," says Veronica, mother of nine-year-old Jason. "But after a while I started to get irritated about little things, and was often struck by how different he was, in his interests, his way of talking and being. He didn't have that 'part of me' feeling that my other kids, adopted as infants, do. Not that he wasn't a great kid; he just didn't feel like *mine* yet. But slowly I can feel that attachment growing. He is adapting to our family and vice versa. His frequent rapping doesn't irritate me anymore, since it's now familiar, and getting to feel like part of us now. There are still times when I get too impatient or feel myself getting irritated and pulling away from him, but it's much less frequent now, after three months. And I can see the same process going on in our son."

The things that make parents and kids feel like strangers are numerous. One thing that families mention often is smell. Trina, adoptive mother of three, says, "It was almost like my system had to acclimate, both my household system and my inner emotional system. The kids smelled differently, and until I got rid of their outgrown clothes and replaced everything with stuff I had bought and I had washed, it just wasn't the right smell. Even now, a full year later, it sometimes feels like they are just visiting and will eventually go home."

Olivia and her husband adopted an eight-year-old child from Vietnam over twenty years ago. She says, "Andrea and I were talking and she said to me, 'Mom, I remember you meeting me at the plane and I remember that you had red hair and you had a gift box for me with new clothes and stuff, but you stunk like milk.' And I said, 'I remember a little eight-year-old girl who had clothes and shoes on that were way too small for her and she was so dirty. Her body had never had a full bath and she had lice in her hair.' We both loved each other, but the thing that we can both remember is that she stunk to me and I stunk to her, but it was two different kinds of stink."

Aaron, age eight on arrival, doesn't go to sleep when he goes to bed and hates to get up in the morning, which has been difficult for his mother because she is used to kids who get up early. "I think he just isn't a morning person. I don't think it's an adoption issue. It's one of the few things I can point to that says, 'He is out of sync with the rest of this family,'" says Deanna.

Any number of things may throw you off balance. It might be facial expressions, speech patterns, gestures or appearance. Your son may have a haircut you hate, or your daughter's favorite clothes may be distasteful to you. Whatever it is, you and your new child will have to find ways to acclimate to each other. Remember that your child has emotional and behavioral systems, too. You will have to find a way to blend the two together so that you *both* change in acceptable ways.

Having reasonable expectations helps. Social worker Sandra Russell says, "There are people who think the child is going to get off the plane, they're going to put tennis shoes and a pair of jeans and a T-shirt on them, and they're going to be American. I think it's real important that they can accept the child as the child is. And then work on maybe their habits and mold the child, but know that it's going to take a while, it doesn't happen overnight. Choose your battles wisely."

Choosing your battles wisely is good advice for all parents, but especially those who adopt older children. There is no way you will be able to change everything you dislike about your son, nor would you want to. Don't we all want others to accept us as we are? You will likely learn as much about yourself in the first few months after adoption as you will about your child. You will find out what is really important to you and what you can let go. Remember that this is a time of immense change for your whole family. Give yourself and your family a break.

One thing that makes the first few months so difficult is the exhaustion that accompanies older child adoption. You will likely be as tired as you've ever been in your life. If your child has sleep problems, the exhaustion may be physical, but more often it is emotional exhaustion in response to the enormous changes in your household. Don't be surprised if you find yourself doing strange things. One day, in a state of total exhaustion, I put vegetable oil instead of vinegar into my mop water and washed the kitchen floor with it.

Brent, a single father of two boys, said getting enough sleep at the beginning was very difficult. "I definitely had times when I was more tired all the time, like during medical residency, but the difference was there was always a day [back then] when you could sleep in and make it up, but that doesn't happen anymore. A lot of it is emotional exhaustion, too, and you think, 'Thank God it's only thirty minutes 'til bed.' When [Austin] first got here I had to go to bed when he did because I was so exhausted."

The most obvious solution to the strain of the initial adjustment is time. Your agency will likely require, or at least suggest, that you take time off if you work outside the home. It is incredibly hard to adjust to a change this big while simultaneously juggling work, school, and other obligations. You may also find it helpful to limit other activities. The housework will still be there a month from now.

Social worker Teri Bell says about parental leave: "I really believe that each child is so different that there cannot be a standard amount of time. Some children start school full time right away and an at-home mom/dad isn't always that necessary for the majority of the day. Having said that, six months would be optimum, three months would be great and one month should be planned. Some children, however, need that mom at home for a year." Her agency's policy is that a working parent should take off a reasonable amount of time when the child arrives to provide a stable and secure environment.

Experienced families have differing opinions on how much time off is necessary. "I wouldn't mourn the lack of intense one-on-one time that you would have had. I found that stage to be almost artificial. It is the simple, ordinary, everyday shared experiences that have helped our son bond to our family," says Veronica, who adopted nine-year-old Jason.

On the other hand, Allison, who has adopted three older children, believes the kids need intense time with their parents. "It's so across the board that I can't imagine otherwise. People who adopt should have a need to be with that child and should be able to find a way to do it. I think if a person has a career that they have to go back to in six weeks, this is not for them." Perhaps the only absolute is that each child and each family are different.

Virtually all parents agree that assigning your child chores from the beginning is a big step in helping him feel like one of the family. Start as you mean to go. The longer you treat your child as a guest, the longer he'll feel like one. Obviously, he will not know all the rules of the house or exactly what you expect of him, but participating is the biggest thing initially. As soon as you're sure your child knows what to do and how to do it, then you can begin enforcing consequences for not doing it properly.

Deanna says, "I would say, 'Oh good, Aaron is doing the dishes tonight. He is not complaining, he is washing them and that's the end of it,' whereas if Leah did them that way, I would hand her back the plates."

Be prepared for the fact that your children, both new and old, will be intensely attuned to the "fairness" of everything at first. They will be quick to point out who is doing more and how unfair it is. Although all siblings do this, it may be very intense with an older adopted child. It will eventually lessen, as the new child becomes more secure. Even normal sibling rivalry issues will feel like a relief after the intensity of the initial adjustment. Also, your new child may be trying to be perfect and may find any amount of correction or guidance evidence of failure. A little additional leeway and a gradual push for improvement should help a great deal.

One thing that may catch you by surprise is how many unspoken rules you have in your household. If you have other children, your rules are usually already firmly in place. Your kids may know that they're not supposed to run in the house, or talk to Mom before she's had her coffee, or eat without praying, but your new child won't. You will find yourself not only teaching your rules, but *explaining* them, too.

"Having other kids meant that we couldn't be flexible because the other kids would immediately see the double standard, but that helped him [Jason] see what the rules were," says Veronica. "All our rules are pretty spoken. My other son is a pretty high-energy child who loves to test limits, so having him was really helpful because it means that we were very structured as a family. Some families don't have to talk about the rules all the time, because they don't have kids who break the rules."

Deanna says it was hard on her kids at first because her daughter's theory was that Aaron "should just *know* what was right." Remind yourself and your other children that we all had to learn the rules. We don't expect kids who have never ridden a bike to be able to do it the first time, so why would washing dishes or making beds be any different?

As the newness wears off and you find yourself falling in love with your new son or daughter, you'll probably experience intense feelings about their earlier lives. While this is the part of older child adoption that most people think about, you may be caught off guard by how deeply you feel their pain and sadness. The starkness of their early lives, their experiences of abuse or pain, and the depth of their anger can strike you forcefully. With them comes the realization that you can't fix or change what has happened to them.

"One night we were talking about the orphanage and he said he was pretty happy there. Then he said, 'The night I went there was number one time I not hungry in bed,' " Tara says about her son Simon. "My heart just broke for him—and for all the other kids who go to bed hungry at night."

Trina, whose children were badly neglected in their previous homes, says, "This is what got me through all the extreme highs and lows. Take a step back and disassociate yourself for just a minute. Try to remember that you didn't create this situation, you are not responsible and that you are here to help, not control. I found that when I removed myself and accepted that I was not to blame, I was better able to cope."

At the same time that you are experiencing this kaleidoscope of emotions and adjustment, so are your children. How does the new arrival affect the children you already have?

Getting a New Sibling

Most kids are excited about a new sibling joining their family. But after the initial excitement wears off, the real work of becoming a family sets in. Sharing not only their houses, but also their parents and belongings, can be a shock. And regardless of how much time we spend preparing our children for their new sibling, they may still have unrealistic expectations. Veronica says that one day after Jason came home, her other son said, "Mom, I didn't want this kind of a new brother. I wanted the kind of brother that was going to share his toys!"

Sometimes our kids expect the new kid to act better than they do. Deanna says her daughter Leah got mad at Aaron one day. "I asked her what it was this time and she said, 'He treats me the same way I treat Caleb!' She had no idea what she had just said."

"We were sitting at the table with one of our teenagers and Simon was misbehaving," says Tara. "Our daughter says, 'I can't believe he is acting like this, he should be so *grateful*,' and I just busted out laughing! We asked her, 'When have *you* ever been grateful?' "

Yes, just like some parents, some children expect their new sibling to be so grateful that they never cause any trouble. Gently pointing out the unfairness of that thought usually helps. However, you should also try to remember that their whole world

❖ What I Didn't Know ❖

I did NOT know that I wouldn't bond the minute I laid eyes on them.

I did NOT know that it would take so darn long to put this many kids to bed.

I did NOT know that some American kids could have ever not had a doughnut.

I did NOT know that I would so resent the best intentions of my friends who have no clue what is going on in my house.

I did NOT know that my other children would accept them before I did.

I did NOT know that I would be so aggravated about giving up my private time.

I did NOT know that a small child could consume so much fruit.

I did NOT know that I would never get the chance to be intimate with their bodies at this age. I wouldn't know each little toe like it was my own.

I did NOT know that I would be so afraid of them.

I did NOT know that I would be angry at my husband because he is *not* afraid of them.

I did NOT know that social workers could take them away, but if I wanted to give them back that's a whole different story.

I did NOT know that I was crazy not to meet them first.

I did NOT know that I would feel so responsible for them.

I did NOT know that they wouldn't know how to live with a dog.

I did NOT know that I would have to teach the House Rules long after I had actually forgotten what those rules were.

I did NOT know how much all this would cost.

I did NOT know how much people would stare at his disabilities.

I did NOT know that it would be this much trouble to get them enrolled in school.

I did NOT know that social workers leave out crucial details.

I did NOT know that I would doubt myself so much, especially in the middle of the night.

I did NOT know they would be so happy with us.

—Trina, adoptive mother of three

has turned upside down, too. When we are tired and strung out, it would be wonderful if our other children were on their best behavior. But they too are tired and on edge. They're wondering, just like your new son or daughter is, how the new arrival will change their place in the family. Allison says she didn't even think about the effect the new kids would have on her other kids. "I was too busy worrying about whether the Russian kids would adjust. And you would think that after watching each of my kids dissolve when another was born into the family that we would have thought about that! It had more of an effect than I anticipated. If there are children at home, biological or not, be very, very understanding and patient with them because I don't care if you bring in an infant, as I did with three bio kids, or you bring in older children, it's going to knock the kids in the home off balance."

Some families have found books that deal with the subject of new babies to be helpful. They can usually be adapted to fit the older child situation, and they do address many of the fears that your children will have. For kids older than eight or nine, though, it will fall on your shoulders more to talk about the changes. Sometimes simply acknowledging how difficult it is to get a new brother or sister can ease frustration. If you talk about how tough it is, your children will feel more comfortable discussing their troubles too. Sometimes our fears about whether we made a good decision prevents us from talking to our kids about their negative feelings. However, if we let our children drive their feelings underground, those feelings will resurface in bad behavior, upsetting the family even more.

Tara says that her son Simon was very upset when his younger brother Adam came home. "One day I said to him, 'It's tough getting a new brother, huh?' and he broke down and cried. He had been trying so hard to be happy and upbeat that he was holding it all in. Then we talked about ways he could relieve the pressure. He hadn't felt like he could go off and do something alone; he thought he needed to make sure Adam was included. So, we talked about how *he* was important, too. After that, he enjoyed his time with Adam more, because he did things with him when he wanted to, not just because he had to." Experienced parents recommend that you set aside some time to spend with each of your children, both new and old, alone. Doing so can ease the competition between them.

One fear that most kids have, whether they were born to the family or adopted, is that their parents will love them less when the new sibling arrives. This feeling can be exceptionally scary to kids who have lost families before, especially if they were separated from their siblings. My son was petrified that we wouldn't need him or want him anymore when his younger brother arrived. Even though part of him knew that wasn't the case, the other part of him was sure it was. We talked to him about it often and assured him of our love, but it took time for him to really believe it. This fear may subside only *after* everyone is settled in. About six months after his arrival, I asked him how he thought our family had changed. He replied, "It really hasn't. I was worried that you wouldn't have time for me anymore but that hasn't happened and I'm still here. It really helped me feel better about never having to leave. Having him only made things better."

Some kids are concerned that their place in the family is being threatened. Giving up their space as the youngest may be hard, especially if they've held that spot for years. Some families find that giving the child an extra privilege or responsibility to emphasize her older status helps her have more positive feelings.

Other people may unintentionally make the situation worse. Friends and family often come bearing gifts for the new arrival, but forget to include the others. You may want to keep some small gifts aside for just this situation. If you feel that it is more important to emphasize that fair does not mean equal, you should discuss the possibility ahead of time with your children. You can then remind them of how many things they have received in the past from family and friends.

But for some kids, the hardest part is the attention the new arrival draws to the family. This is especially true if the children are preteens or adolescents. At that age, it can be terribly awkward to feel that everyone is looking at you. Deanna says, "Leah is the one who has had to explain to her friends what he is doing here, and every now and then the office at school calls her down to help them figure out what is going on with him. The whole thing has just really been hard on her." Not only do kids have to explain the new arrival to their friends, but they may find themselves answering a stranger's questions in public, especially if the new brother or sister is of another race. We adults find that hard to deal with sometimes and it can be much more difficult for a child. Once again, time seems to be the best healer in this regard. Parents report that they have had to be hyperalert to the situation, especially in public, and that they often let their child go off for a "forgotten" item if the family is cornered in a store or other public place.

If your other children also were adopted, be prepared for the new arrival to bring their adoption issues back to the surface. Even if you have prepared yourself and your child beforehand, actually dealing with it can be much more difficult. Theresa and her husband Alan adopted a sibling group of four several years ago, and the birthmom kept a younger child. Their latest adoption, of an unrelated infant, brought up a lot of memories for the four about leaving their brother behind. "We've gotten a lot of questions like, 'Do you think our old Mommy is being mean to Blake, too?' " says Theresa. Another mother said her son's adoption also raised questions for her daughter, who was adopted from Korea as an infant: "A lot of her questions and feelings had to do with where you make the distinction between buying a child and paying adoption expenses. It also brought up how much better it is to have a birthmother who can't raise a child and decides to place him for adoption than the mother who just sort of 'mislaid' the child."

Some families have had to deal with full-blown panic. Stan says, "Tony went ballistic one week and misbehaved in ways he never had before. He was hitting his siblings and screaming at us. He was tearing things up. It was wild. It finally hit me that he was just afraid. Afraid of losing us, afraid of being sent away. I think the new arrival provoked a lot of memories of his moves. The day he finally talked to us about it, he lay on the floor and cried for almost thirty minutes."

If at all possible, try to set aside fifteen to twenty minutes each day to talk with each of your children one on one about their feelings toward the new arrival. We often get so wrapped up in how our newest child is doing that we ignore blatant signals that our other kids are in crisis.

There's No Place Like Home?

Most of us agree wholeheartedly with this sentiment. But to the newly adopted child, home may be a scary place indeed. You and your children have chosen to add a new child to your family, but in most cases, the adoptee doesn't have a choice, and he may not be sure at all that he really wants to be here. You may have had a chance to meet and visit with him, and that may help. However, the day he moves in, it all becomes real.

Nancy did an independent international adoption and was able to meet and actually live with her son's birth grandmother for almost a month before bringing him to the States. She says, "He was very blasé about this and I was not really sure he was getting it because he was all excited about going to America. We had a going-away party and he was fine. We went to the airport and he was saying 'bye, bye' and I was crying. His grandmother and great aunt were allowed in the airport up until we got to this last point, where we had to go through a set of guards and up an escalator, and I was thinking, 'This is just too easy.' All of a sudden he looked around and it hit him and he screamed bloody murder, dropped all his stuff and *ran* for all his little legs were worth screaming, 'Grandmother, Grandmother!' He was running down the 'up' escalator and the whole airport was staring at us." Nancy finally got him and the guards let the aunt in with them until they boarded. "I was sweating bullets, and he was sobbing and hanging on to his aunt for dear life and I went over and just peeled him off her. When we got to where he could see airplanes, he was okay. We both laugh about it now."

Even if your child is not visibly screaming and kicking, he may well be doing so inside. Few of us can imagine how difficult it must be to be moved somewhere against our will. When my younger son came home, he had been with one adoptive family and that placement had disrupted. The report stated that the doctor detected "a possible stubborn streak." I thought, "What if I had been married to someone for four years and then one day my husband said, 'I can't take care of you anymore, so I'm taking you to somebody who can,' and dropped me off. And then they told me that soon a new husband would pick me up and everything would be good but that husband took me to a new country where everything looked different and smelled different and tasted different and I couldn't understand anyone. And then he decided I wasn't really what he wanted so he sent me somewhere else. I'd probably be a tad oppositional, too!" Given our kids' history, is it any wonder that they may not think we are really going to be their parents either?

Liam says of his new son, Colin, age twelve, "He *knew* it was just a matter of time before he left and he was going to go out on his own terms and he was going to cause as much trouble as he could so that he would be justified in leaving."

Sometimes things your child has been told in previous homes aggravate these early problems. "Apparently he was told if he was bad that he was going to have to go back and so if I got upset at him or yelled at him, he would lose it," says Brent about his son Austin. "I also think he was told he had to do good in school, because when we got in the cab to go to the airport, he started reciting his ABCs and counting to ten."

Nancy adds, "I worked with Nicholas a lot about grieving because his grandmother had told him all that good Asian stuff—you know, don't cry, don't be sad."

Kids who are loaded down with all the fear and anger of previous families and rejections are not easy to love. They likely have deeply entrenched coping skills. Social worker and adoptive parent Sandra Russell says, "I think the one thing we have to remember is that older children are the survivors—the fittest of the fit. If you get a child who is over the age of three, he has survived hell already. Not that he's tough, not that he's worldly, but he survived. And not always do survivors have some of the best habits or some of the best perceptions of the world either. But we have to respect that and if we can't accept it and respect it then we shouldn't be parents. [There is] very much an independence in these kids. One minute they are the child who wants to cling to you and wants all your attention and the next minute, it's 'I can do it myself!'"

This pull between independence and dependence is the hall-mark of newly placed older kids. They may be desperate for love and acceptance and at the same time petrified to trust that you will be able to care for and provide for them. During the first few weeks, or perhaps months, they will attempt to present their best side—the side most easily lovable. They feel it is safe to do so then, because they don't have any real bond or attachment to you yet. However, when your child begins to grow attached to you, the less desirable behavior, and the feelings behind it, often become more obvious. Some feel that at this time the child is testing you to see if you will still love her when she is bad. Perhaps a better explanation is that she feels torn between wanting to love you and being safe. She may be feeling love for you and so pulls closer, then decides it is too scary and pulls back. At times her control over her feelings may slip, allowing you a glimpse of the pain within—but then she will cover up with bravado and outward shows of independence.

Olivia says that when she met her daughter at the airport, "she walked around our brand new, expensive car and looked at it like, 'Well, I'm not sure that's good enough to ride home in.' And she wanted to know where all the color TVs were and why there wasn't one in every room, and where the maid was to make her bed in the morning, and the closet full of clothes and everything because the streets are paved with gold in the U.S. It was like, 'I'm not sure this family is good enough for me.' "

When you've scraped and saved to adopt and then survived the wait, the "It's not good enough" attitude can really chafe. It may seem like everything you do or say, or anything you give them, will just not be good enough for them. In fact, the feeling may really be that your child doesn't feel good enough. Ted thinks there were times when his new son felt uncomfortable or unworthy, especially when Ted was buying things for him, and would act out, trying to get the new father to reject him. "Sometimes they do things that really irk you, but when you think about it, it makes sense," he says.

Kids also act out because they may not be committed to the relationship at first. Many of these kids have never had a full commitment from a parent and may doubt that you will stick by them. "It is getting that child to commit to the adoptive parents which is sometimes a problem—you have to earn it," explains Sandra Russell. To the child, his previous home was a comfortable, familiar place, and he doesn't know you. "All of a sudden he's got two parents telling him what to do and having great expectations of him and he's not sure he is even committed to this relationship yet. All of a sudden he is expected to be this charming child." When the family tries to set "normal" boundaries, she adds, the kid's response is, "Why do I want to be here?"

Helping Your Child Bond

Although the weeks and months after your child comes home can be trying, most families and children do bond. Getting past your child's fear and anger may take time, but you will likely succeed. It is the small, everyday occurrences and rituals that

---

❖ Building Attachment ❖

I asked many experienced families how they had helped their child bond. They shared these suggestions:

Read a bedtime story every day, perhaps as part of a larger, elaborate bedtime ritual.

Have family meetings where you discuss such things as what everyone in the family is doing, and what gifts the children have and how they can use them.

Put on kids' music and sing and clap to it.

Have a new family portrait made early on.

Have fun together. Play in the snow, make hot cocoa, see a movie.

Rock them to sleep.

Put up any valuables you don't want broken, so that nothing interferes with your good feelings toward them.

Establish set routines, especially at mealtime and bedtime.

Don't try to change bad behaviors all at once. Allow time for bonding first.

Let the housekeeping go and focus on your child.

Find opportunities to touch: tickling, back rubs, feeding each other ice cream.

glue families together, and the same is true for families formed through older child adoption. Perform bonding activities on a regular schedule. These rituals will help your child feel more secure and more quickly find his place in your family.

Sometimes, big experiences help strengthen ties. "Dylan had to have surgery shortly after he arrived, and I was worried about the effect it would have on the bonding," says Ted. But he thinks the experience actually helped his son learn to trust him because Ted was there for him. Other families have found that going on vacation and returning home together helps reassure the child that he isn't going to have to leave or be left behind someplace.

Some families have welcome-home parties or showers for their children. It's probably best to wait a while after your child arrives, however, so you don't overwhelm her with too much pressure. But being included in extended family gatherings and being accepted by your extended family will likely also help her attach to you.

By Any Other Name?

Professionals and families alike are divided over the wisdom of changing your child's first name at the time of placement. Some kids eagerly accept a name change, feeling that their new name is a symbol of being claimed by the family. Others hang on to their old name as a way to keep distance between them and the family, or to retain ties to their past—or maybe just because they're used to the name and like it.

Veronica says nine-year-old Jason is determined not to take his new family's name. "He wants to keep his original first, middle and last name and not add anything. He has had two other pre-adoptive placements that did not work out, so twice he had changed his name and then the families sent him back." She thinks he may be afraid that if he changes his name, this adoption won't work out either.

Some families hesitate to change their child's first name. Deanna says, "We've taken this child from everything he knows, packed him up and taken him halfway around the world and dropped him into this mysterious family and a whole new culture. How can we take his name away from him?"

Like many parents, she chose to give her son a new middle name while keeping his original first name. Some families give their child a new first name and keep the original name as a middle name. Most feel it is necessary to keep some part of the child's original name. Indeed, one of the first questions that kids adopted as infants usually ask is, "What did my birthmother name me?" Their name is part of them and their history.

Even parents who feel that retaining a name is important sometimes have to make adjustments. One girl's Korean name was Mee Joo. Her mother says, "It didn't seem right that a child raised in a mostly Jewish home should have to spend time telling people her name was 'Me Jew.' It seemed like a perverted version of 'Who's on First.' " She and her husband did give their daughter another Korean name.

It may be difficult to get schools and doctors to use your child's new name until the adoption is final. Parents suggest asking teachers to use the child's new name in informal situations, even if his legal name still appears on official documents. At times, a statement from a counselor or therapist stating that it is in the child's best interests to do so may be helpful.

Sometimes parents have no choice but to change a name because the child's safety depends upon it. Birthparents who have had their rights terminated for abuse or neglect may try to abduct a child. In this case, you must be firm with the school system and other authorities and demand that the original name be removed from their records. Trina was worried that her new son's mother might try to find him. She says, "I called a meeting at the school, gave everyone a business card from my lawyer with a secret password written by me on the back. I told them that anyone who called on the telephone about Ryan, wrote a letter about Ryan, or came to pick Ryan up would have one of these cards with the name on the back in my handwriting. It was not enough to just say the password, they had to have the card with the password written on the back. Then I gently reminded them that if they did not follow this one basic instruction, and anything went wrong, the name on the *front* of the card would be calling them immediately."

Many children, including those who change their names willingly at the time of adoption, want to begin using their birthname again in adolescence. Most professionals agree that the only *right* answer about whether to change your child's name is the answer that both you and your child come to together.

"What If I Don't Love My Child?"

For some parents, the initial adjustment period does not result in a loving attachment. This may especially be true if your child has serious behavioral difficulties or if your personalities simply do not mesh. Some parents may even consider disrupting (ending) an adoption because they cannot attach to the child. If your child is doing well in your home it may be even more difficult to deal with your lack of feelings for him.

Experienced parents say that you must distinguish loving from liking and commitment. Most parents will tell you that love takes time. You may be committed to your child for months or even years before you truly love him. If your child hesitates to attach to you, you may find yourself holding back, too. But even if everything is progressing normally, love takes time, and a year or more is not that unusual.

Parents who have children by birth often talk about the fact that they love each of their children differently. At times, a personality clash can mean loving a child you don't really like. Other parents find that they like a child and her personality and behaviors, but don't feel a deep love for her.

Many experienced parents point out that you don't have to love a child to parent him. Parenting is about commitment and support. If you can concentrate on being a "good enough" parent instead of a perfect one, you may be able to have a fulfilling relationship with your child even in the absence of strong love.

Paula says she found it difficult to love one of her daughters. She finalized the adoption anyway, because she was committed to her. Her daughter had some attachment difficulty but after a period of years, her daughter did begin to attach and then Paula began to love her. She says, "Several months later she was in trouble at school for something she didn't do and I immediately felt what I call 'jump-through-fire mother love' for her."

Sometimes parents have to change their definition of what

love is. This may be especially true for people who have never been parents before or for those who always felt an instant connection to their other children. Some parents find that acting loving towards their children can jump-start those feelings. Parents point out that real love is shown in what a parent *does*, rather than what they *feel*.

It may help to talk with an experienced professional about your feelings. Perhaps you are holding back from your child because some of her issues remind you of painful things from your past. Perhaps you are holding back because of the fear that your child will not really love you. Whatever the reason, you can be a successful adoptive parent without professing undying love.

❖ 5 ❖

Settling In

Control is the buzzword for older adopted kids. As much as we parents can understand that, it doesn't make it any easier to live with. Having one person trying to exert control on the rest of the family can create chaos.

Sabrina, new adoptive mother of nine-year-old Holly, says she feels like she has a 4½-foot two-year-old. "I understand that 'no' is a means of control when you are unsure of yourself and your surroundings, but when 'no' is the first and last word on everything, I have to wonder."

Control is the end result of several emotions, but fear and anger are the likeliest culprits. And our kids have those emotions in spades when they arrive. Regardless of how well behaved they try to be at first, they will likely show some measure of the need to control. Sleeping, eating, and toileting issues are generally the first to arise, simply because they permeate every aspect of our lives. Some problems are easily understood and easily handled, while others may have deeper roots.

Sleep Adjustments

Sleep is something we all need and something that most of us can't get enough of during the initial adjustment. Yet, sleeping is one area in which virtually all children experience difficulties, in one way or another. It may be hard for us to believe that our children are not as exhausted as we are. In fact, they probably are, but that doesn't mean sleep will come easily to them. Falling asleep is one of the most difficult things for newly adopted kids to do for many reasons. Foremost is probably the fact that when they fall asleep they can no longer be vigilant about their safety and what's going on in the house.

"Vigilant" describes almost every newly adopted child. Even when they appear relaxed, these kids undoubtedly know where everyone in the household is, what they are doing, and how it affects them. Think back to a time when you were truly frightened. Perhaps you awoke one night to a strange sound in your house. Can you remember the feeling of uneasiness? Do you remember how each sound echoed through your brain, and every movement seemed exaggerated? Was your heart pounding and the hair on your arms standing on end? That is vigilance. A rush of adrenaline caused by fear activates this "fight or flight" response, which prepares your body to protect itself by either fighting the danger or fleeing from it.

Your child is no doubt experiencing this sensation. You may notice that loud noises or sudden movement easily startle her. Or perhaps she gets anxious when there is a lot of noise and activity. One obvious sign of vigilance, though, will probably be a resistance to bedtime.

Your child knows that if he falls asleep, he no longer has any control over what happens to him. Some children may have been moved while sleeping. If this happened to your child, you can be sure that he will resist sleep—after all, how can he be sure he will still be in your home in the morning? Other kids may fear being moved in their sleep, even if they have never experienced it. Children know that being asleep makes them more vulnerable. In most cases, once a child becomes confident that he will not have to leave, the sleep problems subside.

Allison and Shawn adopted two children from Russia at ages four and six. Their daughter Emily had difficulty sleeping. Allison says, "She only cried at bedtime. We weren't sure how much of it was that she was afraid she'd wake up in the morning and this wouldn't be here, or how much she missed having fourteen other kids in the room with her. But she didn't like going to bed and didn't want to cooperate at all. It lasted about eight weeks and then one night when I was putting her to bed she said, 'Emily no go back to detsky dom [orphanage].' I said, 'That's right, Emily stays here forever.' And that was the last time she cried at bedtime. It was *her* declaration. She needed to commit to us."

Kids who have never slept alone may be frightened to do so.

Although this is most obvious with kids from overseas who have lived in orphanages, it can be true for kids adopted domestically, too, who have lived in foster homes with many other kids. On the other hand, some children may be uncomfortable sleeping in the room with someone. Your son or daughter may have been mistreated or abused when sharing a room. Gentle discussion about nighttime fears may reveal such things.

When my children came home, they were both petrified at bedtime. My older son had never slept in a bed alone, never mind in a room alone. There was a trundle bed in his room and for months one of us had to go lie down in there until he went to sleep. As soon as he awoke, he ran to my room to see if I was still there. Our younger son had experienced several moves in a short period of time. He fought sleep for everything he was worth, and only succumbed when he was truly exhausted. His older brother was sleeping in the top bunk, but that wasn't enough. He insisted that someone lie where he could see them until he fell asleep.

Some children resist bedtime because their memories come flooding back when things are quiet and they have nothing to focus on except a blank ceiling. Tara says, "One of our teenage foster kids would fight bedtime—she was always jumping up for one reason or another to put off

> ❖ **No Fear of Strangers** ❖
>
> Many newly adopted kids will walk off with just about anyone. Although indiscriminate affection with strangers can be a sign of more serious problems, it is also common for children without attachment difficulties to do this in the first few months after their arrival.
>
> Remember, even you are a stranger to your child at first, and he may not distinguish between you and others for at least a few weeks. Some kids have lived in sheltered environments and have never learned that some adults are dangerous.
>
> Experienced parents warn that you should keep a close eye on newly adopted children, especially when they are in unfamiliar places, as they may simply wander off or approach strangers. With time, this tendency should pass and your child should begin to show anxiety when separated from you.

going to sleep. She later told me that when everything got quiet, she couldn't keep the memories of her birthmom and everything she had lost from overwhelming her. She would just cry and cry."

Simple things like leaving lights on or allowing your child to take a teddy bear or small blanket to bed may help him get to sleep. Your son or daughter may simply be afraid of the dark. Kids who are older may be ashamed of their fears, and may have been teased about them in foster homes or orphanages.

Kids have many ways of avoiding bedtime. Some refuse to change into pajamas or get into bed. Others throw temper tantrums or begin weeping. Some kids become very interested in talking with their parents all of a sudden. Parents often use elaborate nighttime rituals to ease their kids into bed. Over time these rituals help kids form a pattern of expectations that ease their fears. Allowing children to read, even to the point of falling asleep mid-story, seems to work well for kids who have trouble keeping their memories at bay. Some families use nighttime banter between rooms to make bedtime a time of giggles. We used this in our house, with much success. I think it emphasized that we were close by and had not left. Many children need someone to sleep with them, or at least nearby, at first. Parents are often reluctant to do so, for fear of setting a precedent that will later be hard to break. Although this is understandable, most of these children have experienced serious trauma in their lives and a little accommodation can go a long way in easing their fears. Most families find that their children will learn to sleep alone if the companionship is withdrawn gradually.

The first week after our youngest son, Connor, came home, we allowed his brother, Patrick, to sleep in the same bed with him. The next week Patrick moved to a trundle in sight of Connor's bed. The next week or two, I went in to lie on the trundle, but only until Connor actually fell asleep, and then I would leave, until he became used to waking up without me there. After that, I would read in my bed in the next room, but would answer him when he called. Within six weeks or so, he was going to sleep easily.

Some children enjoy going to bed, although they seem to be rare. Sometimes, they have used sleep as an escape in the past and the pattern continues. This is especially true of depressed children. They may be able to escape feelings of loss and grief through sleep. "A lot of times after he has an emotional blowout he will just fall asleep immediately," says Veronica of nine-year-old Jason, adopted from the foster care system. "He doesn't resist going to bed at all. That is a safe place for him."

Children who fight sleep may be prone to night terrors. They may fall into a deep, exhausted sleep, when night terrors are more likely to occur. Parents often report being wakened by their children's screams. Night terrors are characterized by behavior such as crying, thrashing, kicking, moaning, mumbling, and even running about. They occur during partial arousal from a deep, dreamless sleep. When experiencing a night terror, a child usually appears to be very confused, perhaps terrified, and may scream. The child is likely to breathe rapidly, sweat profusely, and show other signs usually associated with fear. The child does not recognize parents and is likely to push them away. Rousing a child into full wakefulness is impossible and attempts to do so only intensify and prolong the episode. Sleep terrors can last from a few seconds to thirty or forty minutes and usually appear one to three hours after the onset of sleep. When the episode ends, the child is likely to calm, wake briefly, and then go back to sleep, with no memory of the episode in the morning. Normally, night terrors are common only in preschool-age kids. This is just one instance where stress and regression cause behaviors that don't fit the "rules" you'll find in typical child care books.

Parents find night terrors much harder to deal with than their children do. You may have trouble falling asleep, knowing that a screaming child is likely to awaken you. It can be difficult to watch your son struggle with a night terror. Your first instinct will be to help him, but you can't. Night terrors can be especially draining to exhausted new parents. As your child settles in and becomes more secure, they should subside.

Your child's fears and memories might also surface in nightmares. Brent says eight-year-old Austin slept pretty well, but had nightmares. "One morning I woke him up and he said he had

dreamt that I had taken him back to India and he said he didn't
want to go back."

With time, most sleep problems disappear. They may resurface, however, during times of change and stress. Parents often
report sleep difficulties if one of the parents is away on business
or if the family goes on vacation. If sleep problems recur, revert-
ing back to the things you did earlier will likely bring things
back to normal. Some children may need to sleep with comfort
objects such as teddy bears well into their teenage years.

Eating Difficulties

Eating problems range from simply adjusting to new tastes to
serious disorders. Many kids pick food issues as their major control point. As any parent who has raised a child through
toddlerhood knows, there is no way to control what enters or
exits your child's body. If you force peas into your daughter's
mouth, she can throw them right back even more forcefully. This
battle can be impossible to win.

If your child feels the need to exert control over her life,
eating is probably the easiest way to do it. Sabrina describes her
nine-year-old daughter's efforts at control:

"She'll only drink Coke and water, forget juice, and the diet
non-caffeinated stuff. Forget fish sauce and anything typically
Vietnamese, she didn't even eat it there in Vietnam. However,
she'll eat fruit and cabbage four times a day and noodles until
she looks like one." Sabrina says she also gets the big sulk: 'What!
You bought this cabbage? I wanted another kind!' and then the
world falls apart in anger for thirty to forty minutes and then
she doesn't talk to whoever bought the challenged vegetable, only
to eat it two days later!"

Holly may be reeling from the loss of familiar foods, angry
at all she left behind and feeling like it's all out of her control.
Fighting over food may feel like a safe way for her to vent anger
and grief. If your child is this combative over food, the best thing
you can do is not make it a control battle. Some families are
afraid of putting themselves into the position of cooking several
different meals each night. But that doesn't have to happen. If
your child is displaying control issues through food, then give

her the control. Let her shop with you and pick what she wants to eat. If your son hates the food you make and is old enough, let him prepare his own meals. If he's younger and refuses most foods, let him eat fortified breakfast cereal for dinner or bread three times a day if you have to. Your child isn't likely to let himself starve and by allowing him that measure of control, you have made his world a little safer. That frees him up to work on more important feelings.

Problems sometimes arise simply from a difference in tastes. Your son may be used to eating a bland diet while you serve spicy food. Or perhaps your daughter is used to eating only a few comfort foods and has never tried much of what you set before her. This can be especially true of international adoptees. Deanna says her son Aaron likes Cajun pickles, Tabasco sauce, and Thai chiles. "He thinks our food is bland."

Veronica says food has been a big issue for her son Jason. "He was used to a really high-sugar, high-fat, high-salt kind of diet and we are these earthy, crunchy organic-everything kind of eaters, although not vegetarian, thank goodness, because that would have been even worse for him."

Families deal with these problems in a variety of ways. Some parents learn to cook dishes that are very important to their children. This can be an excellent way to incorporate their culture and preferences into your home, and it emphasizes that the whole family, not just the new child, is changing because of the adoption. Profound differences in diet such as the ones Veronica dealt with, however, can require moving your child's expectations and tastes to a healthier level. Veronica explains how her family has done this. "We tried to be as flexible as possible, so he picked out a couple of vegetables that he liked and we served those vegetables. He thinks fruit comes out of a can and I'm not sure he had ever eaten fresh fruit." Parents also stress the importance of letting your child accompany you to the store to help choose what to eat, especially if you're trying to change diet preferences. Children are often more willing to try something they have picked out themselves.

Some families find that their biggest food issue is not really about food, but the way it is eaten. Table manners can be virtually nonexistent. If you can stand it, it may be better to let the problem slide at first. You will undoubtedly have larger issues to worry about. However, for some families the problem is so bad that it has to be addressed right away.

"Whenever they had eaten in the detsky dom, it was a finite amount of food," says Allison about her two Russian children. "You just ate a lot and you ate fast and just shoveled it in and you talked at the same time. It was so bad we had to address it right away." When you begin trying to change your child's eating habits, keep in mind that it won't happen quickly. We often forget that it takes months and sometimes years to teach toddlers good table manners. If your child has never learned them before, it could take a long, long time.

In some cultures, it's considered impolite to talk during meals. Therefore, your child may find dinner conversation intimidating. Some cultures separate the children from the adults during mealtime. Brent says of Austin, age eight, from India: "We went to eat with friends a couple weeks after he was here and he was really intimidated by that and ended up sitting in my lap and just kind of playing with his food. I'd say to him not to eat things off the floor, but [in India] they sat and ate on the floor, and he'd say, 'Why not?' It was actually a good question."

Many families report that their children ate voraciously when they first arrived, and some still do months or years later. Many children have never had enough to eat and will eat tremendous amounts of food as their bodies grow rapidly after their arrival. For the first three months after he arrived, my oldest son ate up to six bananas and four apples a day! He was always hungry and fruit was his favorite treat. As he started gaining weight and filling out, he gradually began eating less.

Theresa and Alan adopted a sibling group of four, ages twenty months to six years, from the United States. The children were so malnourished that the twenty-month-old weighed only fourteen pounds. All of their children ate voraciously. Theresa says, "When we first got them, a couple of times we took them to Ponderosa and we were trying to let them eat as much as they wanted because we knew they were so very hungry. A couple of times Noah, age six, threw up because he ate so much. And I remember distinctly one time when we went out to eat he said, 'I'm not going to eat 'til I'm sick this time.' He was finally learning that there was going to be food every day."

Many kids, however, eat voraciously not because they're hungry but because they're trying to fill an emotional void. They may be experiencing feelings of emptiness from their losses and subconsciously be trying to fill that emptiness with food. It can be difficult to decide which type of voracious eating your child is doing. Keep in mind that kids who are underweight may need to eat more than normal. Also, teenagers can often eat a complete meal and be famished an hour later, and that is not abnormal for their age and growth patterns. Some kids also eat just because it is offered and they don't feel comfortable saying no.

If you think your daughter is eating voraciously to fill emotional needs, try to help her distinguish between physical and emotional hunger. In her book, *Helping Children Cope with Separation and Loss*, Claudia Jewett suggests controlling food intake by handing each diner a plateful of food, rather than passing food at the table. If a child asks for more after he's clearly eaten enough, the adult might ask, "I wonder if you're really hungry,"

❖ A Word About Pets ❖

Many children, especially those who have lived in institutions overseas, have never had pets. Your child may show extreme fear of any animal in your house. Children who are not used to pets may also have to be shown how to treat animals. You may find that your ten-year-old treats your animal like a baby would, pulling its tail and throwing it around.

If you have not had children before, your dog or cat may get jealous. Watch your pet closely in the weeks after your child's arrival to make sure the animal is not behaving aggressively toward your child. With time, most pets and children adjust to each other.

If your child has difficulty with anger or attachment, he may try to harm animals. If your pet has unusual injuries or suddenly starts showing aggressive behavior toward your child, watch for indications that the child is hurting the animal. If you see any such signs, seek professional help.

and suggest that a snuggle, hug, or back rub might feel better.

Children who have gone hungry or who eat to fill emotional needs may hoard food. Theresa says her four children would get up in the night, take food from the cupboards, and put it under their pillows. "I would get up in the morning to get my husband's lunch and the fridge would be hanging open with food hanging out all over the floor," she says. (Theresa's children were malnourished, but their birthmother was not. She had told the agency that the children "stole" her food.) The problem continued until the night that Theresa heard the light switch click and someone dragging a chair, and found one of her sons rummaging in the refrigerator. "I said, 'Trevor, this is not good. You are getting food all over, we're going to have mice and ants, the food gets bad and then I have to throw it away and you can't eat it later. Aren't you getting enough to eat? Am I feeding you enough? Do you like my cooking?' And I think he started thinking about it then. It just seemed like before that nothing was helping. A couple of times they admitted they were taking food to give to the others—they were pretty protective of each other."

Theresa and Alan's children stopped hoarding food that night. For many children, the practice continues for years. Some families have to put locks on the refrigerator or cabinets. For children whose food problems are this troublesome, treating the underlying emotional causes may help. Some kids still have difficulty with food-related issues even in adulthood, but to a lesser extent. Olivia says of her daughter, now in her thirties: "I went to her apartment one day and opened her cabinet and she had thirty cans of tuna fish in there. She still stockpiles mounds of food—it is such an issue for her."

In contrast, some children don't want to eat much at all when they arrive. For some, this is undoubtedly a result of their lack of familiarity with our foods. Brent says of Austin, "When he first got here, he didn't eat much. A lot of it was the packaging and stuff and not knowing what it was. We had toast and eggs for probably a couple of weeks." If you have this particular problem with your child, your best bet is probably to have your child accompany you to the store to pick out things he likes.

Children may have trouble eating because of anxiety, fear, or sadness. If your child is trying to hold in his grief over leaving a familiar place, he may constantly have a knot in his throat or may be nauseated. Most of us can remember a time when we were too upset or scared to eat. If your daughter has no appetite for a few days, try not to push her. Ask her if she has a favorite food or offer to cook something she likes. A temporary lull in eating may not be too worrisome, but you should seek the advice of your child's doctor if it persists.

Sometimes, children who have never had much to eat get used to eating small amounts. It may take very little food to actually fill the child up, and eating may not be comfortable. Most children's appetites will gradually increase, but not always. Nancy, who adopted seven-year-old Colton from Vietnam, has had continuing eating struggles with her son. She says, "When I brought him home, getting him to eat was a tremendous struggle. He was thirty-three pounds at the age of seven. His family said he didn't eat much in Vietnam either. He would eat a few bits of rice and then take off. I tried real hard not to make it a power struggle because I knew the potential of it becoming a full-blown eating disorder was there. I tried not feeding him to see if he would get hungry. Found out he didn't and he didn't even care about food. I tried timing him, but at the end of the time, he could have cared less if you took it away. He desperately needed the calories. I did things like put dry milk solids and heavy cream in things. He has made a lot of progress, but he is still far from big. He just broke forty pounds recently and he is forty-three or forty-four inches tall."

Nancy sought medical advice and physical problems were ruled out, as was anorexia nervosa. It seems that Colton simply has little interest in eating. Obviously, a parent worries more when this applies to a child who is malnourished. The only thing you can do is to attempt to feed the child small amounts, several times a day, emphasizing foods that are nutritious but high in calories, fat, and protein.

Some children vomit when they try to eat at first. If your daughter is trying to hold her grief in, she may not be able to swallow past the lump in her throat. Nancy also had this problem. "Colton started vomiting his food during mealtime, which was real pleasant for everybody," she says. "When we were over there [in Vietnam] one day the aunt asked him if he wanted broth and he said yes because it made it easier to swallow. He cannot swallow anything and I noticed that he chews his food into oblivion. We went for swallowing studies and there is nothing physically wrong. So I started working with him a lot about grieving, because his grandmother had told him not to cry and not to be sad. When he started dealing with that, the throwing up stopped. The last time he threw up was the last time we called his grandmother. He is just now [almost a year later] talking about how he felt when he got here."

Families occasionally report that their child eats non-food items. This behavior, called pica, is rare. Some medical experts believe that pica is simply an outgrowth of the normal toddler tendency to taste everything. Others think it can signal stress, attachment difficulties, or psychosis. If your child does this, seek professional help.

Prolonged periods of eating difficulties such as gorging and pica may indicate deeper psychological problems. In some cases, eating difficulties progress to full-blown eating disorders (see Chapter 11). Usually, though, most eating problems subside after your child feels more comfortable in his new home.

Food carries with it the psychological message of nurturing, too. Serving food, with a smile, is one of the best ways to form an attachment. By providing physical nourishment, you send the message that you are also willing to provide for your child emotionally. Some children may resist this at first, as it implies trust, but over time it will likely aid your bonding. Because of its tie to bonding, you should try not to make food a control battle.

Toileting Problems

One area of adjustment that catches many new families unawares is toileting. Difficulties range from differences in customs to the smearing of feces. This is one that parents find difficult to handle because a child's behaviors or problems may not be age-appropriate. When parents adopt an infant, they expect to change diapers, but they may be unpleasantly surprised when they have to deal with a seven-year-old who soils his pants.

For international adoptees, toileting customs may be a problem. In many parts of the world, a toilet is simply a hole in the ground or floor that the person squats over. Many people consider our custom of sitting on a toilet to be dirty or unhygienic. Your son may have never seen a toilet like the one in your house and may have no idea how to use it. The obvious solution to many kids is to simply climb atop it and squat. Some families have had success simply showing their children how to use a toilet the "western" way. For other families, the children watch the explanations and then proceed to do it the way that is comfortable for them.

"I'm fairly sure that he is still standing on the seat when he uses the bathroom [after almost a year]," says Deanna about Aaron, adopted from Asia at age eight. "I always find his shoes on the floor by the toilet. I figure we have enough to worry about without worrying about what he does in the bathroom."

This is probably a good attitude. With time, your son will likely learn how to sit on the toilet, especially if any of his friends at school see him squatting atop it. Remember, too, that this is a matter of comfort. If you traveled to your child's birthcountry, you may well know how difficult it can be to squat over a hole in the floor. Likewise, your child may find it uncomfortable to sit on the toilet, which forces him to use a different set of muscles.

In some countries, toilet paper is a luxury and many children have never used it. They may not even know what it is. They may be accustomed to using their hands and a pitcher of water, or simply not cleaning themselves at all. Colleen says of her two Russian kids, "We only got the one set of clothes with them. They usually want the clothes back at the orphanage, which is fine because they really stank. They didn't have any toilet paper so it was really bad." You should be prepared, if you adopt from overseas, to do a small educational routine showing the appropriate use of the toilet and toilet paper, and the proper way to thoroughly wash one's hands afterwards.

The effects of institutionalization can be seen in toileting behaviors, too. In many orphanages, the children must ask for permission to go to the toilet. It may take a long time for this habit to change. Allison says, "Children are not encouraged to be 'thinkers' in orphanages. Our institutionalized kids couldn't go to the bathroom without asking permission for almost a year, no matter how often we told them they could just go and didn't need permission." Though it sounds like a little thing, this habit can become quite annoying.

Other kids may have been made to "hold it'" and only allowed to go to the toilet at certain times. Ted thinks this may have been the case with his son, who at first could go from one evening to the next afternoon without urinating. In some foster homes, kids may not have been allowed to get up at night to use the bathroom, especially if the family had many children and imposed strict rules to maintain order.

Bedwetting

Bedwetting (enuresis) is common among both non-adopted and adopted children. It is estimated that ten to fifteen percent of five-year-olds wet the bed at least once a month. Boys are slightly more prone to enuresis than girls. About fifteen percent of bedwetters will naturally develop nighttime bladder control by age six; another fifteen percent by age seven, and so on. Only two percent of twelve-year-olds wet their beds. Ninety-nine percent of children who wet their beds eventually gain nighttime control naturally. The other 1 percent almost always have a developmental or physical disorder.

Bedwetting tends to run in families. Unfortunately for adoptive parents, we rarely know whether our child's birthfamily has a history of bedwetting. This can make it difficult to determine if your son is wetting the bed because he is more prone to it biologically or whether it signals an underlying physical or emotional problem. Many ailments cause or aggravate bedwetting, including diabetes, seizure disorders, sickle cell anemia, kidney failure, spina bifida, mental retardation, and autism. Episodes of bedwetting can be caused by urinary tract infections. Some physicians believe that foods can aggravate the bladder if the child is allergic to them. Prematurity has also been tied to bedwetting problems later in life.

If your child wets the bed for any length of time, you should rule out possible medical causes. Once you have done that, you can safely assume that the cause is psychological. Many adopted children have bedwetting problems. At times, such problems clear up after the initial adjustment period. Perhaps the child is unsettled by the move and regresses in his toilet habits. For other children, however, bedwetting has deeper origins and lasts longer.

Suppressed or ignored anger may be one cause of bedwetting. Some children who experience deep feelings of anger and worthlessness do not feel comfortable showing their feelings in a forthright way. They exhibit anger through passive aggressive behavior. Children who feel worthless may use bedwetting and other behaviors as a means to provoke punishment.

Professionals say children who have been abused may find it difficult to distinguish their body's messages, such as the sensation of a full bladder. If this is the case, the child is likely to have wetting problems day and night. Children who have been abused also may wet themselves as a way to keep people at a distance. They learn that the smell makes people not want to be close.

Dealing with bedwetting may leave you exhausted and angry. One of the first steps that experienced parents recommend is that you teach your child how to strip and remake her own bed, so that you do not have to be awakened each night to do it. You can also show her how to operate the washing machine to alleviate some of the laundry load. Doing so may motivate her to help you in resolving the problem.

If it appears that your child is using bedwetting as a release of anger, dealing with the underlying anger is the best way to alleviate it. You can point out things that are obviously making her angry, by saying something like, "I can see that it makes you angry when your brother says that." Some children have never been able to or allowed to express their anger openly, and may have to be gradually taught how to do so. You can encourage your child to stomp her feet, beat her pillow, take a walk, pound nails, or hit baseballs. As your child finds more appropriate ways to express anger, the bedwetting may stop.

If you think your child is unaware of his body's sensations, you may need to cue him to recognize feelings of fullness, or pain, or the need to go to the bathroom. If your child experiences daytime enuresis, try using a toilet training program similar to one you would use with a toddler. First, teach him to go at set intervals, so that he can learn what it feels like to empty his bladder. With time, he should be able to recognize when he has to go. Remember that toilet training can take a year or longer with toddlers, and it may take time with your older child, too.

Bedwetting problems that subside may crop up again later, especially during emotional crises. For some kids, bedwetting is a way to exert control. "Noah's bedwetting is emotional. He can control it when he wants to—he's even told me he can," says Theresa about her ten-year-old son, adopted at age six. She feels there's no point in badgering him about it, so she just makes him responsible for it. He has to do the laundry and change his bed. She says he's gone as long as three or four months without wetting the bed, then starts again.

Soiling

Bowel control problems may accompany enuresis or appear by themselves. Encopresis, the passage of stool at inappropriate times or places, does happen for physical reasons, although that is rare. Like enuresis, it can occur if a child is not aware of his body and does not recognize the signs of needing to defecate. In rare cases, involuntary bowel evacuation can occur after a long period of constipation. A pediatrician can treat medical causes.

Children can use bowel problems as a means of control. Some parents report that their children smear feces around the bathroom or on the floor and walls. Other kids have purposely stopped up toilets with large amounts of toilet paper, much of it smeared with feces. Family therapist and child advocate Joyce Maguire Pavao says this type of behavior often indicates sexual or physical abuse. You should seek professional help for a child who smears feces. At the same time, you'll need to find ways to deal with the behavior at home.

Molly, adoptive mother of two children (ages nine and eleven), says, "We had a period of the toilet being stuffed to the very brim with wadded toilet paper, feces on the toilet paper, feces on the sink. It could have been hostility to yet another placement, we don't know. We sat both of the children down and talked with them about what was an appropriate amount of toilet paper to use, what you do if your bowels are runny, versus what you do if you are having difficulty evacuating your bowels. How we cope with this in this house, which is make them responsible for cleaning it up. We tried, and I think we were successful, not to be condemnatory or punishing. But it didn't work. We saw that behavior probably a dozen times before it just went away on its own. We had the same conversation three or four times and then one day it just ceased."

Some parents advise putting the child back in diapers, calmly giving her the choice of going in her diaper or in the toilet, and making her responsible for cleaning up any messes.

This type of approach works well for some. However, other children will continue to have difficulties until the underlying issues are addressed and resolved.

Intestinal Difficulties

Many families report that their children have intestinal problems upon arrival. Constipation is common, especially among international adoptees. One reason may be that long plane rides can seriously dehydrate the body, with constipation as a result. The difference in diet probably contributes as well. Making sure that your child drinks enough water and eats foods with fiber generally clears up constipation.

A more common problem is diarrhea. In some cases, this is probably the result of the fear and anxiety that accompany a move to a new home. However, if it persists there is probably an underlying cause. Some children may have undiagnosed food allergies, or lactose intolerance—the inability to digest the sugars in milk. Lactose intolerance is very common among Asians, Latin Americans, Native Americans, African-Americans, and people of Mediterranean descent.

Many children, whether adopted internationally or in the United States, have parasites on their arrival. If your child has persistent diarrhea, have your doctor test for parasites. For a more detailed discussion of these problems, see Chapter 12.

❖ 6 ❖
Grief and Change

Kelly got a shock when she opened the biography report from the orphanage that her sons had left four years previously. In it, her youngest son was described as "happy and silent." Kelly queried her older son and was told that the day they were left at the orphanage, Jonathan stopped speaking, and he kept silent for the two years the brothers were there. Kelly had noticed that he didn't speak when she picked them up, but he started speaking about two weeks later, about the time he started clinging to her for dear life. "Even though the boys have been home for four years and are doing really well, it is still sad to think of my little boy spending two years without talking," she says. "Now he is a chatterbox, but he still goes silent when sad or in trouble."

All adoptions are caused by loss. Regardless of age, the reasons for the adoption, or the rightness of the placement, the child will grieve. If your child has suffered multiple losses and has waited for some time for a new family, she has probably already grieved. However, grieving is not a straight line. Children may go back and grieve the same loss over and over. Whatever your child's previous experiences, when she moves to your home she will likely deal not only with *this* loss and *this* move, but with all her previous losses and moves as well.

When you think of grieving, what comes to mind? Do you think of your child sitting next to you, letting you hold her as she sobs? Most people associate this image with grief, and grieving in this manner is good for both you and your child as it reinforces your relationship and allows you to help her work through her grief. However, not all children, or adults, grieve this way. Many children, especially those who have experienced moves like ours have, show their grief in ways—such as keening (wailing), rocking, head banging, or clinging—that are not conducive to building your relationship. Others show their grief through misbehavior, some of which may be as ugly as their grief. It's not always easy to distinguish between behaviors caused by grief and loss and behaviors that are typical to all children (or to your child). However, learning about grieving may help.

The Stages of Grief

Elisabeth Kubler-Ross identified the five stages of grieving—denial, anger, bargaining, despair, and resolution—in 1975. Psychology professionals have come to accept this model as the normal way a person, child or adult, grieves. If the loss has been sudden, as in the unexpected death of a parent, the child may grieve visibly. Losses buried below a mask of indifference or bravado are harder to recognize. Our children may experience different stages of grief at the same time, as they generally have suffered multiple losses.

Denial

Denial is the natural response to profound loss. Without the ability to deny the pain, we would likely cease to function mentally or physically. Denial enables us to make funeral arrangements and entertain guests immediately after the death of a loved one. Denial enables our kids to eat, smile, play, and sleep after leaving everything familiar and dear.

Anger, Bargaining, and Despair

These stages often go hand in hand. As the denial wears off, we often feel intense anger. When we lose a loved one to death, we may feel angry at the person for leaving us. Likewise, your child will likely feel anger over his losses, and will probably take it out on you. Bargaining follows soon after, as the child attempts to change things to reverse the loss. When that fails, despair sets in. Despair is what we most often think of when we think of grief.

Resolution

As we come to grips with our losses and their effects, we hopefully move into resolution: accepting and integrating the loss into our lives and personalities in a way that allows us to move on. Our children will likely resolve their multiple losses over a long time. Some losses, such as familiar sounds and smells, will be more easily integrated than the loss of birthparents. The profound losses of adoption may not be resolved until adulthood. Even after a loss is accepted, it can rise again later for more processing and resolution.

The Behavior of Grieving

Children have less mature coping skills than adults, and may spend only a few minutes at a time thinking about their grief before moving on to another emotion. If they didn't handle grief in this way, it would swallow them. But because kids tend to move quickly through it, their grief is easily disguised.

"Behavior is the language of children. They tell you things by the way they are acting—developmentally and emotionally they often don't have the words yet to describe their feelings, but actions speak for them," says adoption therapist Joyce Maguire Pavao. Although the behaviors discussed can be found in all children, our children are more likely to be driven by inner turmoil. Some parents and professionals have described it as normal behavior that is a bit skewed. It can be hard to describe the difference, except to say that the behavior may be more intense or long-lasting than you would normally expect and may not respond to the types of discipline you'd normally use.

Each child displays grief in his own way. However, there are some behaviors obviously related to a particular stage of grief. The most difficult aspect of addressing our children's grief, however, is recognizing it. Our children have likely experienced multiple losses and may rapidly swing from one stage of grief to another.   As parents, our first instinct is often to address the misbehavior and try to end it. However, if the underlying emotions are not addressed, the behavior may get worse.

Nicole says that when her three domestically adopted children moved in, "we looked at just about everything as a behavior issue and did a lot of timeouts and a lot of room groundings, and gradually [we] started realizing that some of these behaviors were really and truly out of their control and it wasn't fair to punish them on top of all their grief." Parents and children can get caught in a vicious cycle of escalating behavior. This is where intuition comes in. If you can figure out where the behavior is coming from, you maybe able to better address it.

Disassociation

Some children who have suffered losses drift blankly and automatically through the days, moving from one activity to the next with little emotion or awareness. They're trying to distance themselves from pain. Families may see this tendency to disassociate right after their child moves in. Children who are disassociating may be clumsy, bumping into things or tripping a lot as if unaware of their own bodies. They may show little interest in activities, and may not recognize sensations such as hunger or pain.

Children who are hypervigilant may also seem exceptionally clumsy. Hypervigilance is the result of the fight-or-flight response to danger. The traumatized child fearful of rejection or pain may live in a perpetual state of fear following his arrival. If your son is jumpy and responds to every sound and movement, he may walk into walls and trip as his attention is directed elsewhere.

"He wouldn't cry when he first came home," says Allison about her son Tyler. "He fell on the street, tore his knee up and laughed hysterically. He couldn't cry. He kept saying, 'I'm okay. I'm okay.' When I looked at it, I said, 'That hurts!' and he let go. He cried like his heart was broken." She thinks her kids had such a strong hold on their emotions because they were afraid of how much would come up if they let go.

Children who are disassociating may physically withdraw. They may hide in closets or under blankets. Children who have learned self-coping behaviors or who have had no one to calm or comfort them may withdraw in more extreme ways. Some families report that their children engage in head banging or rocking. Children are apt to engage in self-soothing behaviors as a distraction as well—especially during times they are supposed to be quiet, such as at school or naptime. By engaging in rhythmic activity, they can keep their sadness at bay.

If your son has experienced times where he had no caretaking adult to rock or soothe him, he may have learned to rock himself. Many children rock only when visibly upset. For example, if they're disciplined, they may retreat to their room and rock themselves. For most children, the rocking stops when they become comfortable in their new families and learn to rely on their parents for comforting.

Head banging can also be a way to soothe oneself, as hard as it is for parents to believe. Banging his head on the wall or another hard surface, and sometimes moaning as well, allows the child to concentrate on the motion only and to drown out outside stimuli. He may bang his head because of grief and unmet emotional needs. However, it can also simply be a habit he acquired in an orphanage or group home. In some orphanages, many children bang their heads at night. While this behavior is an after-effect of institutionalization that will probably go away eventually, it can recur when the child is under emotional stress.

"She'd go into a bedroom, sit in a corner, keen [cry piteously] and knock her head against the wall," says Olivia about her daughter shortly after her arrival. "If you tried to stop her she'd knock the crap out of you. She'd rock. There was no way to console her."

Masturbation is another common self-soothing behavior. Your child may masturbate continuously whenever he's tired or upset. It may have become an unconscious habit. Obviously this may embarrass the family, and you will need to address it as soon as possible. Many professionals urge parents to redirect children to the privacy of their rooms if they wish to masturbate. After the child's need for self-soothing behavior declines, you may wish to further discuss it if you have a moral or religious objection. Children who have been sexually abused commonly masturbate. If you think your child may have been abused, seek professional assistance.

Your child may display excessive giddiness in an attempt to keep sadness or anger firmly contained inside. As her disturbing feelings rise to the surface, she may try to force herself to be happy, resulting in inappropriate gaiety. The giddiness itself may escalate, with her activity becoming more and more frantic as her attempts to disassociate from the pain and sadness fail. Often, the attempts at cover-up eventually fail, and the sadness or anger comes rushing out. After an outpouring of grief or anger, she may revert to giddiness. Sometimes episodes of giddiness progress to true hyperactivity.

Hyperactivity and Disorganization

In a misguided attempt to make the sadness "go away," some kids engage in limitless physical activity such as running, jumping, banging, tapping, or squirming. Others watch TV endlessly, finding it distracts them from their disturbing thoughts. Older kids may use headphones or loud stereos for the same purpose.

Jack, who was adopted at the age of three and is now nine, tried to comfort his mother after she had a car accident by saying, "Just don't think about it." He told his mother that although that is sometimes hard to do, if you keep doing "stuff" you don't have as much time to think.

Some studies have shown that adopted children are much more likely to be hyperactive. While this is often due to a condition such as attention deficit hyperactivity disorder (ADHD), it's possible your child is inattentive or hyperactive because she is grieving, especially if she has recently joined your family. (For more on ADHD, see Chapter 11.)

Kids may also become forgetful or have trouble concentrating. This can cause problems in school and at home. At times, "forgetting" may look intentional. Sometimes it is, but it can also mean the child is distracted by troublesome thoughts. Disorganization, or "spaciness," is the state of mind that results from the inability to gather one's thoughts and feelings. When a person loses someone close in death, we often allow a significant amount of time before expecting them to get back to normal. Our children likewise need time to be able to fully grieve their losses and integrate them into their lives.

The problems of hyperactivity and disorganization can appear in any stage of the grief process. Often, parents mistakenly feel that all is well after the initial flurry of grieving is over and don't understand why their child still can't follow directions or complete schoolwork. In fact, she may continue to have difficulty concentrating whenever a new feeling or thought comes up or an event triggers a memory.

One mother says that every time her son starts forgetting to do his chores, or starts missing problems in the middle of worksheets, she knows that he is thinking about something disturbing to him. The change from his usual conscientious behavior is a clear sign that he is distracted.

Regression

It's common for children who have experienced losses and are overwhelmed by change to regress to a younger age when their needs were met or can be met. This is usually unconscious, but sometimes children do knowingly regress. Your child may quit dressing himself or start sucking his thumb or soiling his pants. Often parents fear that their child will permanently regress, but that is unlikely.

Many parents report their child returned to toddler-like behaviors such as whining, throwing tantrums, and wanting to be dressed and fed. This can actually be healthy as it encourages you to do more hands-on parenting as you would with a younger child, thereby reinforcing your attachment to the new child. Some children regress to infantile behaviors to recreate the bonding experience of infants and mothers. At the same time, regressive behaviors can be frustrating to parents and embarrassing to children. You may have to set limits or introduce more appropriate ways for your child to have his needs met. Regression can occur throughout the grieving process, but is most likely at the early stages when the child is feeling overwhelmed and insecure.

If your daughter acts like she's two today, she may act like an infant tomorrow and a five-year-old next week. Professionals advise that children sometimes cycle through ages rather quickly, trying on behaviors of many ages in the same day. Some children regress only in certain situations, such as when they're disciplined or overwhelmed by noise and confusion.

Experienced parents say that if your child is acting like a two-year-old, you should handle the behavior as you would with a two-year-old. Only you know how comfortable you are with handling certain regressive behaviors. You may object strenuously to a ten-year-old sucking his thumb, or you may not mind. You might tolerate baby talk in the privacy of your home, but become agitated when your son lapses into it in public. You might not mind feeding your seven-year-old daughter a bottle, or even breast-feeding her, or you might find the idea repellent. You will, however, need to somehow accommodate your child's desire to have his needs met or he may become more insecure. Once he begins to trust in your love and ability to care for him, he'll probably start to act his age.

Natalie's daughter was nine years old when she joined their family, and wanted to breast-feed for several months after her arrival. Natalie felt that her daughter was trying to establish a bond with her and allowed her to nurse when she requested. One day her daughter simply said, "I'm too old for this." Natalie agreed, and the nursing ended. Although many parents would be uncomfortable with this, Natalie knew that women in her daughter's birthcountry often nurse children until they're four or five years old, and she was willing to allow her child to regress to the age she needed to in order to feel secure. This behavior is normal, at least for many kids from overseas. If you are not comfortable breast-feeding your child, you may wish to hold her in the infant position and rock her, or give her a bottle.

Separation Anxiety

Our kids have experienced every kid's worst nightmare: losing their family. Their world will never seem perfectly safe again. Many families report that this is one of their longest-lasting problems. The fear of being abandoned and rejected may haunt our children throughout their lives.

Children often exhibit separation anxiety by excessive clinging. Even teenagers may cling to their parents in public places. This can go on for a year or more in some children. Although it doesn't sound like much of a problem, it can become quite aggravating. Shirley, whose son Brian is eleven, says, "It drives me crazy. Even now after a year, he grabs my arm and hangs on in stores. It's all the time, and I wonder if it will ever stop."

Adds Kelly, "It took several months before [my sons] could bear to be apart from me, so I just let them hang around as they needed. That means company in the bathroom, when doing laundry, when attending conferences, going out to dinner, and so on.

Eventually they felt confident enough to let me venture away without them occasionally."

Some professionals feel that children who experience abrupt breaks from caregivers lose their sense of object permanence. Object permanence is the assurance that something is still there even when you can't see it. Most children learn this during infancy when they play peek-a-boo, or when Mom leaves the room and then returns. Kids whose attachments are abruptly severed may not want to let their parents out of their sight because they fear they may never return. Children who are suffering from separation anxiety may not be able to participate in "normal" kid activities like slumber parties for quite some time. They may be afraid to play outside or even in another room where they cannot see their parents.

My son, almost nine years old at the time of his arrival, would run up on the porch and look in the window every few minutes when he was playing outside, just to see if I was still there. He would come tearing through the house screaming, "Where are you, where are you?" if I was not where he expected me to be.

Separation anxiety can arise virtually anywhere. Kids who go to school or day care have to separate from their parents every day. Some families report having major difficulties in the morning before school, only later finding out that the problem was their child's reluctance to leave home. For children who have been moved many times, sometimes with no warning, any separation from their parents' sight can be too much. For this reason, many parents don't immediately send their children to school after arrival. Waiting a few weeks, or even a few months in some cases, probably won't cause irreversible academic harm, and may help to cement the bonds between parents and child.

"We put Shane in preschool a couple of months after he was home, figuring it would give him kids to socialize with and help him learn the language. He was doing fine for the first week or two, though he always seemed very glad to see his dad at the end of the day. Then one morning William dropped him off and Shane just started sobbing. William wasn't sure why, but decided it was probably best to reassure him, hug him, then leave. After he'd driven home, it finally hit him what the problem was: The teacher had asked him to drop off some spare clothes for Shane. We felt so dumb for not seeing it. Here's a place with lots of kids and cots, and now we're dropping off clothes? It was pretty obvious what must have been going through his mind. We felt awful for him, but decided the best thing was probably to go ahead and leave him there for the day, and pick him up as usual. We figured the only way he would get over the fear of being left was if we dropped him off and picked him up every day, consistently. After that day, he was okay," says Gail.

If you or your spouse have to go away, your child may become frightened that you will never return. When you do return, he might have trouble sleeping at night for a while, or become excessively clingy or irritable. Some kids greet returning parents with anger because of the worry their absence caused. He may also become excessively frightened if you or a sibling becomes ill, thinking that perhaps you will die and leave him alone again.

Children may also grow anxious about their possessions, especially if they were in temporary care for a long time. They may hate to part with clothes or toys, especially if they brought them from a previous home. To children who have lost parents, grandparents, siblings, homes, and schools, their possessions, no matter how threadbare or broken, are the only physical reminders they have of their past.

Anger

Once your son starts to acknowledge his losses, he will likely grow angry. He may be angry at the circumstances that caused his separation from his original parents. He may be angry at the foster care system, angry with the person who abused him, or angry at his feelings of helplessness. No matter who or what he's angry at, though, you'll be the most likely target for his feelings. Parents, especially mothers, represent the most hurtful losses our children have suffered, and you'll probably bear the brunt of the anger he has stored up over the months or years.

Children express their anger in many ways, but most often through actions. A kid who feels free to express his anger may throw and break things, or hit and kick his siblings or you. He may rant and rave about all the horrible things you do to him or don't do for him. If he is not comfortable with expressing anger, he might do so passively by stealing, wetting the bed, lying, or "losing" things. Some children, uncomfortable with anger of any sort, push it down deeper and deeper until they become depressed.

As your child begins to bond with you, she may get scared that you, too, will leave her. Her feelings for you will trigger the feelings she felt for her birthparents or foster parents, along with the pain of losing them. She will probably lash out at you when her feelings scare her. Grief over the people and places she left behind may bubble forth in complaints about how awful you are. Most adoptive parents eventually hear, "You're not my real mother!" Her other house was bigger, her other parents were nicer, smarter, and prettier, and her other possessions were better. The smallest slight in her eyes will trigger cries of "That's not fair!" For children whose lives have been scarred by fear, pain, and helplessness, anger is the safest emotion. When they're angry, they can keep people and things at a distance so they won't get hurt again.

Children of all ages often throw tantrums in the first few months after their arrival. Tantrums are most likely to happen when a child is trying to stuff his anger down, only to have it overflow and explode. As embarrassing as it is to try to calm a screaming two-year-old in a grocery store, it's a walk in the park compared with trying to handle a screaming ten-year-old. Parents have reported multiple temper tantrums in parking lots and stores from thirteen-year-olds. Liam, whose son Colin was adopted at age eleven, says that he had daily temper tantrums at first, then every other day, and so on until a year after placement, when he was experiencing them only about once a month.

The full-blown rages that stem from deep-rooted anger at previous abuses and pain can be truly frightening. Meredith describes one experience with her teenage daughter, several years after her arrival home. "She at one point attacked Edward as we had lunch on a cold, rainy day in our van parked at the beach. She'd hit her brother; we saw it and asked her why she did it. She denied it, and then started screaming, hit my husband on the head with a plastic jar, drawing blood, and then began pounding on the back windows yelling, 'Let me out of here!' She was screaming bloody murder. The van was rocking. She spit in my husband's face, she kicked me in the face and continued raging. It was horrible ... after we came home, she asked me if Dad was alright. I said I thought he was fine and was resting upstairs. She broke down and said she never meant to hurt him and that she didn't know why she did it. I don't think she did know why. She was like a wild animal."

Living with an angry child can be difficult at best. Although nothing makes it easy, trying to empathize can help. We all know how it feels to lose something precious. Perhaps you have lost a favorite piece of jewelry or broken a family heirloom. Our children's losses make these look small. All of us have likely transferred our anger before—perhaps by yelling at our spouses after a hard day at work. Children have far fewer coping skills than adults, so managing anger can be even more difficult for them. However, being on the receiving end of anger, especially when we are trying so hard to give our children a good home and our love, can be tough. For more on how to handle tantrums, see Chapter 7.

Sadness

When children finally begin to allow themselves to feel the pain of their losses, the sadness begins. It can be awful to watch your child suffer through despair. However, she must truly grieve if she is to integrate her losses into her life. Your child may have never been able to cry over the loss of her birthfamily, or over the fear and pain she felt at being abused. Perhaps now is the first time she has been in a safe enough place to let go and cry.

Chloe says her oldest son, who lost his mother at age five, was never allowed to openly grieve her death, largely because of cultural prohibitions. About two years after his arrival, he finally started to really grieve. Anytime someone would say "dead" or "mother," he would break down sobbing. It was heart-wrenching to watch, she says, but necessary.

You'll probably find sadness the easiest manifestation of grief to deal with. When your child lets you share and help ease her pain, you feel needed and loved. First, however, she has to feel safe enough in your home and with your reactions to be comfortable. Sadly, many children never let down their defenses enough to truly grieve. They get stuck in anger or denial. One of your biggest challenges as a parent will be to see through your child's behavior to the pain beneath, and to be able to reach it.

Your child may start searching for the lost loved ones. She may pore over old photos or want to return to places she previously lived in. She may insist she wants to see her birthfamily or former foster parents—even if they were horribly abusive. She may talk endlessly about memories of former homes. Such pining can trigger feelings of jealousy and anger in you.

Your child may search literally by running away from home, trying to return to a place he misses or simply to a place where he feels safe to express his sadness. When adopted people become older, especially in their late teens or twenties, they may search by returning to previous homes or trying to find long-lost family members. As children grieve their losses, they begin to integrate them.

Integration

Our children usually integrate the easiest losses first. Your son may stop talking about his old friends and make a new best friend at school. He may stop wishing that he could have his old toys and begin to play with the ones you've given him. However, the big losses will take time and patience to resolve.

Resolving losses doesn't have to mean that our children *like* what has happened to them, only that they *accept* it. We have to guard against trying to make them forget their losses. As much as we would like to fix it, we can't. We can help them grieve, we can support and love them, but we can't undo the past. Accepting and embracing the fact that our children had lives before they moved in with us will help them pull together the pieces.

For adopted children, learning to accept the fact that they have two, or more, families is the largest emotional task. Hopefully, in time they will realize that they received important pieces of themselves from each family. Your child may find some resolution about this in early childhood, but may have to analyze and come to terms with the situation again in adolescence and yet again in adulthood.

One day Colton, age seven, said to his mother, "Well, America good, but Vietnam not bad." Nancy acknowledged that in fact they were both good, just different. Other children integrate their losses visibly, by displaying pictures of both families in their rooms or wearing their old clothes while sporting a new haircut recommended by her adoptive parents. In adolescence, teens may "try on" different career choices that they feel match the talents or preferences of their birth and adoptive parents to decide which feels most comfortable. As they form their identity, they will likely incorporate some of each family into their lives.

Taking the Lead

Some children arrive in their new families and seem to adjust readily, showing no indication of grieving. Although most can't keep up this facade for long, some children can and do—perhaps because they don't like to display any negative emotion. In some cases, this could be because foster families or orphanage workers admonished the children not to be sad or give their new parents trouble. Other kids grieve only when they are alone.

If your kid is not outwardly grieving, she'll need your permission to express her sadness. Sometimes an indirect remark—"Anyone who's gone through what you have would be sad"—will hit the spot better than a direct question. If your child shows no sign of grieving after the first couple of months, gently question why. Don't mistakenly assume your child is simply super-resilient.

You can't be afraid of your child's feelings if you hope to help her accept and cope with her losses. Many parents hesitate to bring up difficult subjects for fear that they may not know how to handle their child's grief or anger. For many years, agencies unwittingly promoted this behavior by telling parents to simply follow the child's lead. If a child wanted to know about adoption, the child would ask. Marlene's family was told this. She says, "Well, guess what? We had a kid who didn't ask."

Experienced parents recommend that you take the initiative in talking with your child about losses and grief. You cannot go *around* the pain and loss, you must go *through* it. "Kids need permission to feel feelings. I think adults want kids to only have happy feelings. We don't want to acknowledge [their] anger," says Nicole. By discussing your child's feelings and expressing empathy, you validate his experiences and losses and show him that you are truly on his side. Nicole says her son "could not identify why he was so angry, frustrated, confused. He just had all these feelings and no way to process them. So, I would hold him and rock him and tell him, 'I love you. I'm proud of you. I know you are angry and you have every right to be angry. You can scream all you want and I'm just going to sit here and hold you until you have calmed down.'"

Kids who have been traumatized or abused or who simply did not have a stable early life may never have learned how to identify their feelings and their effects. "One night he had been screaming nonstop for over a half hour," says Nicole, "and I was holding him and rocking him and I asked him, 'What's wrong, Alec, can't you tell Momma?' and he said, 'I want...I want...I want *something!*'" Some parents have used posters that display different facial expressions to help children distinguish among feelings. Teach your child the words "angry," "sad," "happy," and "scared." And then point out to him how he is acting. You can help your child see that he may be scared, but he is acting angry, or vice versa. Visual aids and repetition can help him learn to understand his feelings. If you notice a recurring expression or mannerism when your child is anxious or sad, point it out to him. One of my sons wrings his hands when he is nervous. Help him make the connection so that he can learn to identify his reactions. In time, he may tell you what he is feeling before you even notice.

Anniversary Reactions

People who have experienced a profound loss often feel grief and pain on the anniversary date of the event. Many doctors and mental health professionals feel that our bodies store sensory memory and react, even on dates that we don't remember consciously. The experiences of adoptive parents lend credence to this theory. Many children, even those whose losses occurred during infancy, apparently experience anniversary reactions. A kid who is doing well may suddenly revert to clinging behaviors, tantrums, or disassociation on the dates of previous losses. Sometimes, reminders of injuries arise.

"February of the first year I had her she got a terrible strep infection and was sick almost the entire month of February. The second February she got scarlet fever and almost died," says

---

❖ Tips for Handling the Holidays ❖

Make sure you have a support group or respite care and the time to take care of yourself and your relationships.

Start planning and talking about the holidays a month or two ahead of time. Add decorations slowly and gradually.

Write down three to five things your child can do when things get overwhelming and post the list in a place where timeouts occur. Practice by role-playing potentially difficult situations.

Keep it simple. Don't overcommit to parties, elaborate gifts or dozens of gifts, holiday baking, and so on.

Some children function best when family members are apart, so the holiday season may mean doing few "family" things.

Practice how to give and receive gifts. Many of our children have no idea how to respond when given a present. Also, an older child could find a wrapped present threatening. Surprises, in their experience, are not usually good.

Emphasize giving rather than getting.

Open gifts one at a time, and slowly.

Keep visits to other people's houses as short as possible.

Explain to your child ahead of time what sort of greetings will be expected by visiting family members. Many children have difficulty distinguishing between family members and strangers. Will the folks expect hugs, or will a hello and a smile be enough?

Holiday foods can overwhelm kids with abnormal eating habits. Consider packing a favorite snack for emergencies.

Physical exercise is a must for you and your child!

Try to stay on your normal schedule as much as possible.

Honor traditions from your child's past but also make new traditions of your own. The repetition of holiday rituals from one season to the next can provide comfort, structure and predictability, and lessen anxiety for your child.

—from Adoptive Families Together

Olivia, whose daughter, Andrea, was adopted at the age of eight and is now an adult. "There isn't a time [even now] that I talk to this child on the phone in February that she is not sick." Olivia and her daughter later discovered what they believe to be the reason. "Guess when her parents died—February. Every February she lives the battle of her family being killed. It was her mother, her father, her brother, and she was wounded. She still has shrapnel marks in places. She pushes everyone away at that time, too."

Other parents report their children have awakened screaming for their mothers on the date they lost their birthfamily. Many, many children act out on anniversary dates of moves, birthdays, injuries, or other traumatic events.

Try keeping a calendar of behavior for the first year your child is home, highlighting the days when he has difficulty. Do the same thing the next year and the next and see what patterns develop. If your child experiences anniversary reactions, you may have to revert to comforting behaviors or behavior modifications that have worked for you in the past.

Holidays

Grief also tends to resurface during holidays or other significant family events. Many families find holiday time stressful because of all the emphasis on family and togetherness. While you are trying to enjoy the holiday, your child may be grieving for the family he lost. The noise, the crush of people, and the abundance of food or gifts may overwhelm him.

Living with a grieving child can be trying, especially when his behavior seems out of control. Discipline that seems to work with our birthchildren may not work with our adopted children because the causes are different. Recognizing grief for what it is can go a long way toward helping our children cope with the huge changes in their lives.

❖ 7 ❖

Behavior and Discipline

"I did not know that for all the terribly abused and neglected children on the news and in periodicals that break my heart and make me weep, the ones who live in my home might just make me crazy," says Ellen, adoptive mother of two children, ages nine and eleven at placement.

Many adoptive families share Ellen's feelings. We wanted to adopt. We want to parent and parent well. We want to help our children heal from their past hurts. We want them to grow up to be happy, functional adults. But there are days—sometimes many days—when we feel like it was all one huge mistake. Nothing wears down parents more than continual behavior problems, large or small, that require new and innovative responses. Trina's thirteen-year-old son has trouble respecting personal boundaries. "He goes into my desk and uses all the tape, all the glue, all the Wite-Out, all the staples, all the paper, all the pencils, you name it, it's *all* gone. The other night I was hopping up and down with my hands waving in the air like a crazy person." She had to start locking the desk drawers.

All children, regardless of how they joined their families, misbehave. Your child may forget to do his chores, leave his socks on the floor, and daydream simply because he's immature. Parents and professionals who are educated about adoption issues do have to be careful about automatically labeling behavior as adoption-related. You should have a good child-care reference that includes information about children's developmental stages. You may want to ask your friends or family about their experiences, especially if you're a first-time parent. Keep in mind, though, that parents whose kids are not adopted may not be able to see the differences between behaviors that are normal and those that are heightened by adoption.

For example, kids go through a "magical thinking" stage from preschool to about six. During this stage, your child will often find fantastic reasons for things that happen. He may believe that he caused something by wishing it, or that if he doesn't admit he took the cookie then he really didn't. For an adopted kid, the magical thinking may extend to feeling that he lost his birthfamily because of something he did.

In later childhood, children go through a concrete thinking stage when the lines are heavily drawn between good and bad, right and wrong. Thus, your child may react way out of proportion to discipline, because she believes she can't be both "good"

❖ Bonding and Behavior ❖

Before you can change your child's behavior, both you and your child have to be committed enough to the relationship for him to care whether you are happy with him. Nicole says, "A child who is coming from a different home—they don't care if they disappoint you! Rules mean nothing, especially if they've been in several homes where the rules have changed."

Don't try to keep the same clean house you've always had, or follow the same schedule you've always followed. It will simply pile on more stress. Instead, make your child your first priority. Spend time with her, talk with her, do fun things together. Build some good memories, and soon your child will want to please you. If your child's behavior is making it difficult, change what you can change. Put up favorite items so they don't get broken. Adapt your environment to the child. It's unrealistic to expect her to be the only one who has to change.

"In the first year, we had to replace three windows, three lamps and four ceiling lights; 130-year-old tiles were pulled off our fireplace and destroyed. We had to repair several walls with holes in them. It wasn't that the boys were 'bad' or even misbehaved all that much. It was a combination of immaturity and a great amount of insecurity, uncertainty, and confusion," says Nicole.

"If a lot of that behavior is grief-centered, then punishing for it is counterproductive. I think we should give them the tools to understand that they have grief, and give them the tools to understand what is inappropriate. As much as possible, give your child a chance to bond to you."

and "bad," and bad gets you sent away.

Many parents tend to assume their child is merely misbehaving when he is expressing his emotions and experiences behaviorally. This is especially true for new parents, whose fears are already monumental. If your new child begins raging, lying, and testing your boundaries within weeks, or even days, of her arrival you may fear that she is just a "bad" child. In the past, psychological theories and media reports centered on the "bad seed" stereotype. You may fear that the behavior will never change or that it may escalate. Your attempts to address the misbehavior may seem to make it worse, and you may begin to wonder if the adoption was a huge mistake. At this point, you need to try to think methodically instead of merely reacting to your child's behavior.

Marshaling the Forces

As soon as your child begins misbehaving, start gathering information and preparing strategies. At this stage, you'll finally understand the value of having an experienced, helpful agency. If you have chosen your agency well, your worker should be able to provide you with information and support services when your child begins acting out his feelings. Enlist the help of parent support groups, foster and adoptive parent associations, e-mail lists, and patient friends and family. Acknowledge your feelings and fears and talk about them with others. Experienced parents often admit they would have given into their fears without the support of close, knowledgeable people.

If you have prepared well for adoption, you will know about some of the most common behavioral problems older adopted children experience. Now is the time to review that information. Read anything you can find about the possible causes of your child's behavior. Review his case history, if it is available. If you have adopted domestically, ask your worker if she has any information that may shed light on your child's behavior. You may be able to find out if he had similar difficulties in previous homes. Although such information should have been shared with you prior to placement, that does not always happen. If no information is available, seek out parents who have encountered similar difficulties. Their insights can be invaluable.

Some parents find reaching out for support difficult. Perhaps they fear that other families and social workers will think them bad parents for having difficulties. Or perhaps they're afraid to acknowledge their child's problems. Remember that living with traumatized and grieving children can be difficult. In fact, you are likely grieving, too. You may be grieving the loss of your fantasy child or the loss of peace in your home. You may also be grieving because of your daughter's pain. You, too, will likely experience all the stages of grieving and you should try to stay aware of what you are feeling. By doing so, you will help both yourself and your family.

Sometimes parents refuse to acknowledge that their child's behavior may have deeper roots because to do so is painful. It magnifies the fact that our children had former lives and families. It also means that the behavior may last months or even years—a daunting prospect. During times of extreme stress, denial can be a safeguard, and in fact, can help families who would otherwise disrupt placements. However, long-term denial of a child's problems will only aggravate those problems and put the family through prolonged stress. The quicker you can find a healthier way to cope with stress, the better off you and your family will be. If you are having trouble addressing or discussing your child's behavior, it may help to think about the following questions. Writing your answers may help you to release the emotions behind them.

Who could possibly help me with this situation?

If I tell them about this problem, I am afraid they would...

I am afraid they would think I am...

What is the worst thing that could happen because of this behavior?

I am afraid that my child might...

If I don't do anything, the behavior may...

If I do seek help, the behavior may...

You might find it helpful to keep a journal of your child's behavior. This is recommended for many reasons. It can help you to detect patterns of misbehavior and what might be causing it. You can document how you handled the behavior and what the result was, so that you can compare discipline techniques. And perhaps most importantly, it can give you a record of progress. When you're tired and stressed, you may think your child's behavior is getting worse, even if the troublesome incidents are decreasing in frequency. Later, you will be able to look back and see how far you have come.

Often, we react almost instinctively to our children's misbehavior with a reprimand or punishment. Dealing with ongoing behavioral problems, however, requires time, patience, and experimentation. It means acknowledging that our reactions or behavior may be aggravating a problem, and it means dealing with our child's underlying emotions. Most of us take misbehavior personally. But it may not be personal. In many cases, our children are unconsciously acting on their deepest feelings. To resolve the situation, we may have to carefully assess, evaluate, and plan a response to our child's behavior. Some parents do this naturally and can do it mentally. Others find it more helpful to keep a written record.

Step One: Assessing Behavior

The first step in handling difficult behavior is to define it. That's not necessarily as simple as it sounds. For example, you might describe your daughter as "defiant." But what does that mean? For example, does she refuse to feed the dog when you ask her to? Does she feed the dog but give you nasty looks for asking? Does she pull the dog's tail, even after you've repeatedly told her not to, and watch for your reaction? Try to pinpoint exactly what she is doing. Write it down. Then for a period of time, perhaps one week or even one day with a frequent behavior, pay attention to what happens immediately before the behavior and what seems to make it stop. Record what discipline you enforced, and your daughter's reaction.

Step Two: Evaluating Behavior

After you have gathered your notes on the behavior problem, take some time to seriously look at it. Is there a certain time of day that the behavior usually happens? Does it seem to occur at home or away from home? With siblings or alone? When you are busy or when you are directing your attention to her? Does the behavior rise in response to something you or a sibling says or does? Which discipline seemed effective? Do you have an idea about *why* it was effective? After making these observations, think about whether a previous trauma or grief could be causing her behavior. This type of thinking requires practice. It also requires that you take yourself out of the equation.

Step Three: Developing a plan

Deciding how to handle behavior can be difficult. It requires that you think about what you want the outcome to be. Parents generally want to discipline, which means "to teach," and not simply to punish. However, if your child keeps misbehaving in a way that feels personal, your first instinct may be to punish. That's why thinking about the desired outcome can help you decide how to handle a behavior. No parent, regardless of how many children they have raised, always knows what to do. At such times, the best strategy may be to develop a working possibility, such as, "I think this behavior may be caused by _____, therefore I will try to address it by doing _____." Then try it for a week. If it is successful, you'll be thrilled. If not, move on to another possibility.

Often the "right" solution results in an escalation of behavior. This is especially true if your child is using the behavior to cover up a deeper emotion. For example, a child who becomes increasingly giddy because she is trying to keep her sadness locked inside probably needs to be soothed and comforted. However, this may make her very angry and could provoke a tantrum because when she is calmed, the emotions she was repressing rise to the surface. Although her giddiness and tantrums may get worse for a while, she will benefit in the long run by having her emotions out in the open. You can then address the feelings she has been locking inside, instead of simply dealing with the giddiness. In time she will likely become more comfortable with her sadness and learn a better way to deal with her emotions.

Following is an example of this type of discipline approach from my own experience. One of my children developed a habit of lying shortly after his arrival. While lying is typical for a young boy, his behavior was a bit skewed because it seemed to be exaggerated by fear. It became quite a hot issue as his lying and fear escalated. My record looked something like this:

Monday, 10 a.m.: Skates on floor. When asked if he put them there, he won't respond. Asked again. Eyes darting back and forth—saying, "uh, uh...no!" After questioning the other kids and determining that he must have, ask four more times before he answers "yes." Tell him to pick them up, send him to his room. Cries (screams actually) piteously for an hour. Falls asleep.

Monday, 3 p.m.: Argument breaks out between two kids. Sib says he hit him. Tells long tale. I ask him, "Did you do that?" He clamps mouth shut. Turns away, refuses to answer. I ask again, and again, and again. He finally starts crying, then sobbing. Send him to his room 'til he quits crying. An hour later he stops, but when he hears me walking down the hall, starts wailing again. Still refuses to answer. Finally give him the choice of talking to me about the incident or staying in his room. Refuses to answer. Stays in his room until next morning.

Tuesday, 8 a.m.: "Did you brush your teeth?" His reply, "Uh, I don't remember." In five minutes? Ask again, and again, finally says, "No." I make him brush his teeth. For the rest of the morning, he jumps and tenses up whenever I look at him. Finally, he relaxes after I have smiled at him for a while.

Tuesday, 5 p.m.: "Time to put your toys away and wash your hands for dinner." He glances at me, turns his back and continues to play. I repeat it again; he does the same thing. Finally I walk over to him, say, "I told you to get ready for dinner" and he says, "I didn't hear you." I say, "You did too, you looked at me." "No I didn't." "Yes, you did." "No, I didn't." Yelling now, "Well, do you hear me now? Go do it!" He dissolves into a crying (screaming) fit as I send him to his room. He finally calms down—eats at 7 p.m. We eat in strained silence. Beat myself up for being a horrible mother for screaming at him.

Evaluation: It seems obvious to me that he lies most often when he thinks he is in trouble for doing or not doing something. Observe that I have a habit of asking questions that mean he has to either admit wrongdoing and risk punishment, or lie. Decide that the fear (eyes darting back and forth) may stem from the fact that he thinks he is going to be rejected for being bad (he has said he had to leave his other home because they "thought he was bad"). The screaming and crying probably serve the dual purposes of venting his fear and keeping me from talking to him, which may result in rejection. I wonder if sending him to his room sparks' feelings of being "sent away." I decide that if he chooses to scream, he will have to go to his room, because it drives my blood pressure up, but if he responds calmly he will simply have to rectify the behavior. I talk with him about the fact that he is staying here even if he does bad things. Decide I will try not to ask direct questions that tempt lying.

Implementing the plan: On Wednesday, I trip over Legos in hallway. I start to say, "Who left these here," but stop myself. I know from the activities of the morning, it had to be him, so I say to him, "Please pick up the Legos you left in the hallway." His lip starts quivering and tears well up, but he picks them up. Kneeling on his level, I say, "It's okay. Nobody got hurt, but you need to pick them up so no one does, okay?" He nods and wipes the tears, then starts crying again. He starts saying, "I'm sorry, Mom. Sorry. Sorry." I comfort him, assure him we all do things we shouldn't. All is okay.

The next afternoon, we have another sibling problem. He chooses to begin screaming when I try to talk with him. I ask him to go to his room until he stops. When he finally does, an hour later, we talk about the incident and he does not lie. He apologizes to his sister, then leaves his room.

It took several weeks for me to feel comfortable about delivering discipline and at the same time offering comfort. The difference between his reactions—defiance when I questioned him, genuine sadness when I gently directed him—was revealing. I saw that much of his behavior stemmed from the fear he felt when corrected. It took several months for his fear to subside, but the lying happened less and less often from that time on. When he chose to lie, and I knew he was lying, I simply asked him to sit on his bed until he figured out what the truth was. Then he could leave his room and rectify his behavior. The screaming continued for many months, but he finally decided staying in his room wasn't much fun. With time, he stopped that, too.

Trauma's Role in Behavior

Kids who have been traumatized, as most of ours surely have, will usually display some lasting effects. Some children may be diagnosed with posttraumatic stress disorder, which is discussed in detail in Chapter 11. However, even children who don't meet the criteria for PTSD can be traumatized. Any child who has lost his parents has experienced trauma. Professionals who treat traumatized children say they often share the experiences of nightmares, fantasy, shame, and guilt over the incident and what they could have done to prevent it; reenactment or flashbacks of trauma, and repetitive play that mimics the trauma.

Some children do not have visual flashbacks, but show strong emotional reactions to situations or feelings that remind them of traumatic events. Children who were traumatized at a very young age may have no verbal memories of the trauma, but may still react behaviorally. If your child displays a certain behavior repeatedly that seems a little odd, it's possible something is triggering a traumatic memory.

Laura, seven, was adopted as a baby. She reportedly was left at a police station at the age of about seven months. Her mother Gail says, "We took the kids to a playground, and as the three of us were going to the car a bit ahead of Laura, Shane, age five, started teasing her with, 'Goodbye, Laura.' This is NOT a joke we use in this family. They got to the car and she started literally attacking him and sobbing. This fear of being left behind is a deep phobia for her, but maybe phobia really isn't the right word, since it actually happened at one point in her life."

Similarly, smells, sights, and sounds can trigger feelings of loss and abandonment in our children. For children who have been abused, facial expressions or parental reaction can stimulate an intense fear of being abused again. Children whose parents have died from sickness may react strongly to a parent's illness, or to their own. Any of these reactions may be displayed in behavior. If your child repeatedly misbehaves in particular situations she might be displaying a traumatic memory. This is another instance where a written log may come in handy. You can then review behavioral problems to see if there is a recurring thread.

"Samantha does freeze up when her emotions become overwhelming," says Madeline of her twelve-year-old daughter. "She won't move, resists being moved, looks angry and frightened, just isn't 'home' in many ways, and tends to get stuck on one issue. And no amount of addressing that issue seems to satisfy her as she hears *nothing* we say at that point."

Because traumatic memories arouse the "flight, fight or freeze" response, your child may react to her emotions in the same way she reacted to them at the time of the trauma. Many children freeze. Some fight valiantly against an unseen foe, throwing tantrums or engaging in other behaviors designed to push people away. Some take flight, either by literally running away or by "zoning out."

Keeping the child physically and emotionally safe is important. If your child is behaving irrationally or acting on deep-seated fears and feelings, discipline will not be effective until he is calm and in control. For this reason, first try to help your child calm down and assure him of your love and commitment. After he is feeling safe, you will be better able to address his behavior, if you do so in a loving manner. Any attempt to discipline a scared and out-of-control child will likely intensify his fear and his misbehavior.

"We generally try to soothe [Samantha] and get her to accept our comfort, have her cry, and then after that she can come out of it," says Madeline. "Otherwise the anger and irrationality mount 'til she is so frustrated and irrational that she becomes a danger to herself."

Common Behaviors and Possible Solutions

In previous chapters, we discussed many behaviors common to adopted children. The foundation of many of these behaviors is unresolved feelings of grief, anger, and shame. All humans strive for congruency, or agreement, between our inner and outer lives. Children whose inner feelings are chaotic, angry, and painful find congruency when their outer life is that way, too. That is the only time they are truly comfortable—when both sides match. We have to guide and understand the behavior so as to reach the pain beneath it. Only then can we help our children bring their inner lives in harmony with a more peaceful outer life. Although no solution works for every child or parent, the following examples have been helpful to other adoptive families.

Control Battles

Control lies at the heart of many behaviors. Parents, too, can have control issues that aggravate behavior. Learning how to pick your battles wisely is one of the biggest challenges of parenting. One technique that many families use in dealing with control issues is to give choices and let the child take the consequences. A good guide to developing this art is *Parenting With Love and Logic* by Foster Cline and Jim Fay. The techniques Cline and Fay recommend center on allowing our children to learn their own lessons by providing them with natural consequences. If your child loves a good control battle, this book is a must read. Using choices and natural consequences will work in many, if not most, normal adoption behavior situations.

My family encountered a common scenario where natural consequences work well. My son and I were leaving the house in frigid weather. Connor didn't want to wear his coat and argued with me about whether it was really cold outside. I shrugged, said, "whatever," and got in the car. About a mile down the road, Connor said, "I'm cold," through blue lips and chattering teeth. I replied, "I bet you are." Since then, he thinks about it seriously when I suggest that he wear a coat.

Had I continued to argue, Connor would have left the house warm, but very angry with me for making him wear the coat. The natural consequence of being very, very cold taught him the value of a coat more quickly and effectively than an argument with me would have. Cline and Fay insist that for this technique to work, parents must keep their mouths shut about the lesson being imparted. Saying "I told you so" only restarts the battle.

Giving choices can also prevent battles before they start. For example, your son may start a battle every night at dinner when you pour him a drink. If you give him milk, he wants juice; if you give him juice, he wants milk. You will ruin your family's dinner by engaging him in a battle. Instead, you might ask, "Do you want milk or juice?" If he feels like he has a choice, he may become less difficult. Of course, any kid worth his salt will usually reply "water" or not choose at all. Cline and Fay recommend restating the choices, with the implied third choice that if he doesn't decide, you will. Your child will either then make a choice or you will have to choose. Keep in mind, too, that the first few times you do this, your child will invariably protest your choice, possibly quite loudly. If he throws a tantrum then you should resort to your usual discipline for tantrums, and remove him from the table. He can rejoin the family, without comment from you, when he calms down. Some children will fight over control for virtually everything, and you may find yourself becoming quite adept at giving choices.

To be fair, choices that are virtually "do it my way or else" are not really choices. For example, "You may clean your room or be grounded for a week" is a dare disguised as a choice. Instead give your child two choices both you and he can live with, such as "You may either clean your room now or after dinner." With time, the natural consequences of his decisions will likely teach him the lessons you wanted to impart all along.

Kids who have suffered repeated losses often fight mightily for control if their instincts of self-preservation are triggered. Although most kids want control immediately after their arrival when they do not yet trust their parents, the need generally subsides when they become comfortable in their new families. However, even settled kids may attempt to control a situation when they feel threatened or are flooded with memories, conscious or subconscious. Several parents say they believed their children behaved badly in an attempt to be sent away so that the parents wouldn't have the opportunity to reject them. Children attempt to control their environment when they fear that bad things will happen to them. Allowing your kids to control the aspects of their lives that are not essential to their physical, moral, and emotional well-being can help them feel secure and competent.

If your child is fighting everything you ask him to do, try asking, "What do *you* think will work?" One family was having an ongoing argument about their son taking out the trash. His mom finally said to him, "What's going to work here? I need the trash taken out." He replied, "I hate taking out the trash—but

I'd cook!" So, she takes out the trash and he cooks three nights a week.

Testing

Our kids often feel the need to test our love and commitment. Some professionals believe testing behavior is a way for a child to determine if you will still love him when he is bad. All children test, but with our adopted children there is a little quirk. As I explained to a friend who remarked that her kids tested her, too: "The difference is, my daughter [by birth] tests to see if the rule is still being reinforced. My son tests me to see if I'm going to keep him."

Others feel that children use testing behavior to keep parents at a distance when they feel themselves becoming attached. A child who has been hurt by adults in the past may find love and attachment too scary at first and may engage in a cycle of "pulling closer, pushing away." He pulls closer when he wants love and care, and then pushes his parents away when the fear overwhelms him. This is a perfectly normal reaction to being hurt in the past. If your child does this, try having her work side by side with you, which allows closeness without direct eye contact. Some families find that a great time to discuss touchy subjects is while they're in the car, as kids are often more willing to connect to you if your attention is focused elsewhere.

If your child was abused in a previous home, he may try to push you to abuse him. That seems illogical, but in fact, if he can get you to abuse him then at least he'll know what he's dealing with. Most kids fear the unknown more than familiar things, even if those things are bad. Also, kids who were abused often know of no other way to relate to their parents.

Kids who are trying to re-create patterns of abuse, either consciously or unconsciously, tend to escalate their behavior to see if they can goad you into a rage. If your child is scolded for a small behavior, perhaps leaving her toys out, she may respond to your correction by refusing to comply with your instructions. From there she may begin screaming abusively at you or even hitting you. After the incident you may have trouble figuring out how you got from a simple request to a physical scuffle. Kids who display provocative behavior are often masters at getting adults to lose control. You may feel like a horrible parent for losing your temper. And above all, she doesn't learn that parent/child interaction really is different in your home.

Many children begin to re-create past events when their current situation brings up traumatic memories. Your child's behavior may offer insights into the kind of trauma she experienced. If she can cause you to become a screaming, raging person who understands why people abuse children, she may have experienced physical abuse. If she is a master at pitting you against your mate and you often find yourself arguing with each other, you may be seeing a re-creation of the breakup of her birthfamily. If she is sexually provocative with adults or other children, she may have been sexually abused.

Parents who have lived with escalating behavior often find that the only good way to respond is to walk away. Remember that your child may be escalating out of fear that you will abuse him, or because the situation reminds him of his past. Your first priority should be to restore him to a calm, safe place. If you're too angry to do that, remove yourself from the situation. After both of you are calm, you can talk in a relaxed manner. You may be able to get your child to think about why he feels the need to escalate his behavior. Sometimes, kids are able to tell their parents what would help or make them feel safer. Often, the best reactions for us are what our *children* think will work. Your children probably want to feel that you are in control and can handle not only your emotions but theirs as well, and keep them and the rest of the family safe if they spin out of control.

Children can test our limits to the point where we'd swear they're trying to make us crazy. One ten-year-old girl who was told by her father to stay in her room came out as soon as he turned his back. He repeated his request and she responded by sticking her leg out. The next request was met with a foot over the line, followed by a final test of putting her toe over the line. While behavior like this can test your mettle, it also serves a more practical purpose. If our children had been born to us, they would have learned our limits and boundaries gradually from infancy. Instead, they are thrust into our homes with no clue about where our boundaries are and how strongly we feel about them. They have to test every corner to see where the lines are. If you have had other children you understand that every child does this, especially toddlers, but with one rule at a time.

When dealing with a test like this, make sure you care enough about this boundary to defend it. You may feel the need to establish your authority over virtually everything, to show your kid who's boss. This is tough to do with a child who isn't committed yet to a relationship, though, and can start a lifelong battle for control. So ask yourself, "Is this issue important enough to battle over? What is the purpose of the boundary and can I reasonably defend it?" As a general rule, you shouldn't give kids orders that can't be enforced. For instance, if you tell your child he can't smoke, you won't be able to enforce that rule away from home. Your child actually "wins" each time he smokes out of your presence. A better way to state that rule would be: "You cannot smoke in my house, car, or my presence."

That doesn't mean we shouldn't share our morals and values with our children, or tell them what we wish their behavior would be. It simply means that we cannot control their behavior all the time and if we act like we can, we invite their defiance. Some families are pulled into battles over inconsequential things and end up giving in because it really wasn't important in the first place. You will lose ground, however, every time you give in. Even after you stand your ground once, your child will no doubt test that limit a few more times to make sure you mean what you say. If you do give in, be prepared to start again from the beginning.

Temper Tantrums

If your child throws tantrums often, you'll probably end up walking on eggshells trying to prevent them. On some days you may even want to join her kicking and screaming on the floor! While temper tantrums can be trying in two-year-olds, many parents find them absolutely infuriating in older children. While the best cure for temper tantrums is usually helping your child deal with the feelings behind them, a short-term solution is necessary at first.

If you think your child is reacting to memories of trauma or to grief that she has been stuffing, you need to help her calm down and deal constructively with her feelings. If your child is relatively young and is not striking out at you, you may be able to calm her down simply by rubbing her back and talking softly to her. Some parents hold their children and rock them. You may not be able to physically hold an older child, but you can sit by her and try to soothe her if she's agreeable.

Shortly after he arrived home, one of my children would throw what appeared to be a tantrum whenever he was corrected. It was most likely a fear of being rejected for doing something wrong, but he would simply fall apart. When he did, I would pull him into my lap and rock him, gently talking. One night I said, "Oh, you are big sad!" and that started a whole wave of deep sobbing. Putting words to his emotions probably helped him figure out what he was feeling.

If your child is hitting, kicking, and screaming, you won't be able to talk to her until she has calmed down. If she's not hurting herself or anyone else, it's probably okay to just let her vent her emotions. As she starts to calm down, you can talk to her about what she was feeling or thinking. Often, the grief underlying the anger will come to the surface after the anger has been dispensed, allowing you to comfort her. Each time you get to the sadness underneath, you will have a chance to make progress on the underlying feelings. Many professionals feel that the time immediately after a tantrum is one of the best opportunities for bonding between parent and child. If you can hold her and accept her deepest feelings of anger and sadness, you'll win her trust.

About two months after Chase and his brothers moved to their new home, they attended a costume party. Chase's disguise was so effective that his former foster dad, a very important person in his life, didn't immediately recognize him when he ran up. The next night, Chase threw a screaming fit over something small and started crashing into the walls and throwing anything he could get his hands on. His mom, Nicole, says, "I finally picked him up and carried him to our exercise room, placed him in the middle of the room, left, and closed the door behind me. I figured there were fewer things to break in there and I'd let him wear himself out. I sat at the closed door and cried while my child wreaked havoc on the room. Finally when he had quieted a bit, I opened the door, went in and held him and rocked with him. Both of us were crying. I asked him why he was so angry and he said he didn't know. Finally he said, 'Cole [the foster dad] has forgotten me.' I realized that he was a five-year-old who had been through so much he just didn't know how to deal with it." Once Nicole explained to Chase that Cole loved him and had not forgotten him, and why he couldn't adopt him, things started improving rapidly.

Obviously, children also have tantrums because they don't get something they want. This kind of behavior makes parents furious, especially when it happens in public. Experienced parents suggest just stepping back with a bored expression on your face and calmly telling the kid to let you know when he is done. The more you react to his tantrums, the more likely he is to continue them. If you are at home, you may insist that he rage in his room only, again with as little reaction as you can muster. A behavioral tantrum is no fun if it doesn't get you anything, and the less reaction he gets, the quicker he'll let go of this behavior. Unfortunately, getting him to his room may require that you carry him there. If you cannot do that, the rest of the family can leave the room where he is. After the tantrum has ended, calmly inform him of the consequences you have decided upon. This works best if you and the child have agreed upon the consequences ahead of time.

"Ryan couldn't believe it the day I got up from the table at [a restaurant] and just took him out to the car. He was flabbergasted that we were not going back in," says Trina. Her son had disrupted restaurant outings before, so she had planned for such a contingency. She had a good magazine in the car, and her husband ordered a cinnamon bun and tea and had their other son deliver them to her. "I quietly sat and pretended that Ryan was not hysterical in the rear of the van 'til finally he fell asleep and I made my point about how we behave in public. The power of positive discipline."

Tantrums caused by buried or triggered emotions are common in older adopted children. If your child is hurting herself or someone else, you may have to physically restrain her. Some parents subscribe to a type of restraint called "holding therapy." The therapists of the Attachment Center at Evergreen, Colorado, popularized this treatment in which a trained therapist holds the child in the typical nursing position, provoking a rage in him by stimulating the rib cage with his fingers, like tickling. The therapist talks and shouts along with the child as he becomes enraged. When the child begins to rage, the therapist continues to hold him tightly until the rage has passed.

Proponents say the treatment, traditionally used for children with attachment disorders, results in increased trust and intimacy and helps children build attachment. It has its detractors, though, who argue that the results achieved in therapy are not sustainable at home and that provoking rage in a child can further traumatize him.

In recent years, parental holding therapy has become popular, thanks to *Holding Time,* a book by Martha Welch. She suggests that all children can benefit from holding therapy done by the parent. Many parents have used Welch's techniques and claimed success. However, some parents and professionals express concern that if a child has suffered significant trauma in the past, rage or posttraumatic stress reactions could arise which an untrained parent would not be qualified to handle.

Holding therapy is not the same as restraining a child who is having a tantrum. Virtually every parent has had to restrain a child at one time or another. If your child is endangering himself or someone else, you may have to hold him until his anger passes. When he calms down, he is released. This is a natural reaction to an out-of-control child. In contrast, in holding therapy the therapist or parent holds the child to provoke a rage, not to calm him.

If your child is out of control, he may kick, punch, or bite you if you try to restrain him. Many parents have found the best way to restrain a child is to sit behind him with your arms pinning his to his sides, low enough that he cannot bite your hands or arms. You may have to lay your legs on top of his to restrain kicking and movement. Your child may become angrier when you do so, but will usually calm quickly. As soon as he is in control, you can release him.

If you have to restrain or discipline an angry child in public, you may get angry or startled reactions from other people. Sometimes child protective authorities are called. This happened to Meredith and her husband, Edward. Brianna experienced severe rages and often had to be physically restrained. Meredith says, "She ran out the door and down the road. It was ten at night, dark, cold, and rainy. Edward went after her, found her, and brought her home—or rather *dragged* her home. Some passing motorist called the sheriff's office. Three patrol cars converged on our house. What would you think if you saw some balding middle-aged white guy dragging a screaming brown-skinned young woman down a dark rural road at night?"

If you are reported to social services, react in a calm, logical manner and explain the situation. To add insult to injury, your child may falsely claim you were abusing her. If you have been in close contact with your agency, they may be able to intervene on your behalf. In most cases, a simple case of restraint will not result in a prolonged investigation. You should, however, be certain that you are in control of your emotions before restraining a child; losing your temper could result in abuse. If you cannot restrain your child or deal with her tantrums in a controlled manner, walk away and let your spouse or another available adult handle the situation.

Physical punishment is very controversial. Most, but not all, professionals and parents think it's a bad idea, and many would label it abuse. Whichever side of the debate you're on, remember that if the adoption is not yet final, using spanking or similar punishments could cost you custody of the children. Many families also find that physical punishment raises traumatic memories for their children.

If your child has problems with anger, you must give her acceptable ways to express it. Often, kids have no idea what to do with their rising feelings of anger, fear, or sadness. In an attempt to do *something* to dump those feelings, they often choose inappropriate outlets, like tempter tantrums. Tell your child it's okay to stomp her feet, or beat a pillow, or scream at the top of her lungs. You can make boundaries for her by telling her she must do it in her own room or another appropriate place. If you see your child building up to a "meltdown," direct her to her safe place and remind her of the outlets you have designated. With time, she may be able to redirect herself.

Hyperactivity

If your child is hyperactive or excessively giddy in an attempt to suppress his emotions, you may have to try to help him overcome it. This can sometimes be as simple as saying, "Wow, you seem really restless today. Is something bothering you?" However, if your child has been using hyperactivity as a release for quite some time, he may be unaware of exactly what emotions he is suppressing or even that he is doing so at all.

Some parents have found that redirecting their children to a quiet activity that involves parental contact will help. Often, however, once the child becomes still, his anxiety and anxiousness rise. To bring up the topic without putting undue pressure on him, you could say something like, "You know, some kids move and jump around a lot so they don't have to feel the sadness inside them." If your child expresses interest in the conversation, continue by asking him if he thinks he ever does that. You could suggest that perhaps you could hold him and talk quietly and see if any sad things come to his mind.

If your child won't talk about what might be causing his hyperactivity, you may be able to break beyond it by requiring him to take a timeout when he gets out of control. He might then move into an anger/tantrum stage, which may enable you to get to his underlying feelings. It will take patience and intuition not to push him to do so too often or too hard. But as you begin to know your child better, you'll be more likely to see when he needs to release his feelings. After a tantrum or emotional release, you can talk about the connection between getting anxious and hyperactive and feelings. Hopefully, he will learn to express his emotions in a better way. If he becomes stuck in hyperactivity, you may have to seek professional help.

Lying and Stealing

Lying and stealing often go hand in hand. While lying is normal for most young children, it can present a problem if it's persistent or interferes with your ability to get close to your child.

Many children, like my own son, lie to avoid punishment or because they fear rejection. Kids also lie to keep distance between you. Olivia says, "Lying and hiding things you don't want people to know about are common. Much of it is protection because they don't trust you. Lots of times we get a false sense as adoptive parents that 'oh, my kids have been with me for a couple months and they trust me.' "

Kids often steal from their parents and siblings in a misguided attempt to be closer to them, especially if the child is scared to openly show affection. Your child may also steal to bring your attention back after he has pushed you away by other behavior. Sometimes kids steal if they have had few possessions and don't have the impulse control to keep from taking something they want.

Of course, it's common for most kids to steal something, even if it's just candy at the corner store. Approaching a child in anger about his stealing may simply provoke him to lie. You may have better results if you approach him in a calm, non-accusatory manner. Explain why stealing is wrong and together find a way to make it right, which usually involves having the child return the item to its rightful owner.

"Our son stole a cheap trinket from a store when we were out of town on vacation," says one mom. "He insisted that a 'friend' had bought it for him. We were 99 percent sure that was a lie, but he had been talking to other kids in the store, so there was at least a chance he was telling the truth. We gave him the lecture on how stealing is wrong and illegal, and told him we would have to take the toy away because we hadn't actually seen the 'friend' buy it. In the future, we told him, he needed to check with us before letting anyone buy him something."

Lying and stealing can be signs of more serious problems if they continue unabated or if your child consistently lies in the face of the obvious. If you catch your child red-handed at something and he denies it, there could be a more serious behavior problem. However, young children do this often, and lying is considered developmentally appropriate at certain ages. Keep in mind that children from deprived backgrounds, or those who

❖ Handling Persistent Lying ❖

Remember that lying is part of normal development. Just because your child is adopted doesn't make her lying pathological.

Don't tell lies yourself.

Be patient. This problem doesn't have to be solved today, this week, this year. It takes a long time for a child to become a functioning adult.

Keep the communication flowing between home and school to eliminate the "my mom says," "my teacher says" games.

Expect that relatives, baby-sitters, camp counselors, and therapists will get tall tales.

Stay calm and maintain your sense of humor.

If your child has made false allegations of abuse in the past, warn new teachers, counselors, or others of this possibility.

Don't tell your child's friends that he is a liar. This may make your child feel threatened and reinforce the lying.

Don't give your child the opportunity to lie. Instead of "Did you do your homework?" say, "Show me your homework."

When asking a question, tell your child to think about the answer for five minutes before responding. If you still don't get a reasonable answer, give her another five minutes. This puts the child on the "hot seat" but helps her retain dignity.

If your child says something dubious that you can't identify as a lie, respond with a noncommittal, "Hmmm."

If your child tells the truth upfront about a broken rule, make the consequences lighter. If he tries to lie his way out of punishment, make them stiffer.

It's not necessary to get your child to admit to everything. If you know he did it say, "I know you did X, the consequence is Y. I am not interested in discussing it further." Remain calm.

Own your own feelings. Telling a child that lying destroys your trust in her is far more effective than punishment.

Be realistic. You can't detect all lies, so stop trying.

If your child stops lying, it will be because she feels safe enough to tell the truth, so work on the relationship.

Compliment your child and tell others about the good things he does.

Teach your child how to deal with frustration and anxiety.

—from Adoptive Families Together

have experienced trauma, may develop on a different timetable. Rule out developmental delay before you decide your child has a deeper emotional problem.

"You're Not My *Real* Mom!"

Virtually every adoptive parent hears this at one time or another. The first reaction is usually hurt feelings, followed by anger. Parents wonder what they did wrong when their child says this, or figure that the child is trying to use the emotional power of this statement to get something. In many cases, that's true. Kids know it distracts their parents and they are more likely to get what they want if you are feeling bad about yourself. If your child is being manipulative the most often recommended response is, "I am not your *birth*mother, but that is not what we are discussing right now. We are talking about your behavior." If you act defensive, your child will just use this ploy more often.

On the other hand, kids don't say this only when they are trying to wound or distract us. Your child could be thinking about her birthmother and wondering how her life would have been different with her. She may be experiencing a lot of angry feelings about the events leading up to her adoption or with you for being what her birthmother could not be. If you think this is the case, you can say, "Oh, I can see you have been thinking about your birthmom. We can talk about that later, if you like. Right now, however, we need to discuss your behavior." A calm response is probably the best way to stop this taunting exchange.

Your child may need your permission to love her previous family. Although we often assume that our kids know it's okay to love both families, many families have found that their kid did not believe it until they were told that they do not have to choose. If your child keeps throwing "You're not my real Mom" at you or constantly compares you to her birthmom, it may be that she needs to hear, "You can love us both."

"I'm Going Crazy!"

Sometimes, all the behavior techniques in the world don't seem to work. Kids may be stuck in a place the parents can't reach. If your child has experienced severe trauma, he may never come out of that "fight, flight, freeze" mode, making behavior modification impossible.

If your child has long-term problems, your job may seem impossible. At times, you may see no outlet for the frustration and pain you are living with. You must seek support from your agency, from other families, and/or from mental health professionals before you crack under the strain.

"The first months that we spent with [my daughter] were difficult enough that I was thinking that I would either have to be committed or I was going to kill myself," says one mother.

One support group leader says, "I watch stress and pressure fall off shoulders. In one group last year, seven out of twelve of us were in such crisis that they were just exhausted. ... We sat and laughed and used dark humor: 'Is that *all* you're going through? Well, please! You have nothing to complain about, wait until you hear what happened in my house!' On the way out one mother gave me a hug and said, 'You know, nothing's changed. I've laughed and I've cried tonight and nothing's changed and I'm feeling so much better.' "

❖ 8 ❖

Birthfamilies and Culture

Who could ever forget the horror of watching "Baby Jessica" being torn from her adoptive parents or "Baby Richard" screaming in fear and fighting to run back to his mother? Media images like these set adoptive parents' hearts thudding in fear of losing their children. We read stories of young adults searching for and being reunited with their birthparents, while the adoptive parents are barely mentioned, if at all. Is it any wonder that we might be afraid to retain contact with our children's birthfamilies? On the other hand, we wonder what is best for our children. Should children have contact with their birthfamilies? What if their birthparents abused or neglected them? And if the kids don't have contact, will it really matter to them?

Most children adopted at an older age remember their birthfamilies. Some have foster families that they have become close to. All these families played a role in shaping your child into who he is, and how he feels about himself. As you grow to love your child, you naturally want to protect him from possible harm. You may wish you could go back and erase all the difficult things that have happened to him. Above all, you may wish that you could have all the warm, wonderful feelings of being the only one he has ever truly loved. In those fantasies, there is no place for former families. Your child will probably never have those same fantasies. The truth is, adoption is almost never a child's first choice, and most kids long for those left behind.

Ellen, adoptive mother of two, puts it this way: "Where children can't help but expect to be is in the first home, no matter how terrible, and with the people they were born to. No matter how absolutely correct the decision to remove them, the children will *always* feel weird, singled out, separate, and different

151

because they aren't where they expect to be."

This is obviously a loaded subject. Families are often torn between what the parents are comfortable with and what is in the best interests of the child. Situations involving abuse and neglect are even more difficult, as the desires of the child have to be weighed against concerns for her safety. There is no pat answer, but a look at the needs and feelings of both the children and the adults may help you decide what is best for your family.

The Legacy

For many years adoptive parents were told only "to take them home and love them." Professionals and parents alike thought that raising adopted children was no different from raising birthchildren and that children adopted as infants would never know the difference. Likewise, children adopted at older ages would simply be grateful for having new families and once they settled in would never look back. Now we know, from adult adoptees, their adoptive parents, and the professionals who work with them, that those views were painfully erroneous. The losses experienced in adoption do not simply "go away."

"My daughter never talked or wrote about her birthparents, except to say that she wanted to meet them on our trip to Korea," says Erin. "When she met them, one of the first things she said to them was that she thought about them every day. I could have fallen off my chair."

Think for a moment of all the things that you know you inherited from your parents. Do you have your mother's eyes or your father's mannerisms? Do you share a musical talent with a sibling or a grandparent? Do you have a short temper, just like your mom? What do you know about yourself? Do you know where you were born, and at what time? Do you know that your grandfather died of cancer and that heart disease runs in your father's family? Have you grown up hearing about your ancestors who served in wars and suffered hard times? All of these things speak of *who* you are and your place here on this earth. And all of them are things that many people who have been adopted, even at an older age, may never have.

"I never had any idea where or who I came from. It was as if

I just dropped on this earth out of nowhere," says Peggy, an adult adoptee. "My parents had no information on my cultural or ethnic heritage except that I was white and presumably of European derivation. As a child, I remember doing a school assignment in sixth grade about where our ancestors came from... and I felt so uncomfortable that I didn't even know. It felt so strange to not only have no idea who had given birth to me, but to not even know what culture I had come from or what culture had formed my first parents. I think that if I had had more knowledge about where I came from ethnically and culturally, I would not have had such a rootless feeling."

Adoptees who have little idea of what they left behind long for and cherish the scantiest of information. Leslie says, "I was fortunate enough through many letters to get the names and ages of my children's birthparents and just a few facts surrounding the family. That's all I have, but my kids run to this information like a person who has been crawling in the Sahara without water!"

"I was the only redhead in my adoptive family, so growing up I was always asked where I got my red hair. I used to say eating too much ketchup, and sometimes that God gave it to me. That was something that was always embarrassing and always a reminder that I was adopted. Now [after searching] I look in the mirror and I'll know where I got this or that. It always bothered me before. Looking in the mirror was never pleasant," says Faye.

"We know nothing about Laura's birthparents," says Gail, "but we do know that she was born at 10:30 a.m. and she fixates on this every birthday."

You might think that only children adopted as infants or young toddlers lack information about their birthfamilies, but older children may as well. If the adoption is closed (meaning neither the birthfamily nor adoptive family has detailed information about the other), or if your child was left at an orphanage or came into foster care at a very young age, you may know very little or nothing about that first family. Even children who came into care at an older age find that their memories of previous families fade or get all jumbled up, especially if they have lived in several households.

For many families with multiple adopted children, the fact that one child may have more information than the other creates envy and frustration between siblings. There is little parents can do to alleviate this except to make sure that they have pursued every avenue to find information, if not contact, for their child.

Many families find it easy to share basic information with their children. However, for many of our children the questions about *why* they became available for adoption and what their history says about them are even more important. They may wonder which set of parents they're really like, and what that means for their future. The need for information about themselves and their birthfamilies leads many adoptees to search when they are adults.

"I have always felt confused about who I am," says Tori. "Who do I look like? Who do I act like? Why am I the way I am? Am I really a screwed-up person or am I just normal? Am I screwed up because I was adopted? Am I screwed up because I was not nurtured by my natural mother? Do I have separation anxiety?"

Shelley, who searched for and found her birthmom, says, "Sometimes you just need the closure, just to be sure you weren't imagining it. I think sometimes we go through life and we blame ourselves: that there was something wrong with us, so that's why she beat me, that's why she gave me up, that's why I'm adopted. And if you see as an adult that this person is just who they are with all their fallible tendencies, then it's okay—the closure comes—'yeah, I guess it wasn't me.'"

You might find it very hard to share information about the birthparents' lives and decisions, and even harder to allow your child contact with the previous family. Open adoption, where birthfamilies and adoptive families have some form of contact over the child's life, has become common, and many professionals and families feel this has helped adopted children tremendously. Even many international adoptions are more open these days—at least to the extent that the adoptive parents may know the birthfamily's name and place of residence. Still, some parents hesitate to allow contact with birthparents and foster families. They may unconsciously fear that their children will never attach to them as parents if they long too much for previous families. Many parents are uncomfortable about sharing the good things about the birthparents, perhaps feeling that it will make the children want to seek them out more. Or perhaps the parents are so angry about the pain inflicted upon their children that they can't find anything good to say about the first parents. Our children, however, have an intense need to learn about their birthfamilies. They were born to this set of parents and share their genetic tendencies. Who their parents are says a lot about who *they* are.

Marlene, adoptive parent and advocate for openness in adoption, says, "I've learned that life does not begin at adoption. Our children have a history before us and it does not include us. I believe they have a right to the truth, bad or good, of their lives. I believe our kids understand the truth. They know they came from other parents and are part of them. This is not about us and our opinions. It is about our children and what they need. Human beings want to know about themselves and what makes them unique."

Peggy adds, "When I hear adoptive parents or others discounting the importance of the birthfamily, that always seems such an affront to the adoptee. The adoptee is part of the birthfamily and comes from the birthfamily. So, when that birthfamily is discounted then that discounts the adoptee as well."

"When I found my birthmother ... I was positively thrilled at the similarities, especially those of character and taste. I have a great relationship with my family, but I've always felt different. They are all bottom-line type people and ambitious and I'm just *so* not like them," says Tiffany. "And my birthmom—I can't even explain how or what, but it was like, 'That's where I get it from!' Genetics mean something!"

Many adopted children fantasize about their previous lives. Some want to fill in the blanks or make sense of what happened to them. Others choose only to remember the good, and discard the bad feelings about their birthparents. This may stem, in part, from a belief that if the birthparent is "bad" then so are they. Experience shows that even severe abuse does not lessen a child's desire to know about and see his birthfamily.

"Our children remember only the good things about their bio parents," says Dorothy. "They seem to have forgotten being tied to trees or sexually molested or the dark basement they were locked in. In their minds, Mom and Dad are loving parents that miss them and want them to come back someday. This may be selfish and I agree that I may be projecting my own insecurities into this situation, but sometimes my feelings are just as important as the kids'. I don't feel comfortable competing with a fantasy."

Serious abuse must be a factor in determining whether a child has contact with a previous parent. We have to keep our children safe from harm. In cases of serious abuse, it may be detrimental for parents to allow their children contact with their previous families. Children who have been seriously abused may be further traumatized by any mention of—let alone the sight of—their abusers. Even scarier is the fact that some children are in danger of being abducted by unstable birthparents who have lost custody of the kids because of abuse and neglect. Living with this kind of fear can keep adoptive parents on edge. In this case, some families choose to deny contact with the abusing birthparent. In some cases a compromise can be worked out, perhaps by having the adoptive parent, but not the child, remain in contact with the birthfamily. That way, the adoptive family can learn of any changes in the birthparents' lives that affect the children, and can protect their kids at the same time.

Trina, adoptive mother of three children who were abused and neglected, chose this option. She says, "I do think that withholding info if they [the children] ask for it is wrong, no matter what age they are. ... [However], I do not want my child having [contact] with the people who have so efficiently screwed up their lives. ... I think that all adoptive parents who have an opportunity to stay in contact with birthfamily members should do so even if it's inconvenient or stressful. I do not, emphatically, believe that the child should be exposed to this relationship until they are an adult."

Not every parent agrees with this viewpoint, even in cases of severe abuse. Many parents feel that the benefits of some type of contact outweigh the risks. Some families recommend mail contact only, using a post office box or the adoption agency's address; others allow occasional contact by phone. Paula says, "I agree that [birthparents] lost their rights, however there is nothing worse than a child believing they have been completely abandoned and unloved by their birthfamily. If that contact can be positive for them, then regardless of what we think of the birthparents, sometimes it is best for the child to be allowed that privilege." Only the parents can decide what is right. Perhaps the only "must" in the case of serious abuse is that you be willing to change your stance if circumstances change and your child's birthparent becomes less of a threat or your child becomes able to handle limited contact.

The existence of siblings who either stayed with the birthparents or were adopted by another family can further complicate the issue of contact. "My son talked only a little about the adults in his birthfamily," says Gail, "but he was really torn up about leaving his older brother." Kids can grieve even harder for siblings than for birthparents. If at all possible, consider letting your child stay in contact with brothers or sisters.

Talking About Birthparents

Adoption professionals *and* experienced parents feel that some type of contact or at least information sharing is vital for all families. For many families, the biggest hurdle to sharing information is negative feelings for the birthfamily. It is undeniably hard to respect people who have abused and neglected their children, and most us have a difficult time empathizing with parents who "abandoned" their child. However, we must remember that many birthparents have a lot of love for their children, even when they are unable to parent properly.

Marlene says, "I met one birthmom who managed to save a sum of money which she gave to the adoptive parents to help with her kid's college expenses. It reminded me that we do not stay frozen in time. Most of us grow and change with time and opportunity. The point is not who the birthparents are to us, but who they are to *our children*. What would it feel like to think of oneself as a spawn from a 'bad seed' or to look in the mirror and see only evil and failure?"

Parents who did not feel this way when their children were younger often have regrets. Leslie says, "With my three children coming from another country, I thought myself 'safe' from any kind of contact with birthparents. I would never have to go through a Baby Jessica type of thing, and wouldn't have to deal with 'messy' stuff like incorporating total strangers into my idea of extended family. Now that my children are older, it is with *great* sadness that I confront these former beliefs. I never knew how important closing that circle could be to another human being."

Gail says, "Like most young adopted kids, my son thinks he was bad or did something wrong to lose his first family. The fact that they want to stay in touch might help reassure him that that's not true. I can tell him over and over that it was nothing he did, but it has more weight coming from them." Parents and professionals also agree that there is no one better than a trusted parent to share difficult news. If you choose not to share information with your children, they may seek it elsewhere.

Finding opportunities to talk about birthparents is not as hard as it sounds. You can help build positive feelings by commenting on inherited traits. Marlene suggests, "You can acknowledge athletic ability, musical talent, gorgeous skin, a hearty laugh, or sparkling eyes." Other parents speak warmly of the precious gift of life that birthparents bestowed on their children. Many families find that acknowledging the good traits also helps their children be more realistic about the bad experiences. If we acknowledge only the bad, they may feel forever compelled to speak only of the good, and may remain stuck in their grief and loss.

"I remember being a kid and picking on a sibling. It was great as long as I was doing the picking, but when someone else took up the sentiment, I quickly became the defender. 'Okay for me, but don't *you* dare pick on my brother,'" says Marlene.

Many kids feel this way about their birthfamilies. Adult adoptees assure parents, however, that what they want most is to talk about their adoptions, and their birthfamilies, with you.

"Adoptive parents often think their children have no interest in their birthparents because the adoptee never says so. However, many adoptees are *very* interested but don't want to hurt the feelings of their parents or think their parents will be angry and upset. ... For this reason, I think it is important for adoptive parents to be the ones to bring up the subject to adoptees. And to do it more than once as adoptees may feel differently at different stages of their development," says Peggy.

What Adoptees Want Parents to Know

I asked a group of adult adoptees, the voices of experience, what they want adoptive parents to know. They said:

"If I could convey one thing to adoptive parents about growing up adopted it would be that no matter how much a child wants to search or feels the need to know more about where they came from, if they feel it will hurt their parents they will suppress that need to the point where it becomes a wound. Worse, after a while you don't realize where that wound came from unless something or someone points it out. ... It is vital that they know that if they need to ask questions or express feelings they will not be hurting their adoptive parents," says Stephanie.

"I would tell adoptive parents not to be afraid of all this. To know that there *are* issues for adoptees, but not to be fearful of that. To try and understand what our legal system and culture doesn't want to permit: that despite the birth certificates, we don't have *one* set of parents and we *don't* forget that there were other parents. One adoptee stated it well, I think, when she told her adoptive mother, 'It's not the adoption I have a problem with—it's the abandonment before the adoption.' I would recommend reading and educating oneself instead of dismissing or running away," says Tiffany.

"Go into the adoption knowing that your child will want answers to their heritage and be ready to give them those answers. Do not be close-minded about anything and do not assume what your child is thinking. ... If adoptive parents are open and honest with their child right from the start, the relationship they form will be strong enough to weather the normal stages of child rearing and the feelings and emotions that come with search and reunion," says Tori.

"Comments like 'Oh, what a beautiful child! She looks just like her mother' or 'She has her father's eyes' coming from your adoptive parents are a big no-no," says Faye. "It always makes you feel like—or at least it did me—that they would have rather had a child who looked like them and were envious of other parents."

Many adoptees echo Peggy's thoughts: "My need that I had to know about my birthmother and find her has nothing to do with my adoptive parents. ... My search and need to know about my birthfamily is about *me*, not about *them*. I think of the parents who raised me as my parents as they are the ones who filled the parenting role. Sometimes people get into discussions as to which one is my 'real' mother. They are both my real mother in different ways. It isn't a competition where one has to win and the other has to lose."

Culture Shock

Birthparents are not the only ties our children have to the past. Culture can pose obstacles, too. This may be especially true for those who are adopted transracially or internationally. However, for all children, adoption means leaving behind everything that is familiar and starting over in a new place where all the rules and values are different. Cultural changes involve more than the obvious racial differences. There are family culture, income, religion, and class differences as well as the differences in the foods, music, clothing, and activities that were common in your child's former home. Families adopting internationally often find that cultural changes are more difficult to deal with than language.

Some families try to shrug off cultural changes as insignificant. Allison, adoptive mother of four, relates this experience: "My new nephew had been home about a week and we went to Thanksgiving dinner at their house. My first thought was that he must be reeling. They are a very wealthy family and he was rolling in toys and new clothes and living in a five-bedroom mansion. I said to his mom, 'The culture shock must be unbearable for him!' and she said, 'Don't worry about him, he'll be fine. We're going to act like nothing's different.' "

Parents cannot afford to be indifferent to culture shock, because many behaviors can be traced to reactions the child experiences from all the new things in his life. Parents often express the view that they want to raise their families to be "color-blind" or part of a global family. While the sentiment is well-intentioned, it does not always work well. To be "color-blind," we have to deny the differences between our children and us. Instead, we have to be intensely aware of the differences if we are to make the changes in our lives necessary to help our kids build strong racial and cultural identities. Although our families may be mostly free of racial or class prejudice, the world is not, and we must prepare our children to live in the real world. That doesn't mean that we can't share our dreams and hopes for a united, bias-free world, but it does mean that we can't be blind to the reality our children live with every day.

Many adopted children come from poor backgrounds and most are adopted into middle-class homes. Dealing with the sheer number of possessions they now own is one of the most common difficulties, even for kids raised in America. The abundance of clothing, toys, and activities that we're used to can overstimulate and overwhelm them. Many parents have found that limiting the number of things they give their children at first helps them remain calm.

If you are adopting domestically, and especially locally, your child may resist wearing new clothing or showing off new possessions. Chloe and Stan's new daughter was teased unmercifully in the weeks after her placement. Her friends from her old neighborhood accused her of being "stuck up" when she wore new clothing, and she often resorted to wearing shabby clothes to appease them.

On the other hand, some kids express dismay when American life doesn't meet their unrealistic expectations. Colin, adopted from Russia at age eleven, was disappointed that his parents wouldn't buy him a cell phone, beeper and his own TV and VCR. He thought all Americans were rich.

Class differences can become apparent when dealing with educational issues. Some parents want, and expect, their child to do well, but your child may have different ideas. In some cases, former parents did not stress education. Some children from overseas have never attended school. Other kids may not want to put forth too much effort because they are afraid their friends will accuse them of acting like somebody they're not. One man says, "Whenever we talked properly, our friends would accuse us of 'acting white.' " This is another reason it's important that your circle of friends include role models from your child's birthculture.

Family Culture

For many kids, the changes in family culture can be unsettling. Some of our kids come from homes where there was never a father present. Others come from countries where mothers were second-class citizens. For both, listening to and obeying parents in an unfamiliar way may cause problems. Some families have the parent that the child relates to best do the disciplining. While this is a short-term fix, it can ease difficulties during the transition. In some cases, the lack of respect toward women is heightened by the grief and anger our kids feel about their birthmothers.

The differences in how siblings relate to each other in other cultures can also be a problem. In some countries the oldest male sibling has the responsibility and authority to discipline and demand obedience from younger siblings. This can cause a problem for families who change the birth order of their children. The children already in your home will no doubt dash those expectations quickly, but it could cause problems at the outset.

You can save yourself a lot of wondering and frustration by familiarizing yourself with the family culture your child is used to. Without the awareness of how difficult and profound those changes are, you may find yourself disciplining children for things that are entirely appropriate in other cultures. We had this problem with one of our sons. In his culture, people do not often talk about unpleasant things and children are taught not to express negative emotions such as fear or anger. Above all, children are never to argue with an adult. As a result, whenever we were upset with him and tried to talk with him, he would get a blank look on his face that looked like a glare and would refuse to answer any questions. I could literally feel my blood pressure rise in reaction to his "stubbornness." It never dawned on us that this was cultural until I read about "face-saving" behavior in Asian countries. After realizing that he did not feel comfortable arguing with us, we were able to break through the behavior by assuring him that he could tell us what he thought. As long as we remained calm, he felt comfortable talking with us about misbehavior. In time, he stopped "saving face" altogether.

Sometimes behavior that seems unseemly in our country is tolerated in younger children in other countries. Charles and Madeline attended a party held by their child's cultural community shortly after their girls arrived home. Madeline says it was obviously the event of the year. There was a program detailing the order of the meeting. First there were singing and presentations, then a sermon, and a meal. "What was so striking was that no one seemed to feel the pressure to pay attention to anything going on in the front of the room," says Madeline. "People walked around, talked, laughed, walked in and out constantly, chattered. Children walked up to the front of the room and no one seemed to care or retrieve them. ... Children ran and played tag. [Friends] had insisted that the group was informal and that that was the 'Indian way' and boy, did I understand better what they meant. It did help me understand that many behaviors I'd seen from the girls might not be considered rude at all in an Indian context." You may have to repeatedly instruct your son in how you expect him to behave, keeping in mind that it may take quite a while for the new lessons to sink in.

Families may run into religious differences with their older child, too. If your child was raised Roman Catholic and you are Jewish, life could be interesting for a few months or even years! Some families feel that children must worship with the family. Others allow older children to attend religious services elsewhere. If you have strong religious beliefs and expect your child to worship with you, it's a good idea to inquire about your child's religious beliefs *before* accepting the referral. Or, choose an agency with a religious focus that's compatible with yours.

It's the Little Things...

Many families find that their cultural differences come to the forefront in the details of life. We discussed food differences in Chapter 4. Sometimes food remains an issue for kids long after the parents think it should. Make an effort to include your child's favorite foods. Smell is intrinsically tied to memory, and the smell of familiar food is one of the things kids report they miss most.

Music can also be important, especially for teens. Your musical tastes may differ wildly, as is true in most families, but kids can feel really out of place if they arrive in a home where no familiar music is heard. Many families allow their children to buy music they like. For some kids, it is important to see that their families not only allow them food and musical ties, but that their new families also enjoy them. Take an interest in your kid's tastes and see if there are things you can enjoy together.

Some families encounter problems in buying clothing. In some cases, the difficulties stem from differences in taste. Some American kids may at first refuse to wear certain colors or items of clothing that were associated with gangs, and thus dangerous, in their former neighborhoods. Some kids want to wear clothing that parents dislike. Clothing choices create battles in many families, and probably have little to do with your adoption.

If you feel that certain clothing will create problems for your child, explain to him why. Some parents from smaller towns fear that baggy or sagging jeans, for example, will cause the teachers and neighbors to stereotype their child as a gang member. Talk those things over with your child and try to come to a compromise. Remember that many fashions today cross cultural and racial lines, and if you object based only on what others will think, you may need to decide if you are perpetuating racial biases by refusing to allow your child to wear them. On the other hand, kids need to know that some folks will judge them by the way they look, and parents need to emphasize the consequences of their choices.

Many internationally adopted kids are unaware of America's cultural stereotypes. Deanna relates that her newly arrived eight-year-old son wanted to buy hot pink Barbie tennis shoes with silver laces. His sister was aghast. Wanting to spare him teasing at school, Deanna bought him some shoes meant for boys. Aaron was not pleased, and grumbled about his "ugly" dinosaur shoes.

Some girls from overseas refuse to wear anything but dresses. One family adopted sisters who would only wear what they called "frocks," but there were few dresses in the stores that matched their definition. In some countries, children wear only sandals or go barefoot much of the time. For these kids, shoes can be a painful adjustment. Many kids find jeans uncomfortable if they did not wear them in their home country. They may be more comfortable in soft cotton pants when they first arrive.

While most children adjust to the cultural differences of their new home relatively quickly, some have a lot of trouble giving up their former way of life. For the families of these children, culture can remain a frustration for a long time, as the experiences of one family show.

Aaron was adopted at age eight from Vietnam. Deanna, his new mother, had read quite a bit about the culture of Vietnam, but it never occurred to her that it would be as big of a problem as it became. She says, "[I knew that] they probably eat cats in Vietnam, but that doesn't translate to the fact that the kid may not relate well to the two cats that were here!" They had assigned Aaron the chore of feeding the cats, and for a long time he didn't want to do it. Deanna says, "Basically it's why waste all this good food on cats instead of us eating it, and if we were going to be feeding them and one of them is so fat that we can't stand it, then why are we not eating them?"

Aaron's experiences in Vietnam with food and the necessity of catching it turned into discussions about why his family didn't stop to pick up roadkill or try to catch the Canada geese that were flying overhead. One day Deanna was working in the garden when she heard a ruckus. It turned out that all the neighborhood children were gathered at her front door, where Aaron was holding a bird and her daughter was getting ready to open the door. Deanna says, "They were going to take this bird in my house! I started screaming hysterically to let the bird go and his eyes just kept getting bigger and bigger as I yelled louder and louder. He finally let it go." Aaron hid under the bed and sobbed for hours. "Leah was screaming at me, 'Mom! He was so happy! His Vietnamese mom would have been so happy, she would have cooked it and served it for lunch.'" Aaron didn't believe that his mom was really apologetic about it, but they finally worked it out. Deanna adds, "Recently we were talking about the bird again, and he says, 'No birds for American mom' and then does this imitation of me screaming!"

The changes in Aaron's life were profound and he still struggles with some of them. The fact that leaves fall off the trees in the fall was amazing because, "No, no, if the tree has no leaves, then the tree is dead!" One night his family served spaghetti, accompanied by Parmesan cheese in a shiny green can. He watched his siblings shake it onto their food and then began screaming, "No, no! Bathroom, bathroom!" He ran over to the cabinet, pulled out the green can of cleanser, and said, "Bathroom!" His family tried to show him the difference, but he wasn't convinced.

Although Aaron's experiences will provide family stories for years to come, it is clear that coming to America was a huge shock for him. Deanna says she thought she was prepared for culture shock, but it turned out to be a much bigger issue than expected, even larger than language.

Retaining Your Child's Culture

One of the main reasons many social workers object to transracial adoption is the fear that the children will lose a part of their cultural or racial identity. To counter this, most agencies make it a point to educate parents who adopt across racial or ethnic lines about the necessity of helping their children form a positive racial identity. Most families understand the importance of doing so and try to incorporate culture into their child's life.

Some families become quite alarmed if their children seem to reject their culture and/or language shortly after their arrival. For many kids, though, doing so is simply a sign of their desire to be more like their new families. Some children express a strong desire to look like their parents. One of my sons asked me to buy him brown hair dye. One boy adopted at age eight refused to use lotion on his dry skin, simply because he thought his skin looked whiter when it was dry. Comments like these provide parents with a wonderful opportunity to talk about the importance and beauty of all people, regardless of skin color or ethnic heritage. This desire to change their looks usually passes when our children realize that their acceptance into the family does not rely on their appearance.

Many families who have befriended members of their child's ethnic community are puzzled when their newly arrived children do not seem to enjoy visiting or even speaking with them. For many children, members of their ethnic group may seem like a threat. If you are planning to meet people from your children's ethnic community, you may want to prepare the kids ahead of time and reassure them of your love and commitment.

Shawn and Allison took their Russian children to see a local Russian immigrant. The children only answered her questions in English and refused to make eye contact with her. On the way home their son Tyler, age seven, said, "I don't like. Where she come from?" They explained that she had come to America like they had and that she lived here with her husband. Tyler said, "She no take Emily and Tyler to Russia?" Shawn and Allison immediately stopped the car and assured them that no one was ever taking them back to Russia.

In our family, we tried hard to help our older son retain his original language. He, however, had no intention of doing so, even though he had family in Vietnam that he maintained contact with. For almost a year, he refused to speak to anyone in Vietnamese although he would read and speak with us at home. With time, he began speaking Vietnamese again. He says he simply wanted to be more like us, and speaking another language made him "different." Your child's desire to explore his culture will likely wax and wane. At some ages children are more prone to want to "fit in" with everyone else, while in adolescence many kids desire to learn more about their birthculture. For this reason, you should provide opportunities continually even if your child does not show any interest. Your willingness to do so will make it more comfortable for him to accept his birthculture later.

Some families have moved to larger towns with more diverse populations so that their children have more opportunities to associate with people of their ethnicity. Veronica and her husband, who are white, adopted four black children. She says, "We moved to a new town to live in a more integrated neighborhood. There are a lot of racially mixed families and a lot of transracial adoptive families that we hang out with. In their afternoon program there are African-American staff, and 30 percent or more of the kids are African-American."

Children don't usually reject small gestures of cultural inclusion, and in fact may welcome them. Many families incorporate ethnic foods into their everyday meals, and display artifacts or souvenirs from their son's country. Other families attend festivals sponsored by the local community or participate in cultural education days at school. There are culture camps held throughout the nation for international adoptees where kids can learn about their culture and participate in activities that celebrate it. Experienced parents warn against making only "token" gestures of cultural inclusion. If you mention the child's heritage only during holidays or special events, or if you have only one black doll in a sea of white ones, she may feel that her racial identity is just a small piece of her. Another mistake some parents make is assuming that "close enough" is good enough. There are significant differences between Mexicans and Puerto Ricans; between Chinese and Koreans.

Despite social workers' fears, many children adopted transracially have retained their cultural pride. Veronica says of her son Jason, adopted at age nine, "He has not expressed a desire to be more white. All our kids take pride in their African-American heritage. He talks a lot about how he is African and his ancestors came from Africa. We have contact with many other interracial families and with the black community so he doesn't stand out at all."

Not all experiences, however, are so positive. Many adult adoptees speak of the struggle to form a racial identity when they reach their teens. Many kids feel they don't fit in either culture. Some feel that they were not prepared for the way the world views them or for the racism they encounter as they get older. For this reason, parents must make an effort to help their kids make ties with their ethnic and cultural communities. Doing so is not always easy. You may feel out of place—indeed, as out of place as minorities often feel in your community. Attending functions where you are the minority may help you understand your child's position. Many minorities may hesitate to allow people of other cultures to get too close, perhaps as a protection against being hurt later. Regardless, it's important for your family to make the effort.

Judith Ashton, of the New York State Citizens' Coalition for

Children, reminds parents that there is a difference between "self-esteem" and "group esteem." Parents not only need to help their children feel good about themselves, but also to feel good about the group they belong to. She emphasizes that black children must care about what happens to blacks as a group and feel a part of the struggle on behalf of all blacks. She says that a transracial adoptee without a sense of group identity is a major fear among minorities who oppose transracial adoption. Ashton shares the following thoughts for parents who adopt African-American children. Most of these tips are pertinent to any family who adopts transracially.

❖ Have black friends—adults as well as children. Also have friendships with other interracial families.

❖ Realize that in matters of race and culture you will learn the most about parenting your child from black parents and other cultural guides.

❖ Attend integrated schools. Volunteer in your child's classroom and become known throughout the school. Your family becomes normalized the more people get used to you.

❖ Live in an integrated community. Stay in one community so that you and your child don't have to keep starting over. *Important*: Be prepared to move if it means a more affirming environment for your child.

❖ Use black professional and other services. Find black baby-sitters and other family helpers.

❖ Learn how to take good care of your child's skin and hair.

❖ Have black literature, children's books, periodicals, toys, games, and artwork in your home.

❖ Learn and share with your children black history and important current and cultural events. Participate in black activities (church, community centers, fairs, celebrations).

❖ Visit big cities with large African-American populations, museums, and theater.

❖ Be clear with yourself and your child as to his or her racial identity. Your child is black or African-American whether or not he or she has one white parent. Ambivalence—yours or your child's—will not foster positive self-esteem.

❖ Remember that you and your child are minorities. You are forever a minority family.

❖ Be active in social-change groups, such as affirmative action.

❖ Be prepared to, and do, speak up when wrongs occur.

❖ Remember that your advocacy is not only for your child but also for all children and people of color. What happens to *any* black kid happens to *your* kid.

❖ Be an active anti-racist. Understand why we are racists as long as we benefit from a racist system. Talk about racism and let your child know through your words and actions that you are part of the struggle.

❖ Ask for help and keep learning! Read, talk to people and be alert to anything that will help you better affirm your child, support his or her development and become a better anti-racist. Teach what you learn, by example and by sharing what you know with others.

❖ Find ways for your child to learn that he or she is part of the African-American community. Accept and understand that not all of his or her activities will, or ought to, include you.

❖ Always know whose side you're on. *Do not tolerate racist acts or statements.* The hurt and damage are just as great if the acts or statements are based on ignorance or were not done maliciously.

❖ Learn to choose your battles. You can't do everything.

Dealing With Racism

For many of us who adopt transracially, dealing with racism and teaching our children to handle racism is difficult. If you have never experienced racial discrimination, it can be hard to understand how painful it is. Some parents have a tendency to dismiss things that might be racially motivated because they don't want to admit that their child is experiencing racism. It is important to become attuned to the sometimes-subtle messages of racism that our kids receive. Not all racism is negative. Compliments that focus on the color of your child's skin or hair texture can be uncomfortable for parents. Stereotypes like "all Asians are good at math" are just as harmful as negative stereotypes.

In discussing racism with our children, it is unfortunately necessary to remind them that their behavior reflects upon their entire racial group. In America, when a white person does something wrong, it reflects on the individual. When a minority person does something wrong, it reinforces negative stereotypes that whites have. Discussing racism can be uncomfortable for white parents. One reason may be that it emphasizes the differences between our children and us. Another reason is that we feel like part of the problem because it is our racial group that is dominant. Regardless of how uncomfortable it is for you, you *must* prepare your child to handle the racism he will encounter.

Maya, an African-American mom who's part of a multiracial family, says, "Racial discrimination does seem to hurt more. I think because it is directed toward a whole group rather than a few individuals. So I know I have to prepare my kids. I try to do so by making them proud of who they are and where they came from. And the fact that no one is better than them."

Parents and professionals suggest that you teach your child, and yourself, to handle racism in several ways. Many recommend using humor to defuse uncomfortable situations. One parent recalls, "We were in the indoor playground and a guy at the next table told me my daughter would probably be a good violinist. I assured him that Asia has billions of people, and I'm sure at least some of them must be tone deaf, including my daughter, who makes *my* singing sound good. Then I looked over to where she was playing, as usual the loudest kid in the whole place, and said, 'Besides, I think opera would be more her thing.' "

Teach your children to stand up for themselves, even politely confronting authority when necessary. "You know, coach, just because I'm black doesn't mean basketball is my whole life." Report serious incidents to the school authorities, parents, or police. Don't take racism lightly.

Many minority parents say that they teach their children to use ignoring as the first line of defense. Often, a kid who makes racial comments will quit if he gets no response. Practice with your child. Rehearsing how to respond to racial comments can help your child choose the best approach when confronted with a racist remark. Above all, strong self-esteem is the best tool against racism. Minority parents say that instilling the thought that racism reflects more on the racist than on them helps kids to see that they aren't the problem. If you give your children a strong sense of who they are, both individually and as members of their racial or cultural community, you can help protect them against racism's sting.

Maya says that since her sons were toddlers, she has told them they are handsome, smart, "and they can do and become anything they want. This is America. Not perfect, but a place they can pursue their dreams." She also keeps them aware of accomplishments African-Americans have made to this country.

To ready them for racism, she talks about current and past racially related events, such as the Rodney King and O.J. trials, and the lynchings of black men in the past. She and her sons also discuss incidents that have happened to them, and differences in how they are perceived by others: One of her sons is big and strong in appearance; the other is small and wears glasses.

It is also important to emphasize the need to avoid putting people down because they're "different."

Maya says, "I've always told my kids, if there are only three people on this earth, if they do not look exactly alike, there is going to be some type of discrimination. Albeit the color of one's hair, eyes, height, weight, male, female and so on. The only way to not have discrimination is if God had made us all alike in every possible way. I remind them that a lot of people experience discrimination for reasons other than skin color. People who have physical handicaps, may not dress a certain way, aren't athletic, can't dance, are overweight."

Gail adds, "We don't really concentrate so much on one ethnic group. We like to emphasize the human mosaic—that people just come in different colors, shapes, sizes, and so on. And wouldn't the world be really boring if they didn't?"

The Core Issues

Eight-year-old Jack, adopted at age three, went rock climbing with friends. Jack rappelled down a sixty-foot cliff, twice. He handled it with aplomb, showing little fear. However, on the way home he acted out and threw tantrums. It turned out that he had gotten "lost" on his way back to camp for about ten minutes when he failed to wait for his dad. Another member of the party came along the trail a few minutes behind him, but as far as Jack was concerned, that ten minutes was scarier than rappelling could ever hope to be. He said the panic he felt when he thought he was lost brought back the same feelings he had had once before—when he moved to a foster home.

Jack's mom, Tabitha, says, "Isn't it amazing that a kid can face a challenge like a sixty-foot cliff without a second thought, but is scared stiff by a quick flashback to the horrible sense of loss he had to face in his early years? It really brought home just how powerful all those memories are and probably always will be for him."

Jack is not alone. Virtually all adoptees, regardless of their age at adoption, will have recurrent thoughts and experiences surrounding the core issues of adoption. Throughout their lives they will be sensitive to the fear of abandonment and the memories of the losses they suffered. For many, those early experiences will affect their life choices and attitudes.

In 1982, Sharon Kaplan and Deborah Silverstein, social workers and adoptive parents, drew on their work with adoptees and their families to identify seven core issues: loss, rejection, guilt and shame, grief, identity, intimacy, and control. They believe that recognizing the core issues can help adoptees, their families, and assisting professionals better understand each other.

In previous chapters, we explored some of these feelings and the role they play in your child's initial adjustment. Many behaviors stem from these core feelings, and you may find it easy to handle them initially. You may be perplexed, though, when your child reverts to bad behavior months or years after she arrived in your home. Many children resolve their initial feelings of insecurity only to have those feelings rise again much later, as Jack's did. Some core issues seem to be present throughout the lifetime of the adoptee, while others tend to peak at specific times or ages.

"For the most part, I know who I am and what I believe. The part of me I don't know has to do with my adoption," says Jessica. "I feel as though I have this hole that runs through me that is about the size of a silver dollar. It runs from the top of my head to the bottom of my left foot and can only be filled by the birth side of my situation."

Much has been written in recent years about the inner lives of adoptees and the feelings that arise at certain points in their lives. Most professionals agree that adoption issues do not signal problems, but are rather the *normal* effects of suffering serious losses in childhood. I encourage you to read about the core issues of adoption in depth to gain a better understanding of how they affect your children. You'll find a list of recommended readings in Appendix C.

In discussing the core issues, it's important to realize that many people who were not adopted experience these feelings. And many adoptees, including some of those who share their thoughts here, don't feel that their adoptions have much to do with their personality characteristics. They point out that they could blame their problems on their adoptions but choose not to do so. As parents, your role is to discuss with your children how these core issues *may* be related to their adoptions and to provide them a sounding board for their questions and concerns.

Loss

"I would hope that the majority of us were raised in happy homes. I know I was," says Miranda. "But there was always something missing. Birthdays, Christmas, Easter, Valentine's Day always seemed to bring sadness to me. I always felt there was something I was supposed to receive, another gift, but it wasn't there. The gift should have been from my biological mother."

Our children have experienced the ultimate loss—the loss of their original families. Its suddenness and the lack of explanation often compound the loss. For many adoptees, the fear of losing their family again persists throughout their lives, though it may peak and ebb at various times. Most children display a fear of abandonment soon after their adoption through separation anxiety or clinging. With time and comfort, those behaviors usually subside, but they can arise later if something triggers feelings of loss and abandonment. Each child has his own emotional triggers, although a few are virtually universal, such as the illness of a parent or sibling, or a move to a new house.

The reminders associated with these events are obvious. However, your child may react to events that seem minor to you. Deanna says her son Aaron was very upset the day a substitute taught his class. The change in routine and the loss of his familiar teacher disturbed him.

Other kids seem to fear almost any unfamiliar occurrence, reacting as if their very lives were in danger. Allison says her nephew, adopted at age eight from Korea, has had continuing problems with fear. When he was sixteen his mother came home to find him hiding in his room, terrified. He told her that this horrendous truck broke into the basement and shook the house. He thought he was going to die and didn't know what to do. It turned out that an oil delivery truck had made a yearly delivery, one that he had missed the previous seven years in his home. Instead of acting with curiosity as most teens would, he reacted as if his life was in jeopardy.

You may find that your child reacts to any loss with tremendous fear and sadness. Losing a pet or breaking a favorite toy may send her into a tailspin. If she feels that her place in your family is in jeopardy, perhaps because you are angry with her for misbehavior, she may react with strong anger and defiance. Even when things are going smoothly, she may begin to act strangely if she is thinking about a previous loss. She may "see" a similarity in an activity that occurred before her last move and decide that she is going to be moved again. The connection may make sense to her, even if you can't see it.

We went on vacation one year and visited our son's foster family. He eagerly anticipated the trip for months, as he has warm memories of his foster family. However, a few days before we left he started acting strange. He became jumpy and began sneaking around, hiding behind furniture to listen to our conversations. He finally revealed that he thought we were going to leave him at his foster family's house, and was listening to see if that was the case. When I reminded him that we'd told him he was coming back home with us, he replied, "Well, my other family didn't tell me [I was leaving] either!"

He had a point. Just because you know you are going on vacation like you do every year, your child may not know, and may never really believe, that it's just a vacation. To many kids, packing bags brings up feelings of loss and abandonment. Talk about what you will do when you come back from the trip, and emphasize that your whole family is leaving for vacation and your whole family is returning. Your child may not believe it until it actually happens, but you will have done your best to prepare her.

For many adoptees, leaving home for college or their own apartment is especially trying. Some don't want to leave at all. In some cases, this could mean that a child chooses not to go to college or get a job. What looks like lack of interest in their future may indeed be a fear of leaving home. Others physically leave, but never truly separate emotionally.

"Not one of us has totally been able to break away in an emancipation sort of way," says Shelley about herself and her adopted siblings. "I left for twenty years, but I still have a very strong emotional connection. For me, emancipation will come only when I am able to make grown-up decisions and carry them out without even thinking about what my folks will think. I'd like to think that one day I will feel like I own myself, and that I don't have to fear being on my own. ... I would just love to have that grown-up relationship but it's not going to happen because of my own adoption issues of being rejected, abandoned if you will, that will prohibit it. I think I'm holding on for dear life. It's sort of a reverse control. I'm not demanding control, I'm just holding on as a way of survival."

Although you can do much to help your child prepare for events or losses that are sure to trigger emotional responses, there's no way to foresee some situations. In this case, you may have to refer back to behavior modification techniques that worked for you before, with an emphasis on making your child feel safe. After he has calmed down, you can discuss the event and what precipitated his fears. Tying the current problem into his past may help him see why he reacts the way he does. Assure him that his reaction is normal, considering his previous circumstances. If you are able to recognize when he is reacting the way he did to previous losses, you may be able to help him see the similarities *and* the differences between the previous events and the current experiences, helping him to work through the situation in a different way. With time your son may be able to learn to short-circuit his own fears. Professional help from a therapist trained in adoption issues can help.

Rejection

Many adoptees perceive their placement for adoption as a rejection of themselves. They feel that there was something wrong with them that led to their birthfamily's decision to relinquish custody or that caused their parents to abuse them. They may view each subsequent move as a rejection as well, thinking that if they were good enough their temporary placements would have become permanent. Such children can be highly sensitive to feelings of rejection.

"I can remember being scared that my folks would give me away or give me back to wherever that place was that they got me from," says Tori.

"I can remember my father jokingly saying that I could be taken back to the orphanage and replaced when I did something like trip over my own two feet. To him it was a joke, I guess, but never to me," says Faye.

This sense of being rejected may permeate their relationships with their peers. Although every child experiences problems with friends at some point, these tussles may be more traumatic for an adopted child. For example, many parents report that childish arguments over toys or playing become "he doesn't like me" much more often than is considered normal. Kids who are sensitive to rejection may set up self-fulfilling prophecies, pushing their friends away with combative behavior before the friends have a chance to reject them.

"I fear rejection. I avoid arguments like the plague because of this. In fact, my husband of ten and a half years and I have *never* had an argument," says Jessica. "This is because I fear that if I get mad enough I'll say something like, 'maybe I should leave,' as in separation, and he will reply, 'don't let the door...' Don't get me wrong. I've had my fair share of rejection, but it's usually me doing the rejecting. When someone does something that makes me feel like I'm being rejected, I just shut them out. No explanations, no phone calls, no letters."

Children who have a strong feeling of rejection often become perfectionists, thinking that that is the way to ensure never being rejected again. If your child has this tendency, she may be overly sensitive to criticism and may be her own worst critic.

"He really has a difficult time not being perfect," says Veronica of her son, Jason. "He puts a lot of energy into being perfect and the big emotional things we've had were when he was not perfect—he couldn't play his piano piece, or he was disciplined for something or another. We tell him that [he doesn't have to be perfect], but he doesn't hear it."

Deeply entrenched fear of rejection can pose problems when children are adolescents. As they begin to date, the fear of rejection, coupled with problems with intimacy, may keep them from getting close to anyone. If they do begin a relationship, they may sabotage it as soon as they feel it's getting serious.

"I don't allow myself to get that attached. I always have relationships with the wrong guys. ... I choose the people that can't have a committed relationship with me, an intimate relationship with me, because I'm not going to lose that again," says Shelley.

On the other hand, teens and young adults may stay in inappropriate or unfulfilling relationships, with the dual issues of loss and rejection paralyzing them.

Tiffany says, "I was always lucky when I was younger because I was very pretty. But I couldn't *not* 'love' somebody who loved me, or said they did. How can you turn away love? My way of dealing with that is not to abandon the other person first, but I have to be such a bitch that they end it. I *can't* say no to love."

As your children become old enough to discuss why they react in certain ways to situations, you may be able to help them see the thread running between incidents. One of the biggest keys to working on changing behavior is to recognize it. Many parents have success approaching their children with a statement such as, "Many kids who were adopted at older ages get really scared when it looks like someone they like is going to leave them. Do you think that is why you react this way?"

Shame

A deep sense of shame is part of many adoptees' makeup. They may feel that they deserved what happened to them, and are unworthy of anything else. They may feel shame at being different from most of their friends. Some kids carry the shame of their birthfamily's dysfunction. The effects of their shame may be lifelong.

"I have no idea what is the 'core' of me or if there is one. But whatever is there, if anything, if people actually saw it they would hate me and abandon me, so I can't ever show it, and I live in fear of exposure," says Tiffany.

If your child was separated from his birthfamily during the preschool to early elementary school age when kids go through a "magical thinking" stage, believing they directly affect everything around them, he may have linked a random event with his separation. For example, a boy who told a lie and was disciplined and then had to leave his family a week later may think his lying caused the separation. Some children are so certain they're responsible that they never reveal the "sin" that they're sure led to their loss. To do so would be to admit something too terrible. However, if your child does not tell anyone what he thinks happened, he may never be relieved of his shame. Even children who are repeatedly told that the separation was not their fault may not believe it. Nineteen-year-old Chelsea still tells her parents, years after her adoption, "If you ever really knew me, you wouldn't love me."

Some children operate on a pervasive feeling of shame. Chase has a difficult time in school because of this tendency. "He will get himself into a corner at school by doing one small thing that was slightly inappropriate that merely caused his teacher to say, 'Chase, don't do that.' And he will take that one thing and build it into a monster. He reacts in a shame-based way to her having to mention it to begin with and then will proceed to go running around the room like a monkey for the next half-hour, being incredibly disruptive. I think because he thinks he deserves it [punishment]," says his mother, Nicole.

Adoptees who have little self-worth can find it hard to accept compliments or any positive attention. Spencer, who is a very good athlete, often responds to comments such as "Great catch!" with "Well, John is better." However, if Spencer does something wrong and it is pointed out to him, he accepts that without argument.

"Let me just put it this way. If you did something illegal and you blamed it on me, I would feel the responsibility for it and feel as though I belonged in jail, not you," says Jessica.

People who have never lived with a kid like this don't have a clue how disheartening it is. You have to be persistent in giving good messages to your child, at times pointing out how little he thinks of himself and that that's not how others view him. Professional counseling may help a child who struggles with low self-esteem, especially since children tend to believe positive comments more when they come from people outside the family.

The "shame" of being different haunts some adoptees. "I remember writing an assignment for an English teacher about my being adopted and handing in my assignment in an envelope so nobody else could read it," says Shelley.

Adoptees who have experienced traumatic moves may have a hard time planning for the future or imagining their adult life. "I used to be *certain* that I would die young, because I was utterly unable to formulate a picture of myself grown-up," says Tiffany. This feeling can become evident in discussions about career goals or future marriages. I have one child who prefaces every comment about the future with, "When I move again..." Even though we tell him he isn't moving again, in his heart it is inevitable. This is one point where contact with other adoptive families can help, especially if the group includes adults who were adopted. The realization that others have felt that way and have gone on to enjoy success may help your child to become comfortable thinking about her future, too. You may also find it helpful to include the fact that you will still be family each and every time you discuss the future with your child.

"The kids and I have a little game where I tell them that after they grow up and have kids of their own, they'll call me and say, 'Mom, these kids are driving me crazy. Tell me what I should do!' I roll my eyes and they laugh," says Gail.

Grief

Grief can resurface over and over again throughout an adoptee's life. (For a detailed discussion of grief, see Chapter 6.)

"Loss has always been a major theme in my life," says Tiffany. "I cry at everything that touches on it. When I was sick I watched the Disney movie 'Fox and the Hound' and I hated it because it starts out with the baby fox's mother dying. I can't take it. There is a commercial that ends with a father walking his daughter to her room to tuck her in for the night. You see them from behind and she slips her tiny, little hand into her father's big, secure, loving hand and I cry every time."

Adolescents and young adults may display grief through depression. During adolescence, kids gain the ability to think abstractly and to process their experiences through more mature eyes, seeing for the first time how difficult their birthparents' lives and decisions must have been. They may also analyze their own lives more deeply, revisiting old wounds and memories, and for the first time realizing the enormity of their losses.

A teen who can't confide in family or friends may turn his grief inward, causing depression. Many adoptees simply turn off their feelings and disconnect from them. Some teens try to numb their pain through substance abuse. "I did 'stuff' my emotions. I became a workaholic. I simply cut my feelings off, all of them, for a very long time. ... I went through deep depressions between fourteen and sixteen years old. I remember being furious at my birthmom for not having an abortion. My parents either did not know I was depressed or never mentioned it," says Stephanie.

"When I was growing up I used to run away all the time, but I never really knew why. I just had to get away," says Faye.

"Memory is another one. I have none!" says Tiffany. "It's not a total lack of memory. If a question arises about a certain thing or when something happened, I am usually good with that. But it's like I don't remember being a kid. I have pictures, I see myself at birthday parties and such. I believe I was happy in large measure, because I've heard it often enough—'you were a happy child' or 'Tiffany was a happy child'—when people are talking. But I'll have to take their word half the time."

A recurrence of grief in your child will likely be signaled by a change in behavior. For some kids, grief rises out of normal childhood things. One mom's Asian son began behaving badly, seemingly without reason. After several days he confided that another family member had taken him to see the Disney movie "Mulan." The images of an Asian country and people and all the talk about family honor raised a lot of pain for him.

As adoptees grow older, the incidents that bring forth their grief may be more profound. The death of a loved one, especially a parent, may cause adoptees to grieve not only for that loss, but for their previous losses as well. Sometimes they come face to face with the grief of adoption from

❖ Signs of Depression ❖

Pervasive feelings of sadness, loneliness, hopelessness, pessimism

Mood swings

Irritability, hypersensitivity, crying

Feelings of worthlessness

Suicidal thoughts and/or attempts

Agitation

Sleep disturbances

Change in school performance

Withdrawal from friends and social activities

Migraine headaches, abdominal pains with no apparent physical cause

Loss of usual energy and interest in previously enjoyed activities

Unusual change in appetite or weight

the other side of the adoption experience.

Shelley recalls that her true grieving started in college when her best friend placed a child for adoption. She says, "The grief came when my friend gave birth to the baby she relinquished. I was sitting with my dad in the garage and he asked, 'How do you feel about your birthmother?' and I said, 'I hate her,' but within a week, after that baby was born and I saw the reaction of my friend and the grandparents and I saw how much loved this baby was and how horrible it was for them to have to go through life denied her presence, I really went through a grief that [my family] must have had sort of similar reactions and of how sad it was that I didn't know them. I learned that these people weren't beasts that didn't have any feelings at all."

Identity

Adolescence is when all people begin to form their adult identity. For people who were adopted, this age can be especially difficult. One of the primary tasks of adolescence is separating from the family and becoming independent. This can be difficult not only because of loss and rejection issues, but also because in order to develop their own identity, teens have to have some sense of who their parents—both birth and adoptive—are. For many adoptees the information they have is not sufficient to answer their questions.

"At the end of college, I had a big falling out with a close friend. He wrote me a rather nasty letter that he left for me at my house. One thing in it struck me: that I was a veritable chameleon, that I had no 'me.' And that I changed who I was and what I liked and didn't like depending on who I was with at the time, who my close friends were and with whom I was involved. He was right," says Tiffany.

This is the age that many adoptees begin thinking about searching for their roots if they have not maintained contact with their birthfamilies. If no information is available, they may create an imagined identity for their birthparents, and then try to fit that picture into their identity.

Some kids who try to identify with their birthparents do so, often unconsciously, by "trying on" their identity. For this reason, some adoptees get pregnant or father a child in an effort to relate to their birthparents, or to form a biological connection with someone.

"I was pregnant once, when I was seventeen. I enjoyed the irony of it even then. I mean, there was a sense of justice, right? My mother must have been a bad seed and, clearly, so was I. See? I'm dirt," says Tiffany, who later miscarried.

Other adoptees find that class becomes an issue. Most adoptive families are middle-class, and adoptees may assume, rightly or wrongly, that their birthparents were lower-class. If they do, they may begin to associate with other teens that they feel share their birthfamily's economic class in order to get a better feel for their birthparents' identity.

Cultural identity also becomes important in adolescence. At an age where appearance is very important, being different can be excruciating. Transracial adoptees may have a particularly difficult time merging their identity as one race with the features of another. If your child is black, for instance, and your family is white, your child will have to figure out what it means to be an African-American, and what that means to your relationship. Other people will decide your child's race based on what he looks like, regardless of how "white" a family he grew up in.

Transracial or transcultural adoptees have to figure out what it means to belong to two different cultures or nations. For some, this leads to difficult questions about their birthcountries, as well as their birthfamilies. In her book *The Family of Adoption* (Beacon Press), Joyce Maguire Pavao writes about a young boy who was given a geography assignment on his birthcountry, Korea: "He came home from school one day and said to his mother, as he drank his juice and ate his cookies, 'Do you know how many people there are in Seoul, where I was born?' She said, 'No, tell me,' and he told her how many billions. Then he said, 'Do you know how many people there are in the whole country of Korea?' and she said, 'No,' and he told her how many trillions. And then he sat and stared out the window and eventually said, 'I understand how you told me that my birthmother could not take care of me, but what was wrong with all of those other billions of people?'"

Although maintaining cultural identity is vital in the adolescent years, it can be very important to younger children as well. Aaron, adopted at age eight from Vietnam, became an American citizen. His parents discussed what citizenship meant in terms of the opportunities it brings. He missed a day of school to become an American and when he went back he took cake with red, white, and blue frosting. His class had made cards, virtually everywhere he went someone congratulated him on being an American, and his family made a big deal of the event. His mom says, "About a week later came behavior problems out the ears! The sort of thing where, as a mom, I begin to believe there is something happening that is not being said. ... Finally, in a great fit of anger and frustration, Aaron screamed that none of this was fair. He did not want to be an American if it meant he was not Vietnamese anymore. This child had assumed from all the attention his citizenship was getting, that he no longer had any claim to his Vietnamese heritage. He really did believe that we were telling him that all that he had been before he arrived in our home was 'not good' and that he had to be someone else. Many tears later, from *all* of us, I think we have this straight. This child is an American—but he holds a strong claim to the land of his birth and we are not to try to take that from him."

During adolescence and young adulthood, many adoptees seek out members of their own race or ethnic group to date and to marry. Even kids who are raised in a predominantly white culture may be denied the privilege of dating lifelong friends when their friends' parents object. When they approach members of their birthculture, parents may tell them that they are not Asian enough or black enough or Latino enough to date and marry their children. Many adoptees become more active in cultural pursuits during adolescence and they often go through a period where they reject their adoptive parents' culture and immerse themselves in their birthculture. In time, they usually become comfortable in both cultures.

A teen's search for identity can lead to many problems within the family. Your teen may reject your moral values, educational wishes, or family traditions, believing that they do not reflect the "real" him. However, as he begins to merge the two sides of his identity, he will likely incorporate much of your family history into his identity. It helps to remember that this is not about you, but about him and his need to figure out who he is.

Intimacy

The combination of adoption losses, shame, the fear of abandonment and rejection, and the lack of identity seem to all come together in a fear of intimacy. People who were adopted may never feel they really belong in their adoptive home—or anywhere for that matter. They may be so invested in protecting themselves from more pain that they preclude intimate attachments with anyone.

Many children have intimacy problems from the moment they enter their families. They keep parents and siblings at arm's length to avoid being hurt. Even when a child becomes firmly attached, he may always feel "different" and thus not share all of himself. This tendency toward self-protection can become quite a problem when he marries and has children.

"I have been married three times," says Miranda, "the third time for twenty-three years, but there is a lack of closeness. I am afraid to let anyone get too close to me for fear of being hurt. I don't divulge my inner feelings to anyone lest I be rejected."

"When my oldest child was born, I was unable to leave the hospital for the three days he was there. For years I felt guilt that I didn't have the same needs or feelings toward my daughter. Later I discovered that first-time contact with a blood relative may have been the reason for the joy. I am divorced and due to geographical constraints I have not been actively involved in the life of my two children. The oldest and I are able to make contact every six months or so and we connect just like we saw each other yesterday, while the relationship with my youngest has had many ups and downs to the point of losing contact with her. I really do feel that though my actions towards my daughter have not generated this schism, there may be some subliminal message caused by my having lost contact with my [birth] mother," says Seth.

"Relationships? I'm pretty much an 'out of sight, out of mind' type person. I disconnect better than anyone I know. I deaden better than anyone I know. So, if you leave, and I don't see you, you are *gone*. I'm moving on, adapting. Don't expect me to write or call or remember much. And I do that with my parents and brother. I believe that I hurt them terribly when they tell me that I do, but why would I call? And why would it hurt that I don't? I have no impact on anyone, on anything. And don't expect to have much of one on me, either," says Tiffany, adopted as a toddler.

People who fear intimacy develop many safeguards. They may break off relationships early to avoid being intimate at all. They may use abrasive personality traits to keep people away. They may even use their bodies as a shield. Shelley says, "I think intimacy was a significant part of my weight issues. There was a lot of overeating to protect myself from intimacy."

Overcoming a fear of intimacy takes time and determination. Many adult adoptees report spending years in therapy trying to resolve their adoption issues.

Control

Control can remain a key issue throughout the adoptee's life. As children they had no control over what happened to them. Some adoptees try to compensate for that their whole lives, by making sure that they never lose control and become vulnerable again. This form of self-protection can cause many problems for the child and his family.

"In my teenage years I became somewhat rebellious—drinking, smoking cigarettes and pot, having sex and hanging out doing nothing. I verbally abused my parents and totally alienated them. My grades faltered and my attitude really stank. They did nothing to reprimand me or punish me. ... Perhaps they didn't want to come down on me too hard, for fear of my rejection. What led me into drug use? I have thought a lot about this and cannot honestly come up with answers. I suppose one possibility was the need to control my own life. ... I do not believe my drug use and early sex have much to do with having been adopted," says Tori.

As teens, many adoptees rebel, chafing at the limits their

parents set. While most teens do so, the issue of who has control is often more touchy for the adoptee. Often the need for control stems from the desire to try to undo previous losses and protect themselves from more.

"I couldn't let anyone have any control," says Tristan, who was adopted at age nine. "If I gave them a little, they would have wanted more and then eventually they would have had it all and I couldn't do that."

"Yes! I have to control my life. I get totally stressed out if I have to ride with anyone else. When my husband and I go anywhere, I drive. I hate surprises that have to do with my life. I hate last-minute changes such as employers being late, plans being changed. And I internally react with anger when things like this happen," says Jessica.

❖ Signs of Substance Abuse ❖

Track or needle marks

Wearing of sunglasses inside or on cloudy days

Wearing of long-sleeve shirts in warm weather

Frequent tardiness at work or school

Extreme mood swings

Excessive use of breath mints

Unusually poor grooming or unkempt clothing

Profuse sweating, even on cold days

Borrowing or begging for money

Aggressiveness, "uptight" attitude, paranoia

Swollen hands and/or feet

Constant sniffling

Burns, lesions, or sores on mouth, nose, lips, or face

Frequent isolation

Presence of drug paraphernalia, including burnt spoons or bottle caps, knotted strings or pantyhose

Gradual disappearance of valuables

Unexplained spending of unusual amounts of money

Is Professional Help Needed?

Some professionals believe that every child adopted at an older age needs counseling. The issues of adoption can be deep and lifelong and adoptees often find objective parties easier to talk with. Not everyone agrees, however, and ultimately it is up to you to decide if your child needs counseling.

If your child seems to get stuck in a phase of development

❖ What to Ask a Therapist ❖

Before you commit to a course of counseling, a group of parents from Adoptive Families Together suggests you ask the following questions to determine if the therapist is sensitive to adoption issues.

Do you think there is a difference between children born to their families and those who were adopted? If the answer is yes, go on. If no, hang up.

What do you see as different? If loss, identity, etc., are mentioned, go on.

Do you think that children adopted in infancy have similar issues to those adopted at an older age? If the answer is yes, go on.

What training have you had in adoption? By whom? How long ago?

What is your experience with adoptive families? Types of adoption?

Are there families who would recommend you?

How do you feel about working with siblings?

What is your policy on dealing with emergency situations in the home? At a hospital? Are you available around the clock seven days a week, or do you have associates who are? May I meet them?

Do you attend school meetings? Will you comfortably work with a primary care provider/pediatrician?

Do you accept Medicaid?

Who supervises your office if you're late for an appointment?

Do you participate in any extracurricular activities related to your specialty?

Can you prescribe medication? If not, which physicians do you recommend?

Do you have any children?

and can't find a way out, you should probably find a therapist. Some kids, however, reject the idea of therapy, either out of fear or anger. Kids with strong control issues may refuse to talk to someone who may see their pain. They may be too invested in protecting themselves. Or perhaps your child finds adoption difficult to discuss because of his shame. Some adoptees won't recognize the benefits of counseling until they're adults and seek it out for themselves.

In looking for a therapist, find one who has adoption experience. Some families seek counseling, only to have the therapist question their parenting abilities or chalk up behaviors to normal adolescence. A therapist who is not familiar with adoption and its issues may never be able to help you discover the true roots of your child's difficulties.

❖ 10 ❖
Language and School

For many adoptive families, language problems and dealing with school are huge difficulties. The issues of adoption make school harder for many reasons—daily separation from parents, unresolved grieving and anger that distract kids, the loss of continuity from moving several times, being "different," and school assignments such as making family trees or sharing baby pictures. For some kids, having to learn a new language and all that entails makes it even more difficult. In addition, many families find it frustrating to work with schools and officials who seemingly have neither the time nor the desire to help their kids. Advocating for your child can be exhausting and time-consuming.

Language

Parents adopting older children internationally often spend a lot of time worrying about how they will communicate. For the most part, they are pleasantly surprised to find that language acquisition is not that difficult. However, family members do need to learn at least a few key words in the child's language in order to make the first few weeks easier. A simple travelers' phrase book will usually provide those phrases needed for the initial adjustment. Kids, especially those under age ten, learn new languages quite rapidly. When my husband and I traveled to Vietnam to pick up our son, we were amazed at how much we could communicate using gestures and facial expressions. We also purchased a picture dictionary for Vietnamese and English. If we got stuck, we could point to the pictures, and he could show us things as well. Our nine-year-old son could read and write, so the few times we really had trouble understanding each other, he wrote down what he was trying to say and we looked it up in the dictionary. Our attempts to use Vietnamese were initially met with much laughter, but he quickly became used to our odd pronunciations and could understand what we were trying to say. By the time we adopted our second son, my basic Vietnamese language skills had improved enough to carry on conversations about the day-to-day needs of the family. More detailed discussions, however, posed some problem.

Some kids become agitated and frustrated when they need to talk with you and can't. It is difficult to experience such profound changes in your life and then not be able to communicate your feelings and needs. Liam says his son, Colin, eleven at the time of his arrival, "is a very independent, very sensitive soul and he was trapped in a language he couldn't speak." Colin's frustration sparked continual temper tantrums for months after his arrival. Parents often have to experience something similar to fully appreciate what it feels like to be unable to communicate. If you travel to another country to pick up your child, you'll experience some anxiety and confusion being surrounded by people you can't understand. Even if you don't travel, you can get a taste of this feeling by visiting a restaurant in an ethnic neighborhood. Take the time to remember what that feels like and then think about the fact that you knew the situation was only temporary. Your child doesn't have that assurance.

Many families find it helpful to have on hand a local person who speaks their child's language. Having a willing translator can make a tremendous difference with a grieving child who can't tell you what she's thinking or feeling. You can find someone to translate for you by contacting local community clubs, churches, or universities. You may also gain access to community functions and local families by doing so, giving you a base to build links to your child's cultural origins.

Your child will likely begin understanding what she hears before she begins to speak the language herself, so don't assume you can talk about her in her presence. Olivia and her husband adopted three children. One of their children later told them, "I could hear you guys. I knew what you were saying, but I couldn't come back with what I wanted to say!" Another common mistake is talking louder in an attempt to be understood. You've probably seen this happen and found it quite amusing. At foolish as it is, you may find yourself doing it.

Sometimes parents err in the other direction, assuming that their child understands what they are saying. This is particularly true regarding behavioral problems, especially after the child has been home for several weeks. If your child is repeating a behavior, make sure he truly understands what you expect before you discipline for it. We have found that it is confusing for children to hear words like "can" and "can't" that have opposite meanings. They may be unable to tell the difference and do exactly what you don't want them to do.

My husband and I often resorted to "pidgin" English when our sons arrived, leaving out all the unnecessary words. We would say, "No do that!" and then laugh at ourselves. It served a purpose, however, as our kids would often get stuck on the unimportant words in a sentence and miss the point. "Please stop that right now" has too many distracting words; "stop" will do fine. If you choose to use "pidgin," be careful that you don't start a habit that will be hard to break. These allowances definitely have their place in the beginning, but they can hamper the child's language skills if they last for more than a few months.

Kids pick up on our cliches much faster and it won't be long before you find out what things you say repeatedly. "Just a minute" was one phrase that my kids picked up on immediately. The early language attempts can produce funny sayings that will later be warm memories. Marcus recalls, "I still remember Macy's 'How 'bout this?' as she flipped through the TV channels, looked for a spot on the beach, or reached for a dish of food, and Raynah would refuse some food she didn't want with, 'No, how 'bout this!'"

We have many confusing expressions in English. I went to school with an exchange student from Finland. One day we were playing football and the ball was flying straight for his head, unseen. Someone yelled, "Duck!" and he looked around and said, "Where?" The ball hit him full force while he was looking for a duck. Idioms like "killing two birds with one stone" will also puzzle our children. We often don't realize how often we say things like this until our children point them out. There are also nuances of word usage to worry about. Gail says, "My pet name for Shane is 'buddy.' I had told him it means 'friend' so he wanted to call everyone that, including adults."

Kids pick up sayings quickly, and you need to be careful what you let them watch on television—not to mention being careful about your own language. Many newly adopted kids have let loose with embarrassing obscenities or profanities, although they have no idea what they are saying.

It also seems that being around other kids speeds up language acquisition. Kids are more comfortable with other kids and may find it less embarrassing to make mistakes or practice with their peers. On the other hand, children can be cruel and some kids are teased unmercifully for their accents or grammatical errors.

Most kids gain functional fluency, the everyday use of language, in the first year or so. If your child is five or older, she will learn more quickly if she was functionally fluent in her original language. Many children who speak English as their first language still have pronunciation difficulties when they begin school. It's helpful to know what's expected of other children at your child's age. A good child development handbook or a discussion with a speech teacher may help.

You can help your child gain functional fluency in many ways. The easiest way is to explain in detail what you are doing, using words over and over again. For example, you might say, "Do you want a drink? Let's get a glass. I'll pour your milk into this glass. When you are finished, put your glass in the sink." Parents often do this naturally with toddlers, but may not think to do it with older kids. It also helps to explain the function of something or to examine it closely. Allison does this with her daughter Emily, who has some language acquisition difficulties. She says, "We were taking a walk and I said, 'Let's go around the corner' and she said, 'What's a corner?' So, we walked it, touched it, found fifteen more corners. We learned as much as we could about it. It helps memory."

You may need professional help if your child is having great difficulty acquiring functional fluency. In some cases, this can be a sign of a learning disability or prenatal drug and alcohol exposure. Keep in mind, however, that children learn at different speeds. If you have ever tried to learn a new language, you know how difficult it can be. Don't assume your child is being stubborn or lazy just because he can't remember a word today that he knew yesterday. We all have that problem.

Allison, an adoptive mom who's also a specialist in linguistics, says, "The 'experts' say it takes nine times to commit to memory a concept, but there is no magic number. There are differences between children. With Tyler it's one and a half times, with Emily it's three thousand six hundred and twelve!"

It takes a long time for children to learn the grammar of a new language. Some families try to teach good grammar from the beginning, believing that it will be easier that way, while others wait until their child has strong functional fluency. There are arguments for either approach, and only you can decide what is best. If your son is afraid of making mistakes or is overly shy, correcting his grammar may embarrass him into silence. On the other hand, language habits are hard to break once they're set.

English has more connectives than many other languages. For example, the sentence "We are going to the store" may be expressed simply as "We go store" in another language. Some languages don't have different word endings for plurals, using numbers beforehand as adjectives only. Children who are used to speaking a bare-bones language may have trouble picking up the subtleties. In our family, the helping verbs and articles, such as "is" and "the," posed huge problems. One day I sent my son to get his blue pants. He returned and asked, "Is this pant you talk about?" The first one hundred times it is charming; after that you may begin looking for the nearest wall to bang your head against. Try to be patient. This, too, shall pass if you keep working on it. Today my son speaks proper English most of the time.

There is a vast difference between functional fluency and academic fluency, which is required for a child to learn in a language. Most experts say it takes five to ten years for an older child to gain full academic fluency—that is, to have the same level of fluency and knowledge as his peers. Kids may seem deceptively fluent early on but may still have a lot of trouble in school. Teachers and parents often expect children to do more than they are capable of.

ESL (English as a Second Language)

In most communities today, there are numerous choices for ESL (English as a Second Language) students. There are public, private, and home schools. Some schools offer full-time ESL services; others rely mainly on full immersion into an English-speaking classroom, with ESL help on the side. If your public school does not offer ESL services, you may be able to force school officials to meet your child's needs through the special education services. The choice between ESL classes and full immersion is a difficult one for many families. Most families I spoke with feel that the child learns English much more quickly if he's fully immersed in it. They also think their kids have better self-esteem and social skills from being in a regular classroom.

Colleen says, "[Our kids] were in ESL the first year but it was very limited amounts of information, just a very, very basic thing that we were already teaching them at home or they had already learned at home. ... They missed things in the regular classroom. They were exempted from social studies, which we felt was way more important for them than the ESL."

On the other hand, the Jones family had a wonderful experience with their full-time ESL program. Maxine says, "They [the ESL personnel] were personable and loving. They made home visits so they made sure they communicated with the parents. There were a lot of Vietnamese kids there so [our kids] liked that. They held them until they were ready to go into a regular class and then they entered a class in that school."

For many families a combination of the two works best. No program is without its problems. Even schools with well-established programs may have had little experience with older adopted children. Brent, father of two sons from India, says, "Working with the school has been a problem ... most of their experience with ESL was with the kids of grad students and university professors. They don't have as much of the cultural deprivation and are often bilingual, too." Brent says one of the neighbor children skipped a grade after she learned English, and he feels the difference in circumstances makes a huge difference.

Some families find that a combination of resource classes for reading and speech classes works well for improving language understanding and development. Others report, however, that their resource classes consisted of computer games, which did not help their child learn language. Language resources and programs can be negotiated in an IEP [Individualized Education Program] for each child.

Some teachers expect way too much of new English speakers, and spend little time trying to meet the child's needs. Brent says he had no problem with his son doing the same types of assignments as the other students. In fact, he felt that was preferable to being singled out. At the same time, he feels the school should have made more effort to work with his son. "I don't think the teacher had ever [studied] a foreign language before and didn't make any effort to understand where he came from," he says. "Some of the ways he pronounces words make sense, but the school didn't even think about the fact that his language may have had sounds that we don't use, and we use sounds that he didn't use. The teacher says things like 'We've done these words a hundred times and he just doesn't remember them,' but I think that if you take any one of those kids in the class and do to them what happened to him that they're not going to do better. I just don't see it. One of the things that came out of the principal and ESL teacher's mouths was 'Well, we don't really know for sure whether or not he had any brain damage.'"

Nancy has the opposite problem with her son's teacher. The school tends to coddle her son and expect nothing from him academically or behaviorally. "He got in trouble for making an obscene gesture at the music teacher and his teacher calls me and says she doesn't know what to do with him," says Nancy. "I said, 'Look, Mary, if he is Americanized enough to be giving the teacher the finger, he is Americanized enough to be getting in trouble in school!' "

Cultural issues also pop up at school. The whole culture of the American school system—what to call the teacher, when to raise your hand, standing in lines at lunch and for using the bathroom—poses problems for many kids. Deanna says, "If you don't eat sandwiches, what do you take in a lunchbox? Aaron has developed lunches that consist largely of fruit and Cajun pickles. He experimented with hard-boiled eggs but the reaction from his classmates was apparently so offensive that he no longer takes them. Aaron *only* drinks water that has been refrigerated and it took several attempts at buying school lunches to convince the cafeteria staff that he would not dehydrate if he refused to take either milk or juice. All of the issues of what to take or buy for school lunch are compounded by Aaron explaining, 'In Vietnam, 11 o'clock, school done. Go home to eat.' He had never heard anything so silly as eating lunch at school."

Regardless of which school or programs you choose, you'll probably end up supplementing your child's education with at-home activities. You may have to go all the way back to pre-school level for some concepts, to make up for your child's lack of cultural knowledge. Many countries teach children by rote memorization, and children who can multiply may have no idea what five times seven really means. Tutoring programs may also help your child gain academic fluency.

Some families have successfully used after-school learning or tutoring programs. Public schools often offer after-school programs. Colleen says an after-school tutoring program works well for her son, Colin. He can get his homework done without the distractions he encounters at home, and there's a teacher available to help him.

School Choice

You will have to choose whether to send your child to a public or a private school, or to homeschool. There are benefits and drawbacks to each choice.

Many adoptive families teach their new children at home. They cite numerous reasons, including more family time, one-on-one attention, individualized programs, and the lack of negative outside experiences. Allison says, "It wasn't until I began homeschooling that Shawn and I agreed we could do an older child adoption. We knew our kids would come with many issues. The difference in our home and family with homeschooling and having a full-time mom is incredible, even for our birthchildren. How long is it going to take for my children to learn how to be in a family after all their years without one? I knew we needed the time together."

Tara has taught both of her older adopted children at home. She thinks the extra attention helped her son learn to read more quickly. He began reading on grade level within seven months.

Homeschooling also has drawbacks, especially in families where there are few or no other children. Talking with other children speeds up language acquisition, and if you choose to homeschool your child, you may need to enroll her in activities that will encourage her language acquisition and social skills. Some families find the initial adjustment period too difficult to consider homeschooling at that time. The intensity of the relationship is not comfortable for either parents or kids. Too, many kids like going to school. Brent says of his son Austin, "I think for him being with a lot of people is an advantage—it's more what he is comfortable with."

Some families choose private schools. "We enrolled Rachel in the private school because the classes are small—there are only 120 students in the whole school. She gets a lot of personal attention and there are a lot of foreign students there. The teachers love her and she is on the honor roll. It has been difficult, she's had to work hard, but it is worth it," says Maxine.

Most children adopted at an older age attend public schools. The largest advantage that public school systems offer is the availability of special-needs programs. Depending on the local community, public schools may include a more ethnically diverse student population than many private schools. And, of course, they're the only choice if you work outside the home and cannot afford private school tuition.

What Grade?

Whether your child was adopted domestically or internationally, you may face the dilemma of what grade to place her in. Many children who are adopted at older ages have experienced multiple moves, often in the same year. Some children have never attended school. Many are considerably behind their peers academically. For the most part, school professionals believe it's in the child's best interests to place her in the grade that's appropriate for her age, and provide the extra assistance needed.

Children who are considerably older than their classmates may be teased for being behind. On the other hand, children who are not on the same academic level as their classmates may be ostracized. Neither placement seems to be better than the other in this regard. For some international adoptees, the question of grade placement is muddied by the fact that their true ages are unknown. Meredith's daughter, who was nine on paper at the time of her adoption, was considerably behind academically. Meredith placed her in second grade, but was upset when Brianna began to sexually develop the same year.

For many students, the question of grade placement rises year after year. As it can take years to attain academic fluency, many schools pressure parents to keep their children back if they test under grade level. This raises the question of what social repercussions there would be by changing classmates and what progress the child will be able to make by staying in the same grade another year. Often, the delays can be addressed with resource classes or language assistance, and many parents choose to let their children progress. This obviously has to be a case-by-case decision.

Brent says that every year, Austin's school raises the possibility of holding his son back a grade, but Brent resists the idea. He feels there's no guarantee holding Austin back would help him get up to grade level, and his son is already getting plenty of extra help: an aide, speech programs, ESL, and after-school tutoring. Austin also is very social and popular with friends in his class. "He has made some tremendous gains, up to two years or more in the past year. It seems like a punishment to hold him back when he has tried so hard," says Brent.

Ongoing emotional or behavioral problems also can affect grade placement. Nicole says, "We have a complicated kid and some of it is emotional from his past, I'm sure. Academically he is doing fine; socially I will be surprised if he makes it through the year without getting kicked out. It is something we are working with, but unfortunately we keep running into teachers running out of patience before the change can be made that needs to be made." For many children, their behavior is their biggest challenge, and special-education classes may relieve them of the pressure of being in a mainstream classroom. Often, too, regular classroom teachers are not trained to handle special situations, or simply do not have the time to deal extensively with one child's problems.

One mother whose son has autism says, "Based on my experiences and those of my friends, the teachers are not prepared to handle the challenges of our kids, and while it would be great for things to change, my kid is not going to be the guinea pig while they try to get a clue."

Many families choose to have voluntary academic testing done to determine the child's grade level. Public schools are required to do this with good cause, but many families have to fight to get testing done. If your school has a long waiting list for testing, you may wish to have an independent counselor or tester do it. Private testing is expensive, but you may get better feedback as to what would work well for your child and what services to request from the school. If your child does not speak fluent English, it may be difficult to test her. Most standardized tests require language and cultural competence. Your child will likely have to undergo nontraditional testing.

The one constant theme among the families I talked with is that you *must* play an active role in your child's education. You need to actively monitor his placement, academic progress, and classroom experiences in order to make appropriate decisions for him. When it comes right down to it, all of these decisions should be based on the individual child, not on theory.

Nancy says, "My son needed to start at first grade in reading, even though he was in a second-grade room. So I asked that he be sent to first grade. What dismayed me was that the teacher had no idea that she had a non-English-speaking kid coming into her classroom! I had to ask for a meeting for all of us to get together to discuss it. I couldn't believe that they didn't do this automatically." You have to become your child's best advocate because no one else will put her interests first.

Dealing with your local school system can be time-consuming and frustrating. In order to be a strong advocate for your child, you should become familiar with the laws that affect the availability of special services and what your rights are under those laws. To find out what services are available to you, call your school board and ask for information on Section 504 regulations and services available for special needs. If you feel that your school is not being honest about what is available, talk with other parents and teachers. Some parents feel that schools do everything they can to limit the number of services your child receives. Education professionals counter that getting a child certified as disabled is not as easy as parents believe.

IEPs (Individualized Education Programs)

Each child who receives special ed services is required to have an IEP (Individualized Education Program). The IEP is a written statement of an educational program designed to meet your child's needs. The IEP usually covers your child's strengths and weaknesses, educational goals, and services to be provided. The IEP is written jointly with parents, teachers, administrators, counselors, and sometimes the child. Before you sign it, make sure you understand what is being stated, and review the document for errors. The IEP should include short-term goals that can be measured. If the IEP is written before you arrive, it is not the joint document it is intended to be and you should insist upon a new document including your input and recommendations.

Although IEPs and special ed programs are intended to meet the child's needs, parents often wind up at odds with the school over how the plan is implemented. Many experienced parents feel that the school's desire to place children in the least restrictive environment is really a disservice to challenged kids. Parents also have to deal with school personnel who do not take IEPs seriously. Trina says, "The teachers didn't even *read* his IEP until we had a meeting in December—like a 17-page IEP shouldn't have tipped them off? We wrote a whole new plan and then when Christmas was over the teacher in charge of his program had been transferred so nobody was available to *implement* the plan." Trina moved her son to a school for disabled children.

Some parents find that befriending your child's teacher by volunteering at the school is a useful way to get to know staff,

❖ Dealing With Your Child's School ❖

Donate supplies, volunteer, join the PTA, attend board meetings.

Dress for success. Act like a professional.

Give a copy of your child's IEP to her teacher on the first day of school. Don't just assume a teacher has read it.

Set up a time to discuss your child's diagnoses with her teacher(s), including art, music, and physical education; counselors; the principal, and the school nurse. School professionals may not be familiar with difficulties such as fetal alcohol syndrome.

If you feel your child needs a special program or school, then find it and fight for it.

If your family has special needs, then be able to discuss chapter and verse of the special ed law, the Americans with Disabilities Act, Medicaid and its applicable payments to the school system, and who does what in your local school system.

Schedule twice-monthly meetings with teachers, counselors, aides, and principals, and prepare an agenda.

If you make a request, no matter how small, be assertive and back it up with logic and a quote from an expert or two.

Learn the "Silent Smile." State your request and then smile and say nothing more. The silence will eventually be filled and you may get a positive response.

Use body language. Dig in your heels if someone tries to move closer and closer to intimidate you. Use direct eye contact.

Repeat yourself. The other person will soon feel like giving you anything to get rid of you! For example, "I really need that IEP meeting this week…" "Yes, I realize that, but I really need that IEP meeting this week…" "How difficult for you, but I really need that IEP meeting this week…"

Take someone along. Emotional involvement can block your ears.

Keep a written record of conversations and meetings with school personnel. Keep copies of notes from the teacher, resource lists from the counselor and anything that you write to the school.

Think of a positive action that the teacher or principal has taken and send a thank-you note.

If all else fails, you can try the favorite tactic of one parent. She hands school personnel her phone number—on the back of her lawyer's business card.

—from Adoptive Families Together

but experienced parents also point out that you may have to become less friendly and more businesslike to achieve your goals. If you feel that your child needs services that she is not getting or that the school isn't cooperating, you may have to take an assertive stance.

School and Adoption Issues

Sometimes it's the everyday problems of school that weigh a family down. The daily separations are hard for some children who have strong feelings of loss and abandonment. Peer relationships can be difficult for kids who are seen as different. On top of it all, schools often aggravate the situation with assignments that highlight the differences of our families, and raise strong issues of pain and shame for our kids.

One assignment that can create difficulty is the family tree. The biological connections to family trees are often emphasized, making our children feel like "frauds" for completing it with the adoptive family's information, or bringing up their sadness at having little to no birthfamily information. Many schools require this assignment, so be prepared. Parents offer these suggestions:

❖ Ask the teacher to stress that there are many different types of families and that all are appropriate. Kids with divorced parents, stepparents, and others have similar problems with family trees.

❖ Distinguish between genealogy and the importance of blood ties, and family history which affects all members of a family. For example, the place your ancestors settled in may have affected the type of work they did.

❖ Allow your child to include birthfamily history if she would like to. Some kids draw a tree with different branches representing the adoptive and birth families. Others use wheels or other symbols instead of trees.

Not all adopted children have difficulty with this assignment. Many children simply assume they belong on the adoptive family's tree and spend little time worrying about it.

Other assignments and activities can upset adopted children, too. Discussions about genetics and DNA are difficult for adolescents, many children do not have baby pictures to share, and activities with a family emphasis, such as Mother's Day or Father's Day or parent/child events, can renew feelings of loss and shame.

Sometimes vocabulary can unexpectedly trigger inappropriate behavior. Marlene, adoption educator, asks, "Wouldn't it make sense for a kid to be sitting in a classroom and begin staring out the window if the teacher just mentioned 'the father of our country?' 'Father, hmm … I wonder about *my* father.'"

In her book *The Family of Adoption*, Joyce Maguire Pavao tells of a young boy who was having difficulties in school. He was getting help for severe learning disabilities and had behavioral and social problems as well. She writes, "One day, I was playing blocks with him, trying to get him to do a little bit of math indirectly, when he burst into tears and said, 'I can't do subtraction. As soon as they say "take away," it makes me feel really sad.' I understood that Tony's losses had blocked him from doing math from the moment 'taking away' became part of it. He wasn't going to learn in a class that was about loss."

Indeed, school is full of potentially pain-producing words. Math classes move from subtracting to dividing and then to fractions or pieces of a whole. Kids are taught to group math problems and spelling words together into families because they look alike or fit together. And multicultural curriculums can raise uncomfortable questions for transracial adoptees, especially if everyone in the class assumes that your daughter from Colombia knows all about South American history. Many schools have adopt-an-almost-anything promotions from time to time. In addition, some children have difficulties when they begin changing classes during the day, notably during adolescence. The motion of packing up all your stuff and "moving" somewhere else has negative connotations to our kids.

You cannot protect your child from the world, of course. However, the more familiar you are with problem areas and with what your child is doing in school, the better you'll understand what may be causing emotional or behavioral disturbances. If your daughter is acting out of character, ask some pointed questions about school assignments. You may be able to prod her to talk by saying, "Many adopted kids have trouble with school assignments that make them think of their birthfamilies or past lives. Has this ever happened to you?" Most kids will talk when they think that their listener understands them.

Great Expectations

School remains a problem for many older adopted children. Their loss of time and continuity in the classroom can result in delays that are never overcome. Emotional and behavioral problems may further inhibit academic progress. Many children lack the attention necessary to be a successful student because their focus is elsewhere. We may be frustrated that our children do not meet our academic expectations. Birthfamilies encounter the same obstacles, but there is an added component for adoptive families—the effects of the past. Accepting, and helping your children to accept, their limitations can be difficult. You may have dreamed that your son would get a master's degree, but he may be content with a job at the local fast-food restaurant. The daughter you'd envisioned in medical school may decide to move in with her jobless boyfriend at eighteen.

Explore the reasons that you feel so strongly one way or the other about his life choices. If attending college is *your* dream but not your son's, you may be inviting rebellion. Sometimes, parents feel the need for their children to succeed for them to feel successful as parents. Other parents truly believe that a college degree is essential in life. Try to keep in mind that our world runs on working service professions. Very few people in the world are college-educated and our society would not last if the people who perform service-oriented jobs weren't there. Spend some time observing the people you interact with in your daily life. How many of them are blue-collar working folks who make your life run smoothly and more happily?

We all want what is best for our children, but often the only person who can define "best" is the child himself. After a discussion on this topic, the consensus of experienced adoptive parents is that our job is to encourage, offer help and resources, and let our kids be, to explore who they want to become.

❖ 11 ❖

An 'Alphabet Soup' of Diagnoses

Reactive attachment disorder, fetal alcohol syndrome, sensory integration disorder, posttraumatic stress disorder, bipolar illness. Diagnoses like these strike fear in the heart of parents. Many of our children have experienced sexual abuse, have eating disorders, or are diagnosed with attention deficit hyperactivity disorder. As they visit one therapist after another, some troubled children end up with a virtual "alphabet soup" of diagnoses after their name—PTSD, FAS, ADD, SID, RAD.

In recent years, there has been an explosion of information about the emotional and behavioral difficulties adopted children can have. This glut has been good and bad—good because prepared parents make better decisions, and bad because people who have only a little information may jump to erroneous conclusions. Most of the information available is about reactive attachment disorder (RAD), which has come to the attention of many professionals in the past few years. Other disabilities can look remarkably like RAD, and even professionals may diagnose RAD without fully exploring the possibilities. I am including information about several diagnoses in this chapter to provide parents with a range of possibilities regarding their child's disabilities, and to provide resources that can help them help their children.

Reactive Attachment Disorder

According to professionals, attachment between a child and a primary caregiver, usually the mother, must occur in infancy. A helpless infant feels a need, then expresses it, and the parent meets it. For example, a baby grows hungry, cries, and the mother responds with food, calming the child. This cycle of attachment encourages the child to trust other people to fulfill his needs while building love, affection, security, and reciprocation. If a child's needs are not met and he is allowed to cry continuously, he learns to soothe himself and does not form an attachment to a primary caretaker. Likewise, children who are abused or neglected never know what kind of response they will get from parents, resulting in an anxious attachment.

A break in the attachment cycle can occur for many reasons, such as abuse, neglect, repeated illnesses that cause pain a parent cannot alleviate, maternal depression, or breaks in the continuity of care, such as those experienced by many children in foster care. A child who has a strong bond but is then separated from his primary caregiver and moved several times may lose his ability to attach. Some professionals think attachment can be transferred up to four or five times; others believe that estimate is too optimistic. The personality and individual resiliency of the child seem to play a major role. Some parents who have adopted birthsiblings from similar circumstances have found that one has serious attachment difficulties while the other bonds easily to his new family.

One common misconception is that the risk of attachment problems rises proportionately with the age of the child at adoption. This is not necessarily the case. If an older child formed a strong attachment to a primary caregiver in infancy and remained in his birthfamily or with one foster family for several years before being adopted, he may have less chance of RAD than a baby or toddler who has spent the first nine months to two years in an orphanage or a series of foster homes and who never forms a primary attachment. What is true is that most older children have likely been abused and/or neglected either before or after their relinquishment. Their risk of attachment difficulties depends on the strength of their initial attachments and their individual circumstances and personality.

The quality of care in the institution or foster homes that your child was in plays a large part in his ability to carry forward an early attachment. In orphanages with minimal staff and few toys or one-on-one interactions, the child will learn to depend mostly on himself to meet his needs. Repeated moves can make children exceptionally fearful of trusting and loving anyone again. It's important to get as much information as you can about your child's early years.

Many object to the term "disorder," believing that RAD is not a mental illness, but a logical, sensible reaction to abuse and neglect. Whatever you believe, RAD can seriously disrupt the whole family.

You should realize that virtually every child adopted at an older age shows at least one or two signs of attachment disorder on arrival. True RAD, however, has to include many of the generally recognized symptoms and a pattern of behavior over time. Many adoption professionals suggest that parents wait six months to a year after arrival before even considering the possibility their child may have attachment disorder, since many behaviors that look like attachment difficulties are simply normal adjustment.

When our son Connor arrived, he began to show a sign that

❖ Signs of Attachment Disorder ❖

Lack of ability to give and receive genuine affection

Destructive behavior (to self, property, and others)

Cruelty to animals

Phoniness or superficially engaging and charming behavior

Lack of eye contact on parental terms

Chronic lying in the face of the obvious

Extreme need for control

Inability to form long-term friendships

Preoccupation with fire, blood, and gore

Indiscriminate affection with strangers

Little or no understanding of cause and effect

Lack of empathy, compassion, or remorse

Behavioral and academic problems at school

Toileting issues

Speech problems

Parents who appear angry or hostile

could have been worrisome. Wherever we'd go, he would go up to our friends, who were strangers to him, and hug everybody. One of the ten signs of RAD is indiscriminate affection with strangers. So, was it RAD? We didn't think so, for many reasons. He didn't display any of the other signs. He was quite attentive and attached to us as well, and he always kept an eye on us to make sure we didn't leave him. He knew exactly who his family was and he was not eager to go home with anyone else. We saw it more as an indication of an outgoing, loving personality and as a product of his Vietnamese culture, where children are adored and fussed over by all. In time, we were able to help him set some limits, and he became more discriminating in his affection. We also knew that attachment grows in degrees. It does take time for children to trust the new adults in their lives.

Even true attachment disorder occurs on a continuum. Some children set fires and torture animals, while others show only milder symptoms, such as lack of eye contact. Even mild attachment difficulties can be difficult to deal with.

Nancy adopted seven-year-old Haley from the U.S. foster care system. Haley had eleven siblings who had all been removed from their mother's care. For some reason, Haley had fallen through the cracks. She was finally removed from her mother and sent to live with her birthfather. However, the social service agency did not check on her father, and it turned out he was living in a homeless shelter. He handed her over to the man who ran the mission, who then sent her to live with a couple interested in adoption. Her birthfather had unsupervised visitation and sexually abused her. The new adoptive mother was mentally unstable and erratic in her care of Haley. When the couple had a baby, they decided they could not care for Haley anymore. She responded to the news that she was leaving by trying to kill the baby. Nancy was told this, but knowing nothing about RAD at the time, assumed it was just extreme jealousy by a hurt child. Unbelievably, the same social service department that knew of Haley's attempt to kill the baby placed a newborn with Nancy two months after Haley's arrival!

Nancy noticed that Haley had problems from the beginning. On her first day home, she called Nancy "Mommy" and told her that she loved her. Haley could not play with toys and could handle only a small number of possessions without losing control. She ate raw meat from the garbage can. She was destructive. One night she stuffed a roll of toilet paper in the toilet, flooded the bathroom, waited until the floor was covered with water, and finally told her mother that the toilet was overflowing—as water started to pour through the dining room ceiling. When she wanted to make her mother battle her, she would escalate her behavior continually. She always saved the trump card, trying to hurt the baby, for last. Finally, Haley abused her brother, and Nancy had to place her in residential treatment.

One day fifteen-year-old Haley attended a conference with Nancy about attachment difficulties. The speaker was saying that people with RAD should not be held accountable for their actions. Haley confronted him and said, "You're wrong. I absolutely know what I do is right or wrong. I just don't care."

Shannon, adopted from Russia at age four, shows mild signs of attachment difficulties. She has thrown a ball with full force at the family dog when she was angry. She shows some indiscriminate affection, telling strangers, "I'm going home with you." However, she shows appropriate affection with her family. Her mother Janet says, "There are a number of things we know we have to work on with her. We think she has a smattering of attachment disorder." Although Shannon is at risk for developing additional difficulties as she grows older, she is making considerable progress in her home, showing her anger in an appropriate way and bonding to her family. Her family is hopeful that she'll continue to do well.

For many years, children with RAD have been misdiagnosed as having attention deficit disorder or other maladies. Often, several different therapists, unfamiliar with attachment and adoption issues, will fail to recognize the signs of RAD in a child. On the other hand, recent publicity about RAD has resulted in children with other problems, such as sensory integration disorder or bipolar disorder, being misdiagnosed as having attachment disorder. If you think your child may be suffering from RAD, seek a qualified therapist. Reading accounts of RAD (see Appendix C) may also help.

There are various treatments for attachment difficulties. Many consider the Institute for Attachment and Child Development in Colorado the center of attachment therapy. It offers extensive programs to deal with attachment-disordered children. Children with mild difficulties may benefit from play therapies. Most therapies for children have both proponents and detractors. Research attachment difficulties in depth and then make the most comfortable decision for your family.

Attention Deficit Disorder

Attention deficit disorder (ADD) is generally characterized by an inability to concentrate, weak impulse control, and in some cases hyperactivity. What most people call ADD is most likely attention deficit hyperactivity disorder (ADHD)—that is, the child is significantly hyperactive as well as unable to concentrate. ADD without hyperactivity is also common, although kids who have it are less likely to be diagnosed at an early age.

❖ **Signs of ADHD** ❖

Squirms or fidgets excessively

Has difficulty remaining seated

Is easily distracted

Has difficulty following directions

Has difficulty finishing projects

Talks excessively

Interrupts or blurts out answers in class

Loses things

Engages in dangerous activities

Children with ADHD generally do not function up to their ability level in school and often have behavioral problems. They often can't engage in activities that don't interest them because they don't remain focused. They may have trouble learning to read because they can't concentrate well enough to see the patterns of words, or to stick with it long enough to feel some success. Kids with ADHD are often frustrated and angry, and have low self-esteem.

Researchers don't really know what causes ADHD. Some theorize that it may result from head trauma before, during, or after birth, or be caused by brain damage from toxins, bacteria, or viral infections. Some people believe that food allergies or food preservatives and additives can aggravate ADHD symptoms. There is a very strong genetic component to ADHD. Some sources indicate that as many as seventy percent of children with ADHD have a relative with the disorder. ADHD tends to appear in clusters with other disorders such as Tourette's syndrome, learning disabilities, fetal alcohol syndrome, developmental delays, obsessive compulsive disorder, and depression.

Attention deficit disorder has become an increasingly common diagnosis among children, adopted or not, in recent years. Researchers think three to five percent of the general population has ADHD. Adopted children tend to have much higher incidences of ADHD. Theories, but no conclusions, abound on the reason for the higher incidence among adopted children. Some experts think that the genetic component of ADHD likely means that many birthparents of adopted children have ADHD and tend to act impulsively, leading them to more unwanted pregnancies. Others feel that children with ADHD are more difficult to parent and thus more likely to be abused and, eventually, taken into the foster care system. It should also be noted that many symptoms of ADHD are similar to the behaviors experienced in grieving children: lack of concentration, giddiness, losing things, and so on. It's possible that children who have experienced multiple losses remain stuck in their pain and grieving, and do not actually have ADHD. Other children who are diagnosed with ADHD may, in fact, have bipolar disorder or sensory integration disorder.

Before diagnosing a child with ADHD, a physician should rule out physical causes of neurological problems. Because ADHD coexists with and mimics other disorders, a full evaluation should include assessments of the child's medical, neurological, behavioral, and educational functioning. Parents and teachers should be required to fill out an assessment form for behaviors. Educational testing should be performed to measure the child's IQ, reasoning abilities, language skills, and hearing and vision. Be leery of a doctor who prescribes medication for ADHD without doing the appropriate testing. Although no conclusive test exists to diagnose ADHD, much can be determined by the above tests.

Living with a child with ADHD can be difficult. Amy says, "Nicholas was always buzzing around the room, touching things and dropping them, and couldn't watch an entire half hour of TV. He could not play normally, or have friendships with other kids. He was in a self-contained special ed class because he could not focus on anything."

On the other hand, some kids with ADHD are enormously creative. Kerri says her eleven-year-old son, Jonah, is academically and musically gifted and has ADHD. "This makes for an interesting combination. He talks continually but sounds like an encyclopedia, does excellent work in school but then forgets to turn it in, and plays the piano beautifully but pitches a fit when he's told to practice. He's impulsive, argumentative, forgetful, affectionate, empathetic and, over all, a very neat kid."

Physicians and parents often use a multi-dimensional approach, including medication, behavior modification, psychotherapy, and academic accommodations, to treat ADHD.

The use of stimulant medications, such as Ritalin, on children with ADHD is controversial. Some families avoid the use of medication, concentrating on behavioral and academic interventions. Other parents have found medication to be extremely

---

❖ Helping the Student With ADD ❖

Schools can make accommodations for students with ADD that make a considerable difference in academic success. Examples of things they might try:

Allow extra time to complete assigned work

Use a timer

Break long assignments into smaller parts

Pair written instructions with oral instructions

Seat student in a quiet area or near a student who can serve as a good role model

Ignore minor, inappropriate behavior

Praise good behavior instead of correcting negative behavior

Allow student to stand at times while working

Provide short breaks between assignments

useful, likening their children's need for it to a diabetic's need for insulin.

"The first day [Nicholas took Ritalin] was the first time he ever played normally," says Amy, his mother. "He built something with blocks! He had never, ever done that before in his life. I cried when I saw what he was capable of." Her son is now in a regular classroom.

There are many books and Web sites available about ADHD and its treatments, with pros and cons; see Appendix C. If you aren't sure your child really does have ADHD, consult your doctor, especially if the medication is not working.

Sexual Abuse

Child sexual abuse is rampant in the world today. It is estimated that as many as one out of every four girls and one out of every six boys is a victim of sexual abuse. Most children are abused by someone they know, such as a family member or friend. Children in group homes, orphanages, or foster homes may be abused by other children.

> ### ❖ Signs of Sexual Abuse ❖
>
> Fear or dislike of certain people or places (often bathrooms or bedrooms)
>
> Sleep disturbances
>
> Excessive bathing or poor hygiene
>
> Constipation or bedwetting
>
> Stomachaches and headaches without medical cause
>
> Irritation, pain, or injury in the genital area
>
> Regression
>
> Depression
>
> Self-destructive behavior
>
> Drug or alcohol problems
>
> Nervous, aggressive, hostile, or disruptive behavior
>
> Sexual play with other children, toys, or pets
>
> Frequent masturbation
>
> Sexual knowledge beyond what's typical for the child's age

Sexual abuse can consist of sexual touching or fondling, exposure to adult sexual activity or pornography, sexual comments, "peeping" on a child during bathing or dressing, and rape. It does not have to involve physical force.

Sexual abuse victims may blame themselves or believe that the abuse was punishment for being bad. Children are often threatened with harm to themselves or their families if they tell. They may be ashamed of the abuse, especially if it resulted in sexual pleasure for them.

If your child tells you that he has been abused, react calmly. Children often misinterpret anger or anxiety as evidence they have done something wrong. Arrange a medical exam immediately and assure the child that the abuse was not his fault. Seek professional counseling, even if the abuse happened in the past and the child appears to be okay. Many children suppress their feelings of pain and fear. Without counseling, abuse victims may remain depressed or traumatized well into adulthood.

Sexual abuse is often one of the reasons children are removed from their birthfamilies, and kids who have been abused are at higher risk of becoming abusers themselves. If your adopted child abuses younger siblings, you need to get professional help for him and for the abused kids immediately. You will also need to keep your other children safe from further harm.

Eating Disorders

Eating disorders often develop as a way of maintaining control over one's life. There are three recognized eating disorders: anorexia, characterized by significant weight loss from excessive dieting or calorie control; bulimia, characterized by a cycle of binge eating followed by purging; and compulsive overeating, characterized by uncontrollable eating and weight gain. There is evidence that chemical imbalances in the brain cause eating disorders. You may wish to talk to your child's doctor about using antidepressants to help with eating disorders.

Anorexia Nervosa

People with this disorder are often perfectionists who may feel that the only control they have in their lives is in the area of food and weight. They feel powerful when they can control their bodies. Anorexics are often motivated by a strong desire to become thin and may still feel fat when they are dangerously thin. An estimated ten to twenty percent of anorexics will eventually die from related complications. People with anorexia often resist treatment because they do not want to be forced to eat. However, once an anorexic admits a problem and seeks help, treatment incorporating psychological, nutritional, and medical care is often successful. Medical professionals warn against setting up control battles over food with your child. These battles may

---

❖ Signs of Eating Disorders ❖

Anorexia Nervosa

Noticeable weight loss

Excessive exercise

Fatigue, muscle weakness

Excuses for not eating, or unusual eating habits (cutting food into tiny pieces, crumbling food)

Complaining of being too fat even when thin

Restricting food choices

Evidence of vomiting or use of laxatives, diet pills or diuretics

Irregular menstruation or loss of menstruation

Depression, irritability, or mood swings

Fainting spells and dizziness

Pale complexion, skin problems

Shortness of breath and irregular heartbeat

Cold hands and feet

Hair loss

Bulimia Nervosa

Binge eating

Evidence of secretive eating

Bathroom visits after eating

Vomiting

Use of laxatives, diet pills or diuretics

Swollen salivary glands

Broken blood vessels

Mood swings

Severe self-criticism

Tooth decay

Fatigue, muscle weakness

Weight fluctuations

Frequent sore throats

Substance abuse

Compulsive Overeating

Binge eating

Depression

Self-deprecating comments after overeating

Withdrawal from activities because of embarrassment about weight

Frequent dieting

Intense focus on weight and body image

Belief that being thin will make them a better person

actually worsen the problem. Seek professional help as soon as possible if you suspect your child has anorexia.

Bulimia Nervosa

People with bulimia binge on food and then purge it from their bodies by the use of laxatives, diuretics, or vomiting. Bulimics often have low self-esteem and may strive for the approval of others. After a binge, a person with bulimia typically feels extreme self-hatred and disgust. Unlike anorexics, bulimics are aware that they have a problem, but may not seek help. People with bulimia tend to have poor impulse control in other areas of their lives as well, and may abuse drugs or alcohol. The cause of bulimia is unknown, but there may be a genetic component. Treatment involves medical and psychological interventions, often including behavior modification.

Compulsive Overeating

Compulsive overeaters use food as a way to cope with stress, depression, and life conflicts. They are usually aware of the problem. Compulsive overeating often begins in childhood when food is used as a way of coping with stressful situations that are out of the child's control. Some sexual abuse victims gain weight to protect themselves from further abuse, thinking that people will find them unattractive.

If you think your child has an eating disorder, approach the subject carefully. Never try to force your child to eat, which can make the problem worse. Seek professional help for your child and avoid talking about weight and food with him. Assure him of your love and concern. Sometimes hospitalization is needed.

Sensory Integration Disorder

Sensory integration disorder, also called sensory integrative dysfunction, is a difficulty in processing information received through the senses: sight, touch, sound, taste, smell, and awareness of body movement. It results when the brain cannot organize or analyze sensory input. Normally, the brain interprets data received and responds unconsciously; this is called sensory integration. This process does not work well in children with SID.

Many things are thought to contribute to SID, although researchers have reached no consensus. Children who have experienced a lack of sensory input, such as children in orphanages who have had little stimulation or movement, seem to be at particular risk. Other risk factors may include prematurity, autism or other developmental disorders, parental substance abuse, stress-related disorders, and brain injury. Some researchers think that up to seventy percent of children classified as learning disabled may have sensory integration problems.

According to Carol Kranowitz, author of *The Out of Sync Child*, sensory integration disorder often coexists with syndromes such as attention deficit hyperactivity disorder or learning disabilities. Because ADHD and SID show similar symptoms, some children with SID are misdiagnosed as having ADHD. The child with SID may also have auditory language, vision, or speech difficulties. A multi-dimensional approach works well with children with multiple diagnoses.

It's also easy to see how SID can be confused with reactive attachment disorder. Some kids with RAD show a lack of conscience and a tendency to harm animals or young children. A child with SID may do the same thing because the correlation

---

❖ Signs of Sensory Integration Disorder ❖

Over- or undersensitivity to touch, movement, sights or sounds
Tendency to be easily distracted
Social or emotional problems
Unusually high or low activity levels
Physical clumsiness or apparent carelessness
Impulsivity
Poor self-concept
Delays in speech and language development
Delays in motor skills
Difficulty making transitions from one activity to another
Poor academic achievement
—*Sensory Integration International*

between his actions and the results does not always compute. He may not recognize that the cat's hissing and arched back correspond to his pulling of the animal's tail. Therefore, he may repeat the action over and over, leading his parents to wonder if he has a conscience.

If you suspect your child has sensory integration disorder, consult an occupational therapist. The therapist will evaluate your daughter's fine and gross motor skills, and sensory perceptions. If your child is diagnosed with SID, occupational therapy, often in combination with speech or vision therapy, can help her learn to integrate sensory information.

Fetal Alcohol Syndrome

Fetal alcohol syndrome (FAS) is one of the leading causes of mental retardation in the Western world. Some 5,000 children are born each year in the United States with FAS. Thousands more are born with FAS throughout the world. FAS is a cluster of birth defects that result when a woman drinks alcoholic beverages during her pregnancy. Although the exact role that alcohol plays in the development of FAS is not known, researchers suspect it may be caused by acetaldehyde (ACH), which is the primary product when alcohol is metabolized. Fetal malnutrition may be a factor, especially if the mother is undernourished. A lack of oxygen or a disturbance of prostaglandins may also be involved. A person who shows some, but not all, of the signs of FAS is said to have fetal alcohol effect (FAE). An estimated 10,000 to 50,000 children are born each year with some effect of prenatal alcohol exposure. Children with FAS may have facial abnormalities, central nervous system dysfunction, prenatal and postnatal growth deficiencies, minor bone abnormalities, and major organ system malformations.

❖ **Signs of FAS** ❖

Microcephaly (small head size)

Small eyes or short eye openings

Underdevelopment of the upper lip with flat upper lip ridges, thin upper lip, and a flat maxillary (between the nose and upper lip) area

Developmental delay or neurological impairment

Children with FAS have a distinctive look that professionals and informed parents often find easy to spot. Some of the facial characteristics of FAS lessen with time, although most developmental, emotional, and behavioral disabilities do not. If you are browsing photolistings of children available for adoption, you may notice the facial characteristics of children who are identified as having FAS. Many times, the facial abnormalities are present in other children not noted to have FAS. It's a good idea to inquire about possible fetal alcohol effects. Children with FAE do not always have the distinctive facial characteristics of kids with FAS.

The effects of prenatal alcohol exposure range from hearing and visual problems, attention deficits, and memory dysfunction to behavioral problems, impulsiveness, deafness, epilepsy, cerebral palsy, and sociopathic behavior. Children with FAS also tend to have difficulties with sensory integration (SID) and attention deficit hyperactivity disorder (ADHD) as well as oppositional defiance disorder, which is characterized by a pattern of defiant behavior over a period of time, and conduct disorder, which is oppositional defiance disorder with the added component of illegal activity. The broad-ranging effects of FAS can lead to a variety of diagnoses for the child.

Parents report that their children with FAS exhibit mood swings, engage in impulsive behavior, don't accept responsibility, can't focus, and are self-centered, engaging, charismatic, excessively vulnerable to peer pressure, sexually impulsive, and defiant. Parents whose children have milder effects of FAS/E often say the kids can't remember anything taught to them in school and have big difficulties with language and visual processing.

The long-term outlook for people who have FAS is not hopeful. In a study of 473 people on the effects of FAS and FAE, funded by the Centers for Disease Control and Prevention, Dr. Ann Streissguth, a professor of psychiatry from the University of Washington, found the following statistics:

❖ IQs range from 29 to 120 for FAS patients, with a mean of 79. FAE patients have an IQ range of 42 to 142, with a mean IQ of 90. (The mean for the population at large is 100.)

- ❖ Ninety-four percent of the tested group had mental health problems.
- ❖ Forty-three percent of youths had been suspended or expelled from school.
- ❖ Sixty percent of patients twelve and over had been confined for mental health or alcohol and drug problems or had been incarcerated for crime.
- ❖ Forty-five percent of patients over the age of twelve displayed inappropriate sexual behavior.
- ❖ Thirty percent of patients age twelve and over experienced drug and alcohol problems.
- ❖ Eighty percent of adult patients remained in dependent living situations.
- ❖ Eighty percent of adult patients had difficulties with employment.
- ❖ Thirty percent of the females of childbearing age had given birth, forty percent drank during pregnancy, and more than half no longer had their children in their care.

If you suspect that your child may have FAS or FAE, seek out a competent specialist. Ask your physician for a referral to a geneticist. The National Organization of Fetal Alcohol Syndrome (see Appendix C) provides a directory of treatment centers and support groups. Early intervention is crucial in helping a child succeed in life. While serious FAS is often easy to diagnose, milder effects may go undiagnosed for years, leading to school and behavioral problems.

Their difficulties aside, children with FAS often do have the capacity to love their families and friends.

Treatment and therapeutic interventions must focus on all areas of development, not just the child's behavior. A full exam by an occupational therapist and a speech therapist is recommended for optimal learning. The child may also need neurological, psychological, and physical therapy. For many children with FAS, a vocational educational approach, centered on life skills rather than academics, works well. Therapy can help even very young children. Preschool programs that follow individualized education plans are helpful, as are small classroom settings and intensive remedial education. Children with FAS have problems structuring their time, and parents and teachers have to impose external structure. Patricia Tanner-Halverson recommends that people working with FAS/FAE children use structure, consistency, variety, brevity, and persistence. Because of serious attention deficits, it is important to provide only brief explanations or to use other techniques to keep their attention. In addition, parents and helping professionals must be willing to repeat what they want the child to remember over and over again.

The vast array of behavioral, emotional, and intellectual problems common to FAS place heavy demands on the whole family. Children often require constant supervision, daily therapies and continual behavioral modification. If your child has FAS, maintain reasonable expectations and enlist all the resources you can find. On the other hand, you, too, have needs. Find a support network of families dealing with like problems where you will be able to obtain information on treatments, learn from others' experiences, and above all know that you are not alone. Respite care, short-term baby-sitters that allow you time away, may be vital to your well-being.

Bipolar Disorder

Bipolar disorder, once called manic-depressive disorder, occurs in 1 to 5 percent of the population. It's characterized by mood swings resulting in either a manic, or highly active, episode or a depressive episode. Many people cycle rapidly between the two states, making bipolar sometimes difficult to diagnose.

The causes of bipolar disorder are unknown, but there seems to be a strong genetic link. At least one professional who works with adopted children thinks bipolar disorder is often overlooked. Psychiatrist John Alston, a consultant to the Institute for Attachment and Child Development, believes that many children who are diagnosed with ADD in conjunction with reactive attachment disorder actually have bipolar disorder.

In his report on the correlation between bipolar disorder and reactive attachment disorder, Alston proposes that many children being treated for ADD may be bipolar. He writes that four types of parents generally abuse and neglect their children: those with antisocial personality disorder, those with disorders of cognitive perception (such as paranoid schizophrenia), those who abuse alcohol or drugs, and those with bipolar disorder. His experience suggests that parents with bipolar are the most likely to abuse and neglect their children, and that many children with RAD inherit bipolar disorder.

There are strong similarities between ADD and bipolar. Alston maintains that while both are prone to sleep difficulties, children with bipolar are more likely to have nightmares. Children with both disorders have a tendency to throw tantrums, but kids with bipolar tend to rage for prolonged periods and their rage tends to erupt from behavioral limits rather than from overstimulation. Most ADD kids are not considered moody, but bipolar kids are. The misbehavior of ADD kids seems to be more accidental, due to inattentiveness; bipolar kids tend to be more deliberately destructive. Alston recommends that children whose ADD is not improving with medication be assessed for bipolar disorder.

Bipolar disorder is generally treated with a combination of medication, hospitalization, and psychotherapy. Lithium is used

❖ Signs of Bipolar Disorder ❖

A manic episode is characterized by:
Decreased need for sleep
Increased talkativeness
Grandiose ideas or racing thoughts
Inflated self-esteem
Increased activity
Involvement in high-risk activities
Irritability

A depressive episode is characterized by:
Persistent feelings of sadness or despair
Recurring thoughts of suicide
Fatigue and loss of interest in normally pleasurable activities
Difficulty concentrating
Disturbances in sleep or appetite

to successfully treat many bipolar patients. Many repeat episodes occur because the patient does not remain on medication. Psychotherapy teaches the patient to predict his own fluctuations in mood and conveys the need for continuing medication. Hospitalization is sometimes needed if the patient experiences a severe episode, leading to suicidal thoughts or attempts.

A recent study showed that a disturbance in sleep routines might bring on manic episodes. In the study, 65 percent of the patients experienced a manic episode after missing sleep, compared to 20 percent who did not experience sleep disturbances. Periods of high stress can also trigger manic episodes.

Adopted children who have bipolar disorder often aren't diagnosed until adolescence. Because it is often misdiagnosed, children may be treated for depression when they really have bipolar. Some parents report that antidepressant medications brought on their children's bipolar episodes. If you feel there's a chance your child has bipolar disorder, discuss the wisdom of taking certain medications with your doctor. Remember that children who are grieving or experiencing behavior problems related to abuse histories may swing between moods, and this doesn't necessarily mean they have bipolar disorder.

Posttraumatic Stress Disorder

Trauma occurs when a sudden, unexpected event overwhelms a person's defenses, leaving him feeling terrified and helpless. People experience trauma when loved ones die unexpectedly, natural disasters strike, they become victims of or witnesses to a crime, or they're in a war.

Posttraumatic stress disorder was first identified in war veterans when it became obvious that the shock of war experiences *caused* what used to be called battle fatigue. Previously, doctors and therapists felt that only people with pre-existing psychological problems remained traumatized after the event, and that sending soldiers home would resolve the problem. Now we know that the effects of trauma can remain for years.

Many of us have experienced traumatic events in our lives. In all likelihood, *all* of our children have experienced trauma. Kids who have lost their homes through repeated abuse and neglect, parental death, or other circumstances have experienced every child's worst nightmare. If the psychological effects of trauma remain with the child for longer than a month, he is said to have PTSD.

People with posttraumatic stress disorder may experience flashbacks, reliving the event as though it were happening again. Professionals think many children continually experience repeated visual memories of traumatic events. They don't always share these memories with their parents, and may only show them in behavior. Likewise, certain sights, smells, and sounds—which may seem perfectly harmless and ordinary to an observer—can trigger a posttraumatic reaction. During a flashback the child may feel he is really in danger. He may experience increased anxiety and try to protect himself.

One of my children has PTSD and I have seen this reaction many times. If we enter a room where there are long tables with chairs, he instinctively stiffens and clings to me. He remembers a room like this where he was relinquished for adoption. The sight of that room brings up the fears and sadness he felt that day.

Some children who have been traumatized act recklessly; others become enraged and turn into class bullies. Some children who have felt helpless and out of control often become overly controlling and angry, determined never to feel that way again.

❖ Effects of Trauma in Children ❖

Sleep and toileting disturbances

Hyperawareness

Startle response to loud or unusual noises

Behavioral and mood changes

Repeated telling of events

Reenactment of events in play

Separation anxiety

Flashbacks to the event, often in response to sensory triggers such as smells, sights, or noises

Avoidance behaviors

Others place the blame squarely on themselves, becoming depressed and suicidal. Our children's traumas are often multiplied by the fact that the people who loved them most hurt them.

PTSD can occur simultaneously with any of the previously discussed problems. Often, traumatic events were plentiful in our children's lives, occurring repeatedly and making their pain that much greater.

In her book *Children and Trauma*, Cynthia Monahan makes a statement that is vital for adoptive parents to understand. In discussing the death of a parent, she writes, "When the death of a loved one is shrouded in traumatic images and memories, a child must really accomplish two tasks—grieving the loss and coming to terms with the traumatic events and memories. Children who face this dual challenge of mastering loss and trauma often need special help to cope with the trauma *before* they are able to proceed with grieving." For our children, the loss of their parents is like a death, whether the birthparents actually died or not. Our children will not start grieving the loss of their parents, and thus move beyond grieving-based behaviors, until their traumatic memories are lessened.

Parents can do much to help. Professionals suggest you provide lots of comforting and reassurance. Be available and willing to hear about your child's pain, even when the feelings expressed are difficult to listen to. You can correct any misconceptions that your child carries about being responsible for the trauma. Shelter the child from further trauma, providing a safe, calm environment. Often professional assistance is required.

Treatment for PTSD should occur as soon after the traumatic event as possible. Professional treatment of trauma may include play therapy for children up to age eleven, behavioral therapy, and cognitive therapy. Some therapists use art or music therapy, encouraging children to express their feelings through different media. Group therapy can be helpful at times, as can family therapy. Eye Movement Desensitization and Reprocessing (EMDR) is a fairly new, somewhat controversial therapy that proponents say is highly successful in treating PTSD. It is a technique involving rapid eye movement, and is used alongside more traditional psychotherapy.

The purpose of therapy should be to help the child move through his pain. It provides children with relief from posttraumatic behaviors and teaches them how to release their feelings in a safe way. Successful therapy may also lessen feelings of self-blame or fear of the future. As your child begins dealing with traumatic memories, you may notice an increase in disturbing behaviors. This is actually a good sign, in most cases— it means her pain is moving toward the surface where it can be dealt with.

Medication and Hospitalization

All of the problems discussed in this chapter are difficult for both children and parents. Children who have experienced multiple losses may have a string of letters after their names, as therapists struggle to decide what kind of problem the child suffers from and how to treat it. Many therapists recommend that the child be removed from all medications. Sometimes, the true problems a child has can be aggravated or masked by medications and treatment.

Remember, not all doctors are well-trained in the side effects of new medicines or take the time to look them up. Some doctors prescribe medicines without checking what other medicines the child may be taking. Make sure you tell the doctor which medications and dosages your child is taking. Whenever you are given a medication for your child, look up its side effects and drug interaction precautions in a drug reference such as the *Physician's Desk Reference,* available in many libraries as well as some bookstores. Also, your pharmacist should have information on the drug. If your child is on multiple drugs but is not making any improvement, you should discuss with your doctor the wisdom of starting over with a new evaluation of your child's condition.

Be informed on the effects of adoption, grief, trauma, and the various psychological disorders that your child shows. If your child continues to make little progress, look for a well-recommended adoption therapist. Recent years have seen an explosion in the number of adolescent treatment centers and psychiatric hospitals. For many families, residential treatment becomes necessary as their child's behavior and emotional state disintegrates to the point that it is no longer safe for him to remain at home. Some families have found that residential or hospital treatment helps their children. Other families have discovered that their child's need for hospitalization "disappears" as soon as their insurance coverage runs out.

If your child needs inpatient treatment, carefully scrutinize the hospital and seek recommendations from other adoptive families and professionals. Psychiatric treatment and psychotropic medications definitely have their place. Remember, however, to be a good consumer and demand thorough explanations of any recommended treatments.

Some states or counties require that the parents return the child to state or county custody if he requires residential treatment, which the state is financially responsible for. While this may make the paperwork and accounting easier, it forces some adoptive parents to fight the very institutions designed to protect their children.

Audrey, the mother of two special needs children adopted domestically, relates this experience with her son: "When the therapist first mentioned placement she also mentioned our need to declare him a child in need of services. At that time she let us know that the county would demand custody. Our first reaction was, 'NO WAY! We'll find another way.' He hated us and wanted to kill us because we were sending him away." Audrey and her husband felt there was only a chance the therapy would work, and they wanted their son back regardless. They resented the county taking that away from them.

To be on the safe side, check your state and county regulations regarding residential treatment before you adopt.

❖ 12 ❖

Medical References

Adoption raises a crop of medical issues that most birthparents never have to think about. Although our children have the normal medical problems that all kids face, they may also have unusual ones that parents, and even many professionals, may be unfamiliar with. Adopted children may be more prone to many illnesses because of poor living conditions, neglect, poverty, or because their birthparents were also ill and could not care for them.

Medical records are often sorely lacking for older domestic adoptees and may be completely unavailable for international adoptees. Sometimes, medical records that accompany a child from overseas contain erroneous information or diagnoses for illnesses that are not familiar to most American physicians.

Following are some brief summaries of medical conditions that can show up in adopted children. While most are more prevalent in international adoption, some apply to domestic adoption as well.

Medical Exams on Arrival

Jerri Ann Jenista, a physician and expert on international adoption issues, recommends that all newly adopted children be screened for syphilis, tuberculosis, intestinal parasites, HIV, and hepatitis B, and have a urinalysis and a complete blood count done. About half of newly adopted children will have an acute illness within a month of their arrival. Because international adoptees often have problems, such as parasites and malaria, that are uncommon in the United States, doctors and parents often need to look beyond the obvious. You may find yourself studying up on an illness that's endemic to your child's birthcountry, or learning more than you ever want to about prescription drugs. (For example, the commonly used drugs for treating tuberculosis can affect the liver—important to know if there's any chance your child could have hepatitis.)

Hepatitis

Hepatitis is any inflammation of the liver. It's usually caused by a virus, although it may also result from the ingestion of toxic substances. Doctors have classified six types of hepatitis: A, B, C, D, E, and G. Hepatitis A and B are the types most commonly found in adopted children, although hepatitis C is beginning to show up as well. Symptoms of hepatitis include fever, headache, muscle aches, loss of appetite, and an itchy rash, followed a few days later by nausea, vomiting, abdominal pain, joint pain, foul breath, and a bitter taste in the mouth. The liver, spleen, and lymph nodes may swell and become painful. Jaundice may develop, although it is rare in children.

Hepatitis A is endemic in most countries. It is usually acquired through contact with soil or water that has been contaminated by feces containing the virus. In developing countries, lack of clean water for drinking or washing fruits and vegetables results in much of the food supply being contaminated. Hepatitis A can be passed onto others through close physical contact.

Children usually show milder symptoms of hepatitis A than adults do, and symptoms do not always develop. If they do, they usually appear ten to fifty days after the virus is contracted. Hepatitis A infection usually runs its course within a few months, and 98 percent of the patients recover fully. A vaccination is available for hepatitis A that consists of two shots and provides lifetime protection. Parents traveling to foreign countries are advised to get the vaccination before travel.

Hepatitis B is much more serious. About 5 percent of people in the United States will get hepatitis B sometime during their lives. In other parts of the world, infection rates can be as high as 80 percent. Hepatitis B is transmitted through sexual or blood contact. It can be transferred by contaminated needles, surgical or dental instruments, razors, hairbrushes, and toothbrushes. It can be transmitted through saliva, although that is extremely rare. Children can contract the disease from their infected mothers *in utero*. Symptoms usually develop slowly and can appear 50 to 180 days after infection. Because there is no cure, treatment usually focuses on relieving symptoms. The rates of recovery for hepatitis B depend in large part on the child's age at the time of infection. Infants become chronic carriers up to 90 percent of the time; that percentage decreases as the age at infection rises. Only about 10 percent of infected adults develop chronic disease. The hepatitis B vaccine consists of three shots—the first two given one month apart and the third five months later. At the conclusion of the series, most people have achieved immunity. Blood tests should be done, however, to see if a booster shot is needed.

Newly adopted children from both the United States and other countries should receive screening tests for hepatitis. These tests should include HBsAg (hepatitis B surface antigen), Anti-HBc or HBc-Ab (antibody to hepatitis B core) and Anti-HBs or HBs-Ab (antibody to hepatitis B surface). Liver function tests or hepatitis B e antigen tests are not necessary at this time. Don't assume that the results of tests done in another country are correct, or that having the

---

❖ Reading Test Results ❖

Here are the generally accepted interpretations for hepatitis B tests:

HBsAg—negative
anti-HBc—negative
anti-HBs—negative

Never infected, vaccine recommended

HBsAg—negative
anti-HBc—negative or positive
anti-HBs—positive

Immune, will not develop infection again

HBsAg—positive
anti-HBc—positive or negative
anti-HBs—negative

Currently infected, either acutely or as a carrier

HBsAg—negative
antiHBc—positive
antiHBs—negative

May be recovering from a recent infection

hepatitis B vaccine means your child is healthy. Professionals recommend screening *all* children for hepatitis immediately after arrival and again after six months if the first tests are negative.

If your child tests negative, and is not naturally immune, you should have him retested after six months to make sure he does not have an infection that had not shown up yet. You should also have him vaccinated.

If your child tests positive for HBsAg, he is either infected or is a carrier. All family members should then be vaccinated against hepatitis B. A few years ago, hepatitis B vaccine was added to the list of recommended vaccinations for all children, so most kindergarten-age children will have already been vaccinated.

After six months, have your child retested. If he is still positive, then your child is considered a carrier of hepatitis B. At that time, he should be tested for HBeAg and anti-HBe. Some professionals also recommend screening for hepatitis D, especially for kids from the Amazon region, Eastern Europe, and the South Pacific. Liver function tests should also be done, including AST and ALT, as well as a urinalysis for blood or protein.

Children who are diagnosed as hepatitis B carriers should have the tests (with the exception of the hepatitis D test) repeated annually. Some doctors also recommend an alpha-fetoprotein test to screen for liver tumors in all carrier children over the age of ten. Some doctors recommend starting this test in the first decade of life, especially for Asian children. Screenings are recommended every six months for carriers over the age of twenty.

If your child has hepatitis B or is a carrier of hepatitis B, follow the universal precautions recommended for health care workers. Use gloves when handling blood, don't share toothbrushes and razors, and cover open wounds. Contact the American Liver Foundation for more information. (See Appendix C.)

AIDS

AIDS (acquired immune deficiency syndrome) is one of the most feared illnesses in the world. Currently incurable, it kills an estimated 2.5 million people a year worldwide, including more than 510,000 children under age fifteen. Worldwide, mother-to-child transmission has accounted for more than 90 percent of all childhood infections with HIV (human immunodeficiency virus). HIV infection can weaken the immune system so that it has difficulty fighting off infection. A person is said to have AIDS after developing one of the AIDS indicator illnesses as defined by the Centers for Disease Control.

HIV is present in blood and other body fluids which can contain traces of blood, including semen, vaginal fluid, and breast milk. Occasionally the virus is found in the saliva or tears of an infected person in small quantities. HIV is spread through contact with an infected person's bodily fluids. Common routes of transmission are the sharing of needles or syringes, sexual contact, and blood transfusions. Babies born to HIV-positive mothers can become infected during birth or through breast-feeding. Contact with saliva, tears, and sweat has never been shown to result in HIV infection. Nor is there any evidence that it can be spread through food, water, or animal or insect bites.

Adoptive families often worry about AIDS infection in internationally adopted children—with good reason. The lack of medical equipment in some countries means that needles are reused, often without being properly cleaned. After an epidemic of HIV infection in such countries as Romania, adoption agencies began testing more uniformly for the disease. This raised new concerns, however, about the accuracy of the tests and the possibility of children contracting AIDS or hepatitis from the needles used to carry out the tests.

Most parents do demand test results, and most agencies now test routinely, especially in high-incidence countries. In some cases, the U.S. Immigration visa service requires the test, as people with HIV can be barred from entering the country. New laws allow some waivers. It is recommended that you have your child retested after arrival in the United States. Most agencies test routinely and there have been very few cases of children with undiagnosed HIV infection in recent years. Using a reputable, careful agency is the best way to prevent such surprises.

Tuberculosis

Tuberculosis kills more children and adults than any other infectious disease in the world today. It is a bigger threat than malaria and AIDS combined, and kills about 100,000 children a year. Some professionals say the rate of TB in adopted children is 50 to 150 times higher than the rate among the general U.S. population. Serious complications of the disease do occur.

TB is caused by the tubercle bacillus, a type of bacteria found in humans, cattle, and other animals. One third of the world's population is infected with the TB bacillus. However, infected people are not always sick. The bacilli can lie dormant for years. If the immune system becomes weaker, the person will often get sick. Only people who are sick with pulmonary (lung) TB are infectious. Coughing, sneezing, talking, and spitting propel TB bacilli into the air.

In some countries, children are commonly given the BCG vaccine against TB, making diagnosis more difficult because the shot can lead to false positive results. Dr. Jenista recommends a Mantoux skin test for adopted children. Skin test reactions of greater than 20 mm are due to infection with TB, and require treatment. TB is usually treated with prescription drugs. Reactions of less than 5 mm are likely to be induced by the BCG vaccine. Any reaction of greater than 10 mm, or 5 mm in an HIV-infected child, should be evaluated.

Inherited Diseases

Thalassemia

Thalassemia is a group of inherited diseases of the blood. About 100,000 babies are born each year with severe forms of the disease. It occurs most frequently in people of Italian, Greek, Middle Eastern, southern Asian, and African ancestry. Thalassemia includes a number of different forms of anemia (red blood cell deficiency).

Thalassemia minor is also called thalassemia trait and may cause no symptoms, although changes in the blood do occur. In thalassemia minor, hemoglobin production is reduced only slightly and most children are not significantly affected. It is often confused with the mild anemia caused by nutritional deficiencies.

Thalassemia intermedia is also called mild Cooley's anemia.

Hemoglobin production is reduced moderately to severely, resulting in an enlarged spleen and thin bones. It can produce no symptoms or very severe symptoms.

In thalassemia major, also called Cooley's anemia, hemoglobin A production is reduced drastically, causing severe anemia, an enlarged liver, spleen, or heart, overgrowth of the jawbone, a rounded protrusion on the skull, thin bones, stunted growth, and frequent infections. Older children with thalassemia major are often pale, jaundiced, listless, breathless, and fatigued, and have no appetite. Without treatment, they usually live only a few years. With treatment, the outlook is more promising, although most do not live beyond their thirties.

Aggressive treatment of thalassemia major consists of frequent blood transfusions. However, this results in a buildup of iron in the body, which can damage the heart, liver, and other organs. A drug referred to as an iron chelator can help rid the body of excess iron. The drug is usually administered through a pump while the child is sleeping. Iron chelation can require up to twelve hours a day. Children receiving this therapy have lived twenty to thirty years or longer, although that age is expected to rise for patients who have had treatment for most of their lives. Thalassemia has been cured, in a few cases, by bone marrow transplant.

Your doctor will probably test for thalassemia if your child's blood cells look atypical. There are several other inherited hemoglobin disorders (such as hemoglobin E enteropathy) that tend to affect the same population groups. Many are mild, affecting the child's health slightly, if at all.

Tay-Sachs Disease

Tay-Sachs is an inherited birth defect that most frequently affects children of Central and Eastern European (Ashkenazi) Jews. Approximately one out of every thirty American Jews carries the Tay-Sachs gene. A small percentage of French Canadian or Cajun people also have an increased carrier rate. If both the mother and father carry the Tay-Sachs gene, there's a 25 percent chance of producing a child with Tay-Sachs.

Tay-Sachs disease results from a lack of a chemical messenger called hexosaminidase A, an enzyme necessary for the metabolism of substances in the central nervous system. Without hex A, these substances accumulate in the nerve cells of the brain, interfering with their function and eventually destroying them.

Children with Tay-Sachs appear normal for the first six months of life, but symptoms usually occur shortly thereafter. An apparently healthy baby gradually stops smiling, crawling, or turning over, loses his ability to grasp objects, and eventually becomes blind, paralyzed, and severely mentally retarded. Death generally occurs by age five.

There are a small number of people who have hex A deficiencies but do not develop classic Tay-Sachs. Some children develop symptoms between the ages of two and five that resemble the infantile form but progress slowly. Death generally occurs by age fifteen for these children. Symptoms of chronic Hex A deficiency also may begin after age five but with milder symptoms. For these children, mental abilities, vision, and hearing remain intact, but there may be slurred speech, muscle weakness, muscle cramps, tremors, and sometimes mental illness.

Because of the poor life expectancy for children with Tay-Sachs, most older children available for adoption will not be affected. However, a child of Ashkenazic Jewish ancestry may be a carrier and could ultimately pass the disease onto his children. For this reason, parents may wish to have their child screened for the Tay-Sachs gene. Screening consists of a simple blood test.

Sickle Cell Disease

Sickle cell is an inherited disease of the red blood cells that can cause pain, damage to vital organs, and early death. It is most common among African-Americans, although it also occurs in people of Mediterranean, Native American, Latin American, and Asian decent. Approximately 1 in 400 African-Americans has sickle cell disease, and 1 in 12 African-Americans carries the sickle cell trait. If both parents carry the trait, they have a 50 percent risk of passing on the trait to their children, and a twenty-five percent risk of having a child with sickle cell disease.

Sickle cell disease affects the portion of red blood cells called hemoglobin. Hemoglobin carries oxygen throughout the body. Although sickle cell hemoglobin carries oxygen normally, it has a tendency to congeal as it loses oxygen. As a result, red blood cells that are normally round and puffy become crescent- or sickle-shaped. The abnormally shaped cells tend to become trapped in the liver and spleen, resulting in anemia, which can cause a child to be pale, short of breath, and easily tired.

At times, sickle cells become stuck in tiny blood vessels (also called sludging), cutting off blood supply to nearby tissues and depriving them of oxygen. The area then becomes inflamed and begins to ache. This blockage of blood vessels is known as a sickle cell pain episode, or crisis. Pain episodes may be severe and sometimes need to be treated in a hospital, but most often can be treated at home with pain-relieving medication, rest, and fluids. Patients generally cycle between episodes of pain and periods of relative health.

The most common complications of sickle cell disease in children are bacterial infections, which can be fatal. After the age of five, sickle cell disease most often involves repeated episodes of pain. If the sludging occurs in major organs, such as the lungs, it may cause illness. Adolescents with sickle cell disease often experience late puberty. In adulthood, the patient may show signs of chronic sludging in the capillaries of the lungs and kidneys, leading to lung or kidney failure. Other patients experience sludging in the eye, leading to blindness. For the most part, patients with sickle cell disease lead full, productive lives, and most live until their forties or fifties. New treatments can often minimize serious complications, although there is no cure.

Parasitic Infections

According to Dr. Jenista, after hepatitis B, parasites cause the most long-term problems for children. Virtually all internationally adopted children, and many domestically adopted children, will have parasites upon their arrival. Skin conditions such as scabies and lice are common. Intestinal parasites are generally rampant in institutions. Most professionals recommend that three stool samples be taken, no more than a week apart. Follow-up tests after treatment are also recommended. It is not unusual for children to be diagnosed with multiple infections.

Malaria

Malaria is the world's most important tropical parasitic disease, and kills more people than any other communicable disease besides tuberculosis. It is caused by a group of four parasites, with *P. falciparum* the most common, and most lethal, strain. Mosquitoes transmit malaria.

Symptoms include fever, shivering, pain in the joints, headache, repeated vomiting, generalized convulsions, and sometimes coma. If your child is suffering from these symptoms, tell your doctor. You should also inform your doctor if *you* have traveled overseas recently and begin showing these symptoms, even if you have taken medication. Some strains of malaria have become drug-resistant. The Centers for Disease Control recommends that persons traveling to malaria-prone countries take preventive medications. Your doctor can prescribe them.

Scabies

Scabies is a skin rash caused by mites—small, round, four-legged crawling insects. Scabies is not harmful unless it becomes infected with bacteria, but it is annoying. Scabies infection is epidemic in orphanages where clothing and bedding are shared. The symptoms are red, swollen, itchy bumps. Itching is usually worse at night. The standard treatment is a prescription cream. It's a good idea to take scabies cream with you when traveling to pick up your child. If your child does have scabies, wash all clothing, bedding, and toys thoroughly to prevent infecting other family members. Many children with scabies develop impetigo infections from scratching. The swollen red spots that signal scabies can linger for days or weeks after the mite itself is gone.

Lice

Lice are tiny insects that attach themselves to human skin and hair. They suck the blood of their hosts, injecting their own saliva and digestive matter into the skin as they feed. This is what causes the characteristic itching. Lice are visible to the naked eye, but are notoriously difficult to remove. Adult lice live about one month and lay four or five eggs daily. Itching is the most common symptom.

To treat lice, you wash the child's hair with a louse-killing shampoo and then use a special comb to remove nits (eggs) from the hair. You can buy lice shampoo in drugstores. Pay attention to the warnings and use the shampoo exactly as directed. Removing the nits, or nit-picking, is a laborious project, but failure to remove all the nits can cause a reinfestation. Some families have found natural remedies, such as tea tree oil or mayonnaise, to be useful. Alternative medicine stores should have information on such treatments.

Lymphatic filariasis

Lymphatic filariasis is endemic in Asia, Africa, and the western Pacific and in some parts of the Americas. An estimated 120 million people worldwide have this mosquito-borne disease, which is the world's second leading cause of permanent and long-term disability.

Lymphatic filariasis is caused by adult worms which settle into the lymphatic system and mature over a period of three to fifteen months. Females produce large numbers of larvae, which invade the bloodstream. The tiny larvae remain in the body for six months to two years. They cause immune damage, while the adults damage the lymphatic ducts. The illness can cause acute fevers, inflammation of the lymphatic system, and the bronchial-asthmatic condition known as tropical pulmonary eosinophilia. In some cases, it can result in elephantitis of the limbs and hydrocele, an enlargement of the scrotum.

Intestinal Parasites

There are many types of intestinal parasites common to adopted children. Every child should be tested for parasites on arrival. However, if the testing lab does not routinely screen for a wide range of parasites, it may not know what to look for. Parasites also can fail to show up on tests, depending on where they are in their life cycle. Parents report getting multiple negative test results on children with obvious symptoms. With treatment, virtually all those children have been shown to have parasites. For this reason, you may have to be persistent in seeking advice or treatment if your child's tests are negative but infestation is probable. It may help to consult a pediatric gastroenterologist. Some common parasites and their main symptoms are listed below.

Worms

Pinworms: Pinworms are a common parasitic infection in both the United States and abroad. Also called threadworms, they resemble short pieces of white thread. Pinworms are transmitted through food or objects contaminated with fecal matter. Kids often spread them by not washing their hands properly after going to the bathroom. At night, female pinworms crawl out of the intestine to the anus, deposit their eggs near the anal opening, and then die. This causes the characteristic itch of pinworm infection. If your child is scratching a lot in the anal area, consult your doctor. Pinworm infection usually clears up easily with prescription medication.

Ascaris lumbricoides (roundworms): Roundworm eggs are found in food that is contaminated with human waste. In many countries, human waste is used for fertilizer, and vegetables and fruits aren't properly washed. After the larvae hatch in the small intestine, they penetrate into the tissues and are carried by the blood and lymph system to the lungs. In the lungs, the larvae break out into the air sacs, ascend into the throat, and descend to the intestines again, where the worms can grow up to twelve inches long.

Roundworm infection may not be noticeable until a child passes one or more in the feces, or occasionally, one crawls up into the throat and tries to exit through the mouth or nose.

Symptoms include vague stomach complaints such as gas or diarrhea, stunted growth, mild anemia, and bronchial symptoms, including asthmatic symptoms and pneumonia during the larvae stage. If your child has a constant tickle in the throat, test for parasites. Roundworm infection is common in the United States and around the world. It is usually treated with a prescription medicine.

Trichuris trichiura (whipworms): Whipworm infection is spread through food contaminated by human waste. Whipworm larvae do not migrate after hatching but mature in the intestine. Symptoms range from vague digestive tract distress to emaciation with dry skin and diarrhea. Allergic symptoms may also occur. Whipworms are common in the United States and in other countries. They are usually treated with prescription medicine.

Schistosomiasis (Bilharziasis): This is caused by five species of a waterborne flatworm, or blood flukes. Schistosomes enter the body through contact with infected surface water, mainly among people engaged in farming. Schistosomiasis can cause serious illness, including paralysis of the legs or bladder cancer, and death. Children with urinary schistosomiasis often have blood in their urine. It's diagnosed by the presence of eggs in the feces, and is easily treated with prescription drugs. This parasite is endemic to Africa, Eastern Mediterranean countries, the Caribbean, South America, Southeast Asia, and the Western Pacific.

Nanophyetus: Nanophyetiasis is caused by parasitic flatworms found in freshwater fish, and is limited almost exclusively to Russia. It usually causes an increase in bowel movements or diarrhea, abdominal discomfort, and nausea. Some patients report weight loss and fatigue. The parasite is common in areas of Russia where people often eat raw or undercooked fish. It's treated with prescription drugs.

Giardia lamblia

Giardiasis is the most frequent cause of nonbacterial diarrhea in North America. It is common throughout the world. Giardiasis may cause diarrhea within one week of ingestion of the parasite. Normally, illness lasts for one to two weeks, but sometimes infections last months or even years. Giardia affects children more frequently than adults, and is common in child care centers. It is generally associated with the consumption of contaminated water, and possibly raw vegetables. It can spread when caregivers don't wash their hands thoroughly after changing diapers.

About forty percent of those diagnosed with Giardiasis have lactose intolerance during infection and up to six months after. Chronic infections can lead to malabsorption of nutrients and severe weight loss. Giardiasis is usually treated with prescription drugs. Some chronic cases can be difficult to clear.

Entamoeba histolytica

Amebiasis is an infection caused by E. histolytica, a parasite transmitted by fecal contamination of drinking water and foods, direct contact with dirty hands, and sexual contact. This illness is common in the United States and worldwide. Infections sometimes last for years and may be accompanied by vague gastrointestinal distress or dysentery, but may also show no symptoms. People with poor immunity are particularly susceptible. Amebiasis is treated with prescription drugs.

Cryptosporidiosis

Cryptosporidiosis is caused by a single-celled parasite and spread through food or water contaminated by fecal matter. The illness can affect either the intestines or lungs and trachea. The intestinal illness usually shows up in severe, watery diarrhea. Lung illness is associated with coughing and low-grade fever accompanied by severe intestinal distress. This illness has been implicated in several large outbreaks in the United States and is common around the world. The intestinal illness usually lasts from two days to four weeks. There is no effective drug treatment at this time.

Nutritional Problems

When you think of malnutrition, you may think of emaciated, gray-skinned children with protruding stomachs like those we've seen on the news in Somalia or Ethiopia. However, malnutrition often has milder forms that many do not recognize, such as a one-year-old child who weighs twelve pounds or a child who looks seven or eight and is really ten. There are many forms of malnutrition, including protein-energy malnutrition, which is simply not having enough to eat, and dietary deficiency malnutrition, which results from the lack of a specific nutrient or vitamin. Adopted children from other countries are often malnourished on arrival. All too often, adoptees from the United States are undernourished as well.

Malnutrition can stunt growth, reduce a child's resistance to disease, impair his mental capacity and alertness, and lead to developmental delays. Many adopted children arrive home significantly smaller than is normal for their age. Most children experience a surge of catch-up growth after their arrival. For the most part, doctors feel that malnutrition's effects can be reversed by a good diet, but the growth of older children who have suffered years of malnutrition may be permanently stunted.

Rickets

Rickets is a disease of growing bone, usually recognized during periods of greatest bone growth, such as infancy and adolescence. The most common form of rickets results from simple vitamin D deficiency. The risk of developing rickets is especially strong, it appears, for children from China, Romania, and the former Soviet Union, probably because of a high rate of prematurity, lack of fortified formula, and/or long periods of confinement indoors with little exposure to sunlight.

The classic symptom of rickets is bowed legs and knock-knees. Other signs include enlarged joints, stunted growth, multiple fractures, poor dental enamel, delayed tooth development, and sometimes seizures. Most children with rickets respond to a simple vitamin program, and children with mild cases generally recover well. Children with severe rickets may require prolonged treatment with Vitamin D, hormones, and calcium supplements. Professionals believe that children treated by the age of two years have the best prognosis for the correction of bone problems.

Nutrient Deficiencies

Following is a list of some of the most common symptoms of vitamin or mineral deficiency. Most effects of mild malnutrition will fade with proper diet.

Protein: Some children, most notably from Asian countries, arrive home with streaks of red in their hair. Professionals believe this is a sign of protein deficiency. Many parents report their child's hair darkening after a few months of adequate nutrition. Protein deficiencies also result in lack of muscle tone and stunted growth.

Calcium: A deficiency can lead to aching joints, brittle nails, eczema, nervousness, and tooth decay. It has also been associated with cognitive impairment, depression, and hyperactivity.

Iodine: Iodine deficiency causes fatigue, malfunction of the thyroid, and weight gain. It's a big problem in some rural areas of China where there is little iodine in the soil.

Iron: The most common deficiency symptom is anemia, which causes fatigue. Iron deficiency can also cause brittle hair, difficulty swallowing, digestive problems, hair loss, and spoon-shaped nails.

Magnesium: Magnesium deficiency can cause confusion, irritability, insomnia, seizures, and tantrums. It can also cause cardiovascular problems such as arrhythmia, hypertension, and rapid heartbeat.

Potassium: Potassium deficiency causes abnormally dry skin, acne, chills, cognitive impairment, constipation and diarrhea, stunted growth, muscle fatigue, headaches, and diminished reflexes. Potassium plays a big role in the regulation of blood pressure and one of the biggest manifestations of potassium deficiency is irregular blood pressure with weakness, dizziness, and an inability to focus.

Zinc: Zinc deficiency can cause a loss of the senses of taste and smell; thin, peeling fingernails; acne; delayed puberty; fatigue; hair loss, and recurrent colds and flu.

Vitamin A: Vitamin A protects against eye and skin problems. A deficiency can cause dry hair or skin, and night blindness. It can also lead to blindness when the eye does not produce enough mucus, making it more vulnerable to surface dirt and bacterial infection. This condition, called xerophthalmia, has been reported in some internationally adopted children.

Thiamin (vitamin B1): Thiamin deficiency causes constipation, water retention, fatigue, forgetfulness, loss of appetite, poor coordination, and a disease called beriberi which causes impaired growth, muscle wasting, mental confusion, gastrointestinal problems and convulsions.

Riboflavin (vitamin B2): Deficiency symptoms include cracks and sores at the corners of the mouth, inflammation of the mouth and tongue, hair loss, insomnia, and skin rash.

Niacin (vitamin B3): Niacin deficiency can cause canker sores, depression, diarrhea, fatigue, bad breath, headaches, insomnia, and muscle weakness.

Vitamin B6: Deficiency causes anemia, convulsions, headaches, nausea, and flaky skin.

Vitamin B12: Deficiency causes anemia, chronic fatigue, abnormal gait, inflammation of the tongue, moodiness, irritability, and labored breathing.

Biotin: Biotin deficiency causes seborrheic dermatitis, resulting in hair loss and skin problems.

Folic acid: Deficiency can often be observed by the presence of a sore, red tongue, and a deficiency in pregnant women has been linked to birth defects.

Vitamin C: A lack of this vitamin can cause poor wound healing, bleeding gums, water retention, and pinpoint hemorrhages under the skin.

Vitamin K: Deficiency can cause prolonged and abnormal bleeding.

Lactose Intolerance

Lactose intolerance, or the inability of the body to break down milk sugar, is caused by a lack of lactase, an enzyme of the small intestine. Lactose intolerance affects up to seventy percent of adults worldwide, and is especially prevalent in people of Asian, African, Native American (north and south), and Mediterranean descent. Lactose intolerance is sometimes a side effect of infection by parasites. Suspect lactose intolerance if your child has abdominal bloating and gas after eating dairy products. Other symptoms are diarrhea, slow weight gain, and vomiting.

Lactose intolerance often shows up around the age of four. If your child is lactose-intolerant, try giving her lactose-reduced milk, or dairy products such as hard cheese or yogurt, which have lower levels of milk sugar. If dairy products are out of the question, your doctor will probably recommend giving the child calcium supplements and/or calcium-fortified foods.

Early Puberty

Some adopted children show signs of puberty earlier than expected. When this happens, parents often wonder if their child's age is correct or if there are undiagnosed medical problems. Puberty is not considered early in the United States unless it begins before age eight for girls or nine for boys.

Some studies have shown that children adopted after the age of three and those who have dramatic catch-up growth, especially in height, seem to be at an increased risk. Early puberty raises emotional, physical, and social issues. Parents may find precocious puberty disturbing, and it can add substantially to the stresses of having a new child. Some children begin growing breasts or menstruating in second or third grade, considerably ahead of their peers, making them feel even more out of place. Your child may also be expected to act older by those outside your family. The main physical result of early puberty seems to be the effect on adult height. A child who begins her growth spurt early may stop growing early. However, it may be the existence of early malnutrition that stunts the growth. In any case, studies have shown that Indian girls adopted in Sweden grow about as tall as girls who remain in India.

There are several drugs available to suppress menstrual bleeding, but the success of suppressing other sexual characteristics is not great. Most doctors advise against using drugs like these, especially if the age of the child is in question. Growth hormones may work well in the short term, but seem to have little effect on long-term growth. If your child shows sign of early puberty, consult a pediatric endocrinologist.

Determining your Child's Age

Many countries do not accurately record birth data. Although children who are adopted are required to have birth certificates, these are often filled in when the child enters an orphanage. For many internationally adopted children, true age is unknown and the orphanage assigns a birthdate, often based on the child's appearance or on information provided by relatives, which may or may not be accurate. For infants, an error of a few months is not that much of a problem, but for older children, ages can be as much as four or five years off.

If you question your child's official age, start by asking him how old he is. He may not know his true age—birthdays are not routinely celebrated in many countries, especially in orphanages—but his perception may be the most accurate estimate you get.

Many parents seek medical tests to help them determine their child's true age. No tests can accurately pinpoint age. The best you can hope for is to get a range of probable ages. Dental "age" is often incorrect, as malnutrition can cause delayed tooth development, and because children mature dentally at different ages. Bone age tests, conducted by wrist x-rays, are often inaccurate because of the effects of malnutrition and because doctors often measure against North American children. Even the onset of puberty is not a good indicator because of the wide range of ages that is considered normal: eight to thirteen for girls and nine to fourteen for boys.

Although you may want to determine your child's age quickly, it might be years before you can make an accurate guess. Most adoption professionals suggest addressing problems such as school placement based on your child's developmental age. A good child development book will tell you what the average child can do at certain ages. You can also gauge what age group your child appears most comfortable in. As your child catches up and acquires language skills, she can skip grades later if necessary. As her parents, you likely have the best idea about how old your child is. Most parents who think their child is older than the records state do not change the official age, feeling that the extra time gives the child more time to grow and adjust in the family before seeking independence.

If you do decide to change your child's age, you usually need to petition the court for a new birth certificate. You may have to supply affidavits from your doctor. Professionals recommend that you wait at least a couple of years before changing a seemingly erroneous birth certificate, to see how the child catches up in growth and development.

In Closing

While the individual stories differ, one thing stands out among families with older adopted children. These kids *are* our own. Through the good times and bad, the joys and the challenges, our kids become a vital piece of our families. It can be difficult. We are, after all, parenting hurt children. At the same time, our children give us much to be grateful for. They inspire us and they stretch our worlds.

My children have given me so much more than I could ever give them. They are my life, my joy, my future, and my hope. I stand in awe of what wonderful people they are and what strength they show in the wake of such broken, painful lives. They are my gift.

Some of the families that have so graciously opened their lives to me share these closing thoughts.

"It hasn't always been easy—there were days early on when I wondered what on earth had inspired us to adopt again, let alone this weeping, sulking, scared little guy. It seemed like it took forever for him to truly feel like our son. And there's what I call that 'black hole': all of his history and memories of his early life that we can never be a part of. But that's a plus, too. Because he has those memories, no matter how vague, I'm hoping he won't feel as 'cut off' as some adoptees. Another plus is that we got an instant companion for our daughter. They're only a year apart, and they're inseparable. I think getting her a brother was probably the best thing we've ever done for her. And for us. He's a great son, even if he does still sulk!"

—*Gail, adoptive mother of two*

"For me, adoption brought a sense of satisfaction that I hadn't found before. Despite having the M.D., I always felt like I wanted more. I was considering nighttime law school, grad school, and advanced fellowships. ... Well, in essence, fatherhood ended my adolescence, which had been prolonged by further education. A few months after Austin arrived I was watching him play baseball, and a little boy came up to me and said, 'I know you.' I was trying to remember his face and I thought he was probably a patient or the patient of one of my partners, but then he said, 'You are Austin's daddy!' That's when I felt complete."

—Brent, adoptive father of two

"Before we had adopted, I was advocating adoption all over the place. I used to publish a newsletter that I sent out to friends and family and I talked a real good line about how adoption was the 'right' thing to do; how there were so many kids out there that are part of our communities who have no one to call mom and dad. That was my take. Now that we have adopted, I'm not remotely an adoption advocate. I think that it requires huge reserves of strength. It requires wells of strength the size and shape of which you have no idea whether you can possibly have until you are in the situation. Knowing what we know now, and looking at these particular children, we probably would do it again. These children appealed to us for so many reasons around what they enjoyed, their interests. They just seemed to be our kids. But the experience of adoption for us has not been one that I would happily replicate."

—Molly, adoptive mother of two

"One day I was peeling wallpaper off the wall and Chase was helping me and he looked up at me and said, 'When we become a forever family, can I change my name?' I said, 'Well, I suppose you could. What would you change your name to?' He said, 'I want to be [father's name] the third. That would make me daddy's.' He was claiming us. It was interesting sitting and watching when he told his dad what he wanted. I swear my husband just about started crying. To have that kind of impact on a child where they want to take your own name, where they want to be that close to you, where they want to be owned by you, is an incredible impact. And that's a different kind of impact than if you have this little infant in your home and in your arms and you name it. It's a different kind of impact, because this child *chose* to belong."

—*Nicole, adoptive mother of three*

"I wish I could express all that our children brought to us by God have meant to Shawn and me. My father always said that children bring their own gifts to a family. Our children certainly have. Among these gifts have been humor, kindness, patience, beauty, purpose, joy, and most of all, love."

—*Allison, mother of eight children, four of them adopted*

"I look back at our year with very positive thoughts. There have been some struggles, but there have been far more wonderful adventures. We would not have adopted this child if we had not believed that the whole process of becoming a family would work, but I am still often amazed at how quickly and how well most days have gone. All three of my kids are truly siblings, with all the good and bad that entails... This year we really are family."

—*Deanna, mother of three children, two of them adopted*

"Here we are—the very first generation of adoptive parents who have knowingly and willingly sought out and adopted disabled children. What kind of legacy are we going to leave? Oh, this is all so hard—I'm not going to lie. I sometimes lie awake at night wishing that I had never heard of adoption and could just be someone who is without all these problems. Trust me, it's even harder when you have 'perfectly normal' biological children and you have this little voice whispering in your ear at three a.m., 'Couldn't leave well enough alone, could you, chump?' But then I remind myself that every single day when I wake up it could go either way. It could be a good day, bad day, terrible day—or the worst, a day that will be completely unremarkable and one I'll forget as soon as it's over, like last week's

Thursday supper. Is that how I want to live? I'm *feeling* things and I'm breathing deep and thinking hard and sometimes I'm praying hard, but I'm *alive*. At least I can say to myself at the end of my life—it was tough, but I handled it. For that brief time that I was here on this planet, I was paying attention. ... Knowing and watching Ryan cope with his issues has been a real education for me. Even when I'm most angry and least able to cope, I'm still in awe of all he's been through— that all three of them have been through—and how they still smile, laugh, love."

—*Trina, mother of four children, three of them adopted*

❖ A ❖
Adoption Subsidies

Subsidy payments are available to most families who adopt older children from the United States. In some cases, children adopted internationally may be eligible as well. There are several different types of adoption subsidies. The Federal IV-E Adoption Assistance Program; IV-B state programs; medical subsidies, and non-recurring expenses are the most commonly used.

Federal IV-E

The federal Title IV-E program provides payments to the parents of an eligible child. The payments are not designed to cover a particular need or purpose. They can be used for any of the child's needs.

The maximum amount of federal funds cannot exceed the foster care maintenance amount that would have been paid if the child had remained in foster care. Families applying for Title IV-E assistance should be sure to check on the maximum allowable, however, as some children do not receive the maximum while in foster care. Don't just assume that what your child had in foster care is the maximum amount.

In order to qualify for federal funds, the child has to qualify for SSI (Supplemental Security Income) or AFDC (Aid to Families with Dependent Children). To qualify for SSI, the child has to have a qualifying disability that interferes with the normal routines of life. AFDC benefits are paid for children who qualified sometime in the six months before court proceedings to terminate parental rights were begun. To find out if your child is eligible for SSI or AFDC, contact your local Social Security office.

State Programs

State benefits, Title IV-B, provide assistance for children who have special needs. In some cases, children who do not qualify for federal funds may receive state funds. In order for a child to qualify for funds, three requirements must be me:

- ❖ The court has to have determined that the child cannot or should not be returned to the birthfamily.
- ❖ The child has to be defined as a special needs child, as determined by the guidelines of the state he resides in.
- ❖ The agency must show that the child could not have been placed without a subsidy *or* that the placement is determined to be the only one in his best interests.

Benefits vary widely from state to state. To receive a copy of your state's requirements, call your local department of human or social services or the state adoption subsidy office. Generally, state assistance consists of some or all of the following programs.

Support Subsidy

A support subsidy is a monthly cash payment to the parents of an eligible child for the care and upkeep of the child. Special medical or emotional considerations may increase the amount.

Medical Assistance

Children in the federal adoption assistance program are automatically eligible for Medicaid benefits. In addition, states may provide Medicaid coverage for children who receive subsidy payments from the state. Medical subsidies may be given to a child with a specific illness or condition that requires treatment. Medical subsidies cover specific medical conditions that are not covered by the family's health insurance.

Non-recurring Adoption Expenses

Parents adopting special needs children may be eligible for a one-time payment to reimburse them for non-recurring adoption expenses, such as travel costs, legal fees, court costs, or other expenses directly related to the legal adoption of the child.

Payments range from $400 to $2000 per child.

Social Services

Under Title XX, children with special needs may be eligible for social services such as respite care, day care, housekeeping, and counseling. Services vary between states and special services usually have to be negotiated before the adoption is finalized.

Negotiating a Subsidy

Subsidy cases are negotiated on an individual basis. Federal funds are not dependent on the family's financial circumstances. Some state programs may take into consideration the family's situation when negotiating subsidies. Do not rely on what the department worker tells you. Insist on getting the state guidelines in writing. Subsidy rules are often confusing, and mistakes are made. Do your homework. Most subsidies have to be negotiated *before* the adoption is finalized. Agencies are required to tell you what services are available before you adopt your child. If they fail to do so, you may be able to appeal after your adoption is finalized.

When negotiating a subsidy, make sure the agreement is in writing and that you read it in its entirety before signing. It should specify the amount of cash payments, the services to be provided, the date the services begin and are to be terminated, and provisions in the event that the family moves out of state. The agreement should also specify what conditions would make the child eligible for increased services.

If you feel that your child is denied services in error, you may ask for an appeal. You should write a letter outlining the reasons for the appeal, and what you believe your child is eligible for. Most states have deadlines that have to be met in filing an appeal. The appeal hearing is conducted by an impartial hearing officer or an administrative law judge. If you lose an appeal hearing, you can retry the case in court.

Internationally Adopted Children

In most cases, children adopted internationally do not qualify for state or federal funds. Some states allow internationally adopting parents to file for non-recurring expenses. If your child was brought to the United States by another family and that adoptive placement disrupted, your child may become eligible for benefits during the time he is in foster care. This can be true even if the child is in the care of a private agency. Check your state's guidelines.

Information about adoption subsidies can be obtained from NAATRIN (National Adoption Assistance Training, Resource and Information Network); see Appendix C.

❖ B ❖

The Immigration Process

Parents who adopt internationally have to go through the U.S. immigration process for their child, who will become a resident alien or automatic citizen at the time of arrival. The immigration process is one of the most frustrating aspects of international adoption for many people, but the rules and regulations are in place to help protect the children and are necessary.

The minimum requirements for parents adopting internationally are:

❖ At least one parent must be a U.S. citizen.

❖ At least one parent must be twenty-five.

❖ Your income must be at least 125 percent of poverty level for your family size.

❖ All persons over the age of eighteen living in the household must be fingerprinted and cleared by the FBI.

❖ You must meet the pre-adoption requirements of your state (which is usually taken care of in the home study).

One of the most pressing requirements set by the Bureau of Citizenship and Immigration Service (BCIS) is that the child you are adopting meet the U.S. definition of "orphan." According to BCIS publication M249-Y:

Under immigration law, an orphan is a foreign child who has no parents because of the death or disappearance of, abandonment or desertion by, or separation or loss from both parents. An orphan is also a foreign child with only one parent who is not able to take care of the orphan properly and has in writing forever or irrevocably released the orphan for emigration and adoption. For such a child to gain immigration benefits, an orphan petition must be filed before his or her sixteenth birthday. Adopted children who are under the age of eighteen, but who are siblings of a child being adopted (or previously adopted) who is under the age of sixteen may also be eligible for immigration as an orphan.

Approval

Although it is possible to file the child's papers and process your application in one step, the recommended procedure is to file an I-600A (Application for Advance Processing of Orphan Petition) before you are referred a child. You do not need to identify a specific child to file the I-600A, nor do you have to specify a country, and approval is good for eighteen months. Federal fingerprint clearances, however, are valid for only fifteen months from the date they are taken. You will have to be re-fingerprinted after that time. Therefore, it is recommended that you wait until your home study is complete to file the I-600A.

After you send in the I-600A along with the application and fingerprint fees, you will receive a letter telling you where and when to report for fingerprinting. The prints will be sent to the FBI in Washington, D.C., for processing. This process generally takes only a few days. Once your home study is complete, your agency will send it to your state for certification that pre-adoption requirements have been met, and then to the BCIS for approval. After your home study and fingerprints have been approved, you will receive form I-171H (Notice of Favorable Determination Concerning Application for Advance Processing of Orphan Petition).

After you receive your I-600A approval and have received your child's paperwork, you will need to file Form I-600 (Petition to Classify Orphan as an Immediate Relative). If you have not already filed Form I-600A, you will need to submit the fees for application processing and fingerprinting. If you have filed form I-600A, there is no additional charge to file form I-600. With the I-600 form you must include proof of the child's age (birth certificate), and death certificates of the parents or proof that the surviving parent has irrevocably released the child for adoption. If you do not already have approval (the 171-H form), you must file your I-600 in the same BCIS office you filed your I-600A in. If you have approval, you may file your I-600 in the

U.S. Consulate of the country you are adopting from or in your stateside BCIS office if you are adopting from a country that does not require parents to travel overseas. When you have been approved, you will receive form 171 (Notice of Approval of Relative Immigration Visa Petition).

If you have not seen your child prior to the adoption or if only one spouse travels to pick up your child, your child will enter the U.S. on an IR-4 visa, and you must file Form I-864 (Affidavit of Support) to show that you have the means to support the child. The parent completing the affidavit must provide proof, including tax returns and evidence of employment, that household income exceeds 125 percent of the poverty line for the size of the household (including the new child). If your child is being escorted to the States, your agency will tell you when and where to file your I-864. Single parents who see their child before the adoption do not have to file form I-864.

Finalization and Citizenship

Usually when a single parent or both married parents travel to bring home the child, the adoption is finalized in the child's birth country. Many, but not all, U.S. states have laws recognizing foreign adoptions as valid. If the child is escorted to the United States under a decree of guardianship, or both parents have not seen the child prior to the adoption overseas, the adoption must be finalized in your home state. Laws differ from state to state on finalization time and document quirements. Contact your agency or an attorney experienced in adoption for details. Many agencies recommend that you readopt or validate the adoption in your state even if it's not necessary, to get an American birth certificate for your child. If you are changing your child's name, it should be done at the time of readoption/validation.

Children whose adoption is finalized overseas and who enter the country on an IR-3 visa become U.S. citizens upon their arrival. A child who enters on an IR-4 visa becomes a citizen when the adoption is finalized in the United States.

You can obtain immigration forms and more information by calling BCIS or visiting its Web site (see Appendix C).

❖ C ❖

Resources

Books

A Child's Journey Through Placement, by Vera I. Fahlberg, M.D. (Perspectives Press, 1991).

Adopted From Asia: How It Feels to Grow Up in America, by Frances M. Koh (East West Press, 1993).

Adopting and Advocating for the Special Needs Child: a Guide for Parents and Professionals, by L. Anne Babb and Rita Laws (Bergin and Garvey, 1997).

Adopting the Hurt Child, by Gregory Keck and Regina Kupecky (Pinon Press, 1995).

Adopting the Older Child, by Claudia Jewett (Harvard Common Press, 1978).

Adoption: a Reference Handbook, by Barbara A. Moe (Contemporary World Issues, 1998).

Adoption and Financial Assistance: Tools for Navigating the Bureaucracy, by Rita Laws and Tim O'Hanlon (Bergin and Garvey, 1999).

Are Those Kids Yours?, by Cheri Register (Free Press, 1991).

Being Adopted: the Lifelong Search for Self, by David Brodzinsky, Marshall Schechter, and Robin Henig (Doubleday, 1992).

Building the Bonds of Attachment: Awakening Love in Deeply Troubled Children, by Daniel A. Hughes (Jason Aronson, 1998).

The Challenge of Fetal Alcohol Syndrome: Overcoming Secondary Disabilities, by Ann Streissguth and Jonathan Kanter (University of Washington Press, 1997).

Children and Trauma: a Guide for Parents and Professionals, by Cynthia Monahan (Jossey Bass Publishers, 1993).

260

Culture Shock series, various countries and authors (Graphic Arts Center Publishing Co., and Times Books International).

The Family of Adoption, by Joyce Maguire Pavao (Beacon Press, 1998).

Filling in the Blanks, by Susan Gabel (Perspectives Press, 1988).

Gift Children, by J. Douglas Bates (Ticknor and Fields, 1993).

Give Them Roots, Then Let Them Fly: Understanding Attachment Therapy, by Carole A. McKelvey (Attachment Center at Evergreen, 1997).

Handbook for the Treatment of Attachment-Trauma Problems in Children, by Beverly James (Lexington Books, 1994).

Helping Children Cope With Separation and Loss, by Claudia Jewett-Jarrett (Harvard Common Press, 1994).

Hope for High Risk and Rage Filled Children: Reactive Attachment Disorder, Theory, and Therapy, by Foster W. Cline (HC Publications, 1992).

How It Feels to Be Adopted, by Jill Krementz (Knopf, 1982).

I Wish for You a Beautiful Life: Letters from the Korean Birth Mothers of Ae Ron Won to their Children, by Sara Dorow, editor (1998).

Lonely Planet travel guide books, various countries and authors (Lonely Planet Publications).

Making Sense of Adoption: a Parent's Guide, by Lois Ruskai Melina (Perennial Library, 1989).

Older Child Adoption, by Grace Robinson (Crossroad Publishing, 1998).

The Open Adoption Experience, by Lois Melina and Sharon Kaplan Roszia (HarperPerennial, 1993).

Oriental Children in American Homes, by Frances Koh (East West Press, 1981).

Parenting Teens With Love and Logic: Preparing Adolescents for Responsible Adulthood, by Foster Cline and Jim Fay (Pinon Press, 1992).

The Out of Sync Child: Recognizing and Coping with Sensory Integration Dysfunction, by Carol Stock Kranowitz (Perigee Books, 1998).

Parenting With Love and Logic: Teaching Children Respon-

sibility, by Foster Cline and Jim Fay (Pinon Press, 1990)

Raising Adopted Children, by Lois Melina (Harper and Row, 1989).

Real Parents, Real Children, by Holly van Gulden and Lisa Bartels-Rabb (Crossroad Publishing, 1997).

The Scared Child: Helping Kids Overcome Traumatic Events, by Barbara Brooks and Paula M. Siegel (John Wiley & Sons, 1996)

Supporting an Adoption, by Pat Holmes (Our Child Press, 1986)

They Came to Stay, by Marjorie Margolies and Ruth Gruber (Coward, McCann & Geoghegan, 1976).

Toddler Adoption: the Weaver's Craft, by Mary Hopkins-Best (Perspectives Press, 1997).

Too Scared to Cry, by Lenore Terr (Basic Books, 1998).

Travel With Children, by Maureen Wheeler (Lonely Planet Publications, 1995).

When Friends Ask About Adoption, by Linda Bothun (Swan Publications, 1987).

The Whole Life Adoption Book, by Jayne E. Schooler (1993).

With Eyes Wide Open: A Workbook for Parents Adopting International Children Over Age One, by Margi Miller and Nancy Ward (Children's Home Society, 1996).

Magazines, Newsletters, Reports

Adoptive Families magazine
PO Box 5159
Brentwood, TN 37024 (subscription address)
1-800-372-3300
http://www.adoptivefam.org
Magazine that covers all aspects of adoption.

Adoption Today
246 S. Cleveland Ave.
Loveland, CO 80537
(970) 663-1185
http://www.adoptinfo.net
Bimonthly magazine on all aspects of adoption.

Report on Intercountry Adoption
International Concerns for Children
911 Cypress Dr.
Boulder, CO 80303
(303) 494-8333
http://www.iccadopt.org
Annual listing, with updates, of agencies that handle international adoptions, plus articles on adoption issues. To be included, agencies must be licensed, have been in business at least two years, and answer a questionnaire.

Organizations, Support Groups, Government Agencies

Adoption Council of Canada
211 Bronson Ave., #210
Ottawa, ON K1R 6H5
(613) 235-0344
http://www.adoption.ca/
Advocacy group and information clearinghouse for adoption and adoptive families in Canada.

Adoptive Families Together
418 Commonwealth Ave.
Boston, MA 02215
(617) 929-3800
http://www.adoptivefamilies.org
Support group has a Web site and newsletter (included with membership), and an e-mail list for parents dealing with special needs (mostly emotional and behavioral). Lots of good, specific tips on handling behavior in children.

Child Welfare League
440 First Street NW, 3rd Floor
Washington, DC 20001-2085
(202) 638-2952
http://www.cwla.org
Association of more than 1,000 agencies that help abused and neglected children and their families. Publishes books and periodicals, and helps sponsor a child welfare database.

Joint Council on International Children's Services
1403 King St., Suite 101
Alexandria, VA 22314
(703) 535-8045
http://www.jcics.org
Information on international adoption, legislation, ethics, and practices. List of member agencies.

National Adoption Assistance Training Resource and Information Network (NAATRIN)
1-800-470-6665
Toll-free hotline, sponsored by the North American Council on Adoptable Children (see listing), for those who need detailed information on and assistance with adoption subsidies.

National Adoption Center
1500 Walnut St., Suite 701
Philadelphia, PA 19102
1-800-TO-ADOPT
http://nac.adopt.org
Advocacy group. Sponsors the National Adoption Exchange and co-sponsors Faces of Adoption, an online photolisting.

National Adoption Foundation
100 Mill Plain Rd.
Danbury, CN 06811
http://www.nafadopt.org
Makes available grants and loans to cover adoption-related expenses.

National Adoption Information Clearinghouse
330 C St., SW
Washington, DC 20447
1-888-251-0075
http://www.calib.com/naic
A U.S. government-sponsored service that offers comprehensive resources (including agency listings, statistics, and online databases) on all aspects of adoption.

New York State Citizens' Coalition for Children
306 East State Street, Suite 220
Ithaca, NY 14850
(607) 272-0034
http://www.nysccc.org
Group that advocates for improved adoption and foster care services. Offers resources on transracial and transcultural adoption. A video featuring adult adoptees speaking about transracial adoption is also available.

North American Council on Adoptable Children
970 Raymond Ave., #106
St. Paul, MN 55114-1149
(651) 644-3036
http://www.nacac.org
Group advocating adoption of waiting children. Has representatives throughout the United States and Canada. Membership includes a subscription to its newsletter, Adoptalk.

Parent Network for the Post Institutionalized Child
Box 613
Meadow Lands, PA 15347
(724) 222-1766
http://www.pnpic.org
Information and support services for parents of children with institutionalization effects.

Bureau of Citizenship and Immigration Services
http://www.bcis.gov/graphics/services/index2.htm
Information on intercountry adoption. Downloadable forms.

Online Resources

Adopt...Assistance, Information, Support
http://www.adopting.org
Huge collection of Web sites devoted to all aspects of adoption and foster parenting. Includes links to photolistings, a list of agencies, chat rooms and forums, listings of adoption laws, and resources for adoptees and birthfamilies who wish to search.

Comeunity
http://www.comeunity.com
Includes photolistings, a listing of adoptive parent support groups for various countries, and a comprehensive list of adoption-related e-mail lists.

Hannah and Her Mama
http://www.HannahandHerMama.com
Information and resources on older child adoption, single parenting, and attachment disorders.

Yahoo! Groups
http://groups.yahoo.com
A centralized subscription center for thousands of e-mail lists, including hundreds related to adoption, and several specifically geared to older child adoption.

Parents Place
http://www.parentsplace.com/messageboards/
iVillage's resources for parents include several message boards related to adoption, including one specifically for parents who are adopting or have adopted older children.

Rainbow Kids
http://www.rainbowkids.com
Online magazine for international adoption. Includes a store, lists of adoption agencies, a photolisting, an area devoted to older child adoption, and a list of adoption publications.

Medical and Mental Health Resources

American Academy of Child and Adolescent Psychiatry
PO Box 96106
Washington, D.C. 20090-6106
(202) 966-7300 or (800) 333-7636
http://www.aacap.org
Offers fact sheets on various mental disorders that affect children and teens, research abstracts, and descriptions of warning signs of when a child needs professional help.

American Liver Foundation
75 Maiden Lane, Suite 603
New York, NY 10038
1-800-465-4837 or 1-888-443-7872
http://www.liverfoundation.org
Information on hepatitis and other liver disorders.

Centers for Disease Control and Prevention
1-800-311-3435
http://www.cdc.gov
Information on various diseases and their prevention, as well as advice for travelers.

C.H.A.D.D (Children and Adults with Attention Deficit/ Hyperactivity Disorder)
8181 Professional Place, Suite 201
Landover, MD 20785
1-800-233-4050
http://www.chadd.org
Support and advocacy group for people with ADHD. Sponsors the National Resource Center on AD/HD (www.help4adhd.org), a national information clearinghouse for evidence-based information on attention deficit disorder.

Institute for Attachment and Child Development
P.O. Box 730
Kittredge, CO 80457
(303) 674-1910
http://www.instituteforattachment.org
Articles on attachment and attachment disorders, FAQs, and an overview of research and therapies.

International Adoption Clinics
http://www.comeunity.com/adoption/health/clinics.html
Comprehensive list of doctors (including Jerri Jenista, who is quoted in this book), clinics, and hospitals that assess international adoption referrals and treat internationally adopted children.

March of Dimes
1-888-MODIMES
http://www.modimes.org
Offers information on inherited diseases and birth defects.
Has chapters throughout the United States.

National Organization of Fetal Alcohol Syndrome
216 G St., NE
Washington, DC 20002
1-800-66-NOFAS
http://www.nofas.org.
Offers information on FAS and fetal alcohol effect (FAE).

World Health Organization (American regional office)
525 23rd St., N.W.
Washington, D.C. 20037
(202) 974-3000
http://www.who.org
Information regarding infectious diseases and malnutrition.

❖ Bibliography ❖

Books

Bass, Ellen, and Laura Davis. *The Courage to Heal: A Guide for Women Survivors of Child Sexual Abuse*. New York: Harper and Row, 1988.

Bates, J. Douglas. *Gift Children: A Story of Race, Family and Adoption in a Divided America*. New York: Ticknor & Fields, 1993.

Brooks, Barbara, and Paula M. Siegel. *The Scared Child: Helping Kids Overcome Traumatic Events*. New York: John Wiley & Sons, 1996.

Cline, Foster, and Jim Fay. *Parenting With Love and Logic: Teaching Children Responsibility*. Colorado Springs, Colo.: Pinon Press, 1990.

———. *Parenting Teens with Love and Logic: Preparing Adolescents for Responsible Adulthood*. Colorado Springs, Colo.: Pinon Press, 1992.

Estridge, David, and Frederick H. Lovejoy, Jr. *The New Child Health Encyclopedia: the Complete Guide for Parents*. New York: Delacorte Press, 1987.

Fahlberg, Vera I. *A Child's Journey Through Placement*. Indianapolis: Perspectives Press, 1991.

Hopkins-Best, Mary. *Toddler Adoption: the Weaver's Craft*. Indianapolis: Perspectives Press, 1997.

Jarratt, Claudia Jewett. *Helping Children Cope With Separation and Loss*. Boston: Harvard Common Press, 1994.

Jewett, Claudia. *Adopting the Older Child*. Boston: Harvard Common Press, 1978.

Keck, Gregory, and Regina M. Kupecky. *Adopting the Hurt Child*. Colorado Springs, Colo.: Pinon Press, 1995.

Kranowitz, Carol Stock. *The Out of Sync Child: Recognizing and Coping with Sensory Integration Dysfunction*. New York: Perigee Books, 1998.

Leach, Penelope. *Your Baby and Child From Birth to Age Five*. New York: Alfred A. Knopf, 1989.

McKelvey, Carole A. *Give Them Roots, Then Let Them*

Fly: Understanding Attachment Therapy. Kearney, Neb.: Morris Publishing, 1995.

Melina, Lois Ruskai. *Making Sense of Adoption: a Parent's Guide.* New York: Solstice Press, 1989.

————. *Raising Adopted Children: a Manual for Adoptive Parents.* New York: Harper and Row, 1986.

Moe, Barbara A. *Adoption: a Reference Handbook.* Santa Barbara, Calif.: Contemporary World Issues, 1998.

Monahan, Cynthia. *Children and Trauma: a Guide for Parents and Professionals.* San Francisco: Jossey Bass Publishers, 1993.

Moss, Robert A., and Helen Huff Dunlap. *Why Johnny Can't Concentrate.* New York: Bantam Books, 1990.

Pavao, Joyce Maguire. *The Family of Adoption.* Boston: Beacon Press Books, 1998.

Peterson, Janelle. *Tapestry: Exploring the World of Trans-Racial Adoption.* 1995.

Terr, Lenore. *Too Scared to Cry.* New York: Basic Books, 1990.

Welch, Martha G. *Holding Time.* New York: Fireside Books, 1988.

Articles

Alston, John F. "New Findings in Diagnosis: Correlation between Bipolar Disorder and Reactive Attachment Disorder." *Attachments,* Winter, 1996.

Ashton, Judith. "Imperatives for Whites Who Adopt Black Children." Internet (World Wide Web); accessed 3/11/99. Available at http://www.nysccc.org.

Guinta, Carole T. "Fetal Alcohol Syndrome." *Roots and Wings Adoption Magazine, 1995.* Internet (World Wide Web); accessed 1/3/99, at http://www.webcom.com/~webweave/rwfas.html.

Hall, Susan. "Leaves, Shoes and School Lunch." Internet (World Wide Web); accessed 4/3/98. Available at http://www.rainbowkids.com.

Jenista, Jerri A. "Rickets in the 1990s." *Adoption Medical News,* June, 1997.

―――. "Chronic Hepatitis B: Medical Management Issues." *Adoption Medical News,* November/December, 1995.

―――. "Chronic Hepatitis B: Diagnosis." *Adoption Medical News,* October, 1995.

―――. "Infectious Disease and the Internationally Adopted Child." Children Youth and Family Consortium Electronic Clearinghouse. Internet (World Wide Web); accessed 10/21/98. Available at http://www.cyfc.umn.edu/Adoptinfo

―――. "Understanding and Dealing With Early Puberty." *Adoption Medical News,* February, 1996.

Kannemann, Frank. "Attention Deficit Disorder," 1994. Internet (World Wide Web); accessed 1/3/99. Available at http://www.bixler.com/brainnet.

Mahoney, Jim. "Racism Issues and Multiracial Families: Attacking Racism Before it Defeats your Child." Internet (World Wide Web); accessed 3/11/99. Available at http://www.nysccc.org.

McFarlane, Jan. "Building Self-Esteem in Children and Teenagers of Color." Internet (World Wide Web); accessed 3/11/99. Available at http://www.nysccc.org.

McNamara, Barry E. "IEP: Individualized Education Program." Internet (World Wide Web); accessed 1/1/99. Available at http://www.parentsoup.com.

Parker, Harvey C. "Accommodations Help Students with Attention Deficit Disorders," 1998. Internet (World Wide Web); accessed 1/3/99. Available at http://www.oneaddplace.com.

―――. "Facts About Attention Deficit Disorder," 1998. Internet (World Wide Web); accessed 1/3/99. Available at http://www.oneaddplace.com.

Rosenthal, James A. "Outcomes of Adoption of Children with Special Needs," *The Future of Children,* Spring, 1993.

Schwarzenberg, Sarah Jane. "A Brief Introduction to Hepatitis B for Parents of Adopted Children," *Hepatitis B Coalition News,* 1994.

Silverstein, Deborah N., and Sharon Kaplan. "Lifelong Issues in Adoption." 1982. Internet (World Wide Web); accessed 12/19/98. Available at http://www.adopting.org

Tanner-Halverson, Patricia. The National Organization of

Fetal Alcohol Syndrome, 1998. Internet (World Wide Web); accessed 1/3/99. Available at http://www.nofas.org/strategy.html.

Thompson, Colleen. "Eating Disorders." Internet (World Wide Web); accessed 3/13/99. Available at http://www.mirror-mirror.org.

Fact Sheets

504 Accommodation Checklist. Internet (World Wide Web); accessed 1/3/99. Available at http://www.azstarnet.com/~tjk/IDEA504.htm.

Adoption from Foster Care. National Adoption Information Clearinghouse, 1997.

Adoption Issues That Impact Our Children At School. Adoptive Families Together, 1998.

Alcohol Related Birth Defects Fact Sheet. Internet (World Wide Web); accessed 1/3/99. Available at http://www.azstarnet.com/~tjk.

Bad Bug Book. U.S. Food and Drug Administration. 1991-1992. Internet (World Wide Web); accessed 1/7/99. Available at http://vm.cfsan.fda.gov.

Behavioral Symptoms of Adolescents With FAS/E Through the Eyes of Parents. FAS Family Resource Institute. Internet (World Wide Web); accessed 1/3/99. Available at http://www.accessone.com/~delindam/symptom.html.

Bipolar Disorder—Manic Depressive Illness, Mayo Clinic, 1998. Internet (World Wide Web); accessed 1/4/99. Available at http://www.mayohealth.org.

Centers for Disease Control. Fact sheets on hepatitis A, hepatitis B, and HIV/AIDS. Internet (World Wide Web); accessed January 1999. Available at http://www.cdc.gov/ncidod/diseases.htm.

Child Sexual Abuse, National Committee to Prevent Child Abuse, 1996. Internet (World Wide Web); accessed 3/13/99. Available at http://www.childabuse.org.

Child Sexual Abuse. The Sexual Assault Crisis Center of Knoxville, TN. Internet (World Wide Web); accessed 3/12/99. Available at http://www.cs.utk.edu/~bartley/sacc/sacc.html

Childhood Depression, Warren A. Weinberg. Learning Disabilities Association. Internet (World Wide Web); accessed 3/12/99. Available at http://www.ldanatl.org.

Disruptions in Sleep May Lead to Mania in Bipolar Disorder, Mental Health Net, 1997. Internet (World Wide Web); accessed 1/4/99. Available at http://bipolar.mentalhelp.net.

Educating Children with FAS/FAE, Internet (World Wide Web); accessed 1/3/99. Available at http://www.taconic.net/seminars/fas.

Fetal Alcohol Syndrome (FAS) & Fetal Alcohol Effects (FAE), 1998. Fronske Health Center. Internet (World Wide Web); accessed 1/3/99. Available at http://www.nau.edu/fronske/fas.html.

Health Insurance Coverage for Adopted Children, Rathburn Lynn and the Joint Council on International Children's Services, 1997.

HIV/AIDS Statistics, National Institues of Health, February 1998. Internet (World Wide Web); accessed 1/7/99. Available at http://www.ama-assn.org/special/hiv/support/aidstat.html.

How to Handle Persistent Lying: Parenting Tips and Techniques, Adoptive Families Together, 1998.

If You Are a Hepatitis B Carrier, Hepatitis B Coalition, 1996.

Information About Child Sexual Abuse, Sexual Abuse Victim Advocate. Internet (World Wide Web); accessed 3/13/99. Available at http://www.fortnet.org/sava.

MalnutritionL Determinants, Extent and Effects. Internet (World Wide Web); accessed 1/7/99. Available at http://www.odc.com/anthro/tutorial/tunit18.html.

Malnutrition in the World, Global Child Health News and Review. Internet (World Wide Web); accessed 1/7/99. Available at http://edie.cprost.sfu.ca/gcnet/ISS4-33a.html.

March of Dimes Fact Sheets on Thalassemia, Sickle Cell Disease, and Tay-Sachs Disease, 1994, 1997. Internet (World Wide Web); accessed 1/7/99. Available at http://www.modimes.org.

Mental Health Net. Fact sheets on bipolar disorder, posttraumatic stress disorder. 1996-1999. Internet (World Wide Web); accessed January 1999. Available at http://mentalhelp.net.

The Multiethnic Placement Act (MEPA) Fact Sheet, Office for Civil Rights, U.S. Department of Health and Human Services, July 1998.

New Study Finds Brain Structure Difference in Children With Attention Deficit Disorders, CHADD, 1995. Internet (World Wide Web); accessed 1/3/99. Available at http://www.chadd.org.

Newsletters, Spring 1995. The Parent Network for the Post Instutionalized Child. Internet (World Wide Web); accessed 1/3/99. Available at http://www.pnpic.org.

Questions Frequently Asked about Hepatitis B, Hepatitis B Coalition, 1994.

School Tips, Adoptive Families Together, 1998.

Secondary Disabilities in FAS and FAE, Internet (World Wide Web); accessed 1/3/99. Available at http://www.azstarnet.com/~tjk.

Signs of Sensory Integrative Dysfunction, Sensory Integration International. Internet (World Wide Web); accessed 1/1/99. Available at http://home.earthlink.net/~sensoryint/.

Some Basic Facts about Eating Disorders, 1997. Eating Disorders Awareness and Prevention, Inc. Internet (World Wide Web); accessed 3/14/99. Available at http://members.aol.com/edapinc/facts.html.

Tell Tale Signs, Substance Abuse Information, Internet (World Wide Web); accessed 3/11/99. Available at http://www.commnet.edu.

Treatment of Children with FAS/FAE, Internet (World Wide Web); accessed 1/3/99. Available at http://www.taconic.net/seminars/fas

Twenty Tips for Surviving the Holidays with an Older Adopted Child, Adoptive Families Together. Internet (World Wide Web); accessed 2/15/99. Available at http://www.adoptivefamilies.org.

What Is FAS? Internet (World Wide Web); accessed 1/3/99. Available at http://www.azstarnet.com/~tjk.

World Health Organization. Fact sheets on tuberculosis, schistosomiasis, child malnutrition, lymphatic filariasis, malaria, and HIV/AIDS. Internet (World Wide Web); accessed 1/7/99. Available at http://www.who.int.

❖ Index ❖

About the author

Trish Maskew is the mother of three, including two boys adopted at ages five and nine. She and her husband have been foster parents, and she has been a program coordinator at an adoption agency. She is the president of Ethica, an independent nonprofit group dedicated to ethical adoption.

CPSIA information can be obtained at www.ICGtesting.com
Printed in the USA
LVOW061811111212

311164LV00008B/881/A